Candlestick and Pivot Point Trading Triggers

Founded in 1807, John Wiley & Sons is the oldest independent publishing company in the United States. With offices in North America, Europe, Australia, and Asia, Wiley is globally committed to developing and marketing print and electronic products and services for our customers' professional and personal knowledge and understanding.

The Wiley Trading series features books by traders who have survived the market's ever-changing temperament and have prospered—some by reinventing systems, others by getting back to basics. Whether a novice trader, professional, or somewhere in-between, these books will provide the advice and strategies needed to prosper today and well into the future.

For a list of available titles, visit our Web site at www.WileyFinance.com.

Candlestick and Pivot Point Trading Triggers

Setups for Stock, Forex, and Futures Markets

JOHN L. PERSON

BICENTENNIAL
BICENTENNIAL
1807
WILEY
2007
BICENTENNIAL
BICENTENNIAL

John Wiley & Sons, Inc.

Published by John Wiley & Sons, Inc., Hoboken, New Jersey.
Published simultaneously in Canada.

For general information on our other products and services or for technical support, please contact our Customer Care Department within the United States at (800) 762-2974, outside the United States at (317) 572-3993 or fax (317) 572-4002.

Wiley also publishes its books in a variety of electronic formats. Some content that appears in print may not be available in electronic books. For more information about Wiley products, visit our web site at www.wiley.com.

Library of Congress Cataloging-in-Publication Data:

Person, John L.
  Candlestick and pivot point trading triggers : setups for stock, forex, and futures markets / John L. Person.
      p. cm. — (Wiley trading series)
  Includes index.
  ISBN-13 978-0-471-98022-3 (cloth)
  ISBN-10 0-471-98022-6 (cloth)
    1. Stocks—charts, diagrams, etc. 2. Investment analysis. 3. Futures. 4. Options (Finance).
I. Title. II. Series.
  HG4638.P468 2007
  332.63'2042–dc22

                                        2006011098

Printed in the United States of America.

10 9 8 7 6 5 4

To my wife, Mary,
who is always by my side and who gave me
encouragement and assistance in completing this book.
Thank you from the bottom of my heart
and with all my love.

Contents

Acknowledgments

I want to thank Pamela van Giessen and Jennifer MacDonald of John Wiley & Sons for allowing me to share my work. I would also like to thank Cindy Cromwell, Mike Felix, Sarah Neis, and Joanna Pak from RealTick Software—what a great team! I also extend my sincere gratitude to Glen Larson and Peter Kilman from Genesis Software for testing my theories and for helping me to develop my trading library on their software. Between these two charting software companies, any serious trader will have the best support and the most advanced trading tools to succeed! I also wish to thank the folks at eSignal.com.

I wish to thank all my past students for taking the initiative to apply these principles and for testing me while trading. I wish you all the very most life has to offer!

To my son John, you have made your father proud! Then to Mary, my wife of 19 years, your help in fixing all my computer and technical issues was instrumental in helping me finish this project, including completing the Pivot Point Calculator CD.

JOHN L. PERSON

Candlestick and Pivot Point Trading Triggers

Introduction

To all the individual traders reaching out to learn how to invest and trade wisely and to all those who are looking for new ideas and who have been around looking to learn a more positive approach, I say that after reading this material, you will find a great approach to trading and will learn the importance of or at least will expand your knowledge on how to develop your personalized mechanical trading system and learn why that is important. You will learn specifically what methods and parameters to use with time-tested material. My first book, *A Complete Guide to Technical Trading Tactics*, was released in April 2004. It was a great introductory on how to incorporate pivot point analysis with other forms of technical indicators and how it related to trading commodities. The foresight that book offered suggested that we would see resurgence in commodity activity and that commodity markets would soon be in vogue. I had chart examples of silver at 4.50 per ounce and gold at 350 per ounce. On page 211, I gave an example of a potentially great scale trading opportunity in coffee when it was as low as 49.00. Sugar was at 7.00. Crude oil was at 21.00. The 30-year bonds were at 111. The Federal Funds interest rate was at 1.0 percent. There were great trading opportunities, many of which I was able to take advantage.

THINGS CHANGE

Times changed, as did prices of these raw commodities. Other hard asset products, including housing and real estate, besides the commodity markets, skyrocketed in value. Things changed; global tensions mounted as we invaded Iraq trying to set a country free. Nations' economies grew as new opportunities emerged in places such as China and India. Global economic growth pushed demand for products through the roof, creating spectacular price gains. Things changed alright, even intermarket relationships. Gold went up on fears of inflationary pressures in light of the Federal Reserve (Fed) raising interest rates. In turn, the U.S. dollar rallied as the interest rate differentials widened here in the United States against foreign central banks.

THE CONUNDRUM

One favorite word among economists in 2005 was *conundrum*, which was used by then-chairman of the Federal Reserve Alan Greenspan. This was the term he used to describe the event of Treasury yields declining while the Fed was raising interest rates. The Federal Reserve moved to raise interest rates 14 consecutive times in 0.25 percent increments in an effort to reduce inflationary pressures. Bond yields, instead of moving in tandem with the Fed's rate hikes, declined. Short-term Treasury instruments were yielding more than longer-term, and what developed was known as a flattening of the yield curve. At some points, we even had an inversion effect, where longer-term interest rate instrument yields were lower than shorter-term. Throughout history, that is a sign that the economy will soon proceed into a recession.

HISTORY SHOULD REPEAT ITSELF

Often it is said that history repeats itself. Economies and the world move in cycles. Based on the market's price behavior and the climb that commodity prices had, intermarket relationships were not moving in a traditional way in 2005, or at least not in a manner in which they had in the past. History should have repeated itself, but it did not; or if it does, it will be a delayed reaction. Due to this keen observation, there was one solid piece of advice I was constantly giving to people through our trading room or in my newsletter advisory service. It was, "Trade the markets independently of each other." One reason for this advice was this: Not much was making sense at times in the traditional way. Let's face it, when crude oil or energies shoot to the moon, it is inflationary and has a taxing effect on consumers. We would have expected stocks to sell off sharply, and they did not (they did not rally much either in 2005). When federal deficits soar, it creates inflationary pressures; when the Fed raises interest rates, yields should go up and Treasury prices should go down. The key word is "*should* go down." What happened was just the opposite. Gold was the only mover that acted in response to investors' demand for protection on resurgence in inflation. In fact, at times, price swings of gold interacted well with crude oil.

DELAYED REACTION

As of February 2006, the U.S. economy was in its third year of an economic recovery. It remained a stock picker's market, as we did see stellar moves from Apple, Rambus, AMD, and other lost hopefuls. But there were other investors who were expanding their knowledge in trading other investment assets, such as foreign currencies. There were others who made fortunes in real estate. Unemployment in January 2006 was reported at 4.7 percent. Times were good and were probably going to remain good forever! Well, that's where I must say, "You can't cheat history." As the old saying goes, if it's got four legs and a tail, it's probably an animal. I see a delayed reaction and an economic downturn. Will it be the end of civilization as we know it today? I doubt it. However, I believe we will go into a period of an economic slowdown. Why? For starters, usually we see energy and commodity prices rally near the peak of an economic upturn. Then, as the Fed fights inflation, they will continue to put the brakes on and continue to raise interest rates. Since no one knows for sure how soon or by how much consumers will adjust their spending habits, usually the Fed will go too far. That will slow borrowing and increase debt payments, especially on all those adjustable mortgage rates (ARMs) that so many people have. Yes, I believe an economic downturn will occur. I just believe it will be a delayed reaction. It seems that most cycles have stretched a little further than people believe. Just ask all the folks who predicted a stock market crash in 1999. They were right, but quite a bit off in their timing. That leaves one to wonder where to go to make money.

TRADING FOR A LIVING

If you don't already know of my past, I started in the business as a runner on the floor of the Chicago Mercantile Exchange back in the late 1970s. I had the privilege of working with a true master trader, George Lane, the creator of stochastics. I had a knack for the financial markets and learned to trade the 30-year bonds. I also discovered how to use pivot points and how to incorporate longer-term time periods in my analysis. Then came options on commodities; and in 1986 I made a fortune for myself and others in the bond market. I gradually improved my techniques; and through the understanding of candle charts while using them in conjunction with pivot points, I have developed quite a methodology that shows a high frequency of recurring patterns. This is what I believe is one of the single best methods for identifying market moves for various trading vehicles. Trading for a living is a fabulous career. Now more than ever, we have global market influences, advanced technology, equal access, market liquidity, and, best of all, diversified markets investment vehicles. We have forex, or foreign currency exchange; futures products to day trade; and commodities that allow speculators to participate in a structured, regulated, open marketplace that offers leverage. Then we have stocks to participate in investing for long-term growth. And there is a new breed of investment asset, exchange traded funds. Most of these products offer options so as to hedge or speculate to fully capture a market opportunity and develop the right strategy to enhance rewards wile reducing risks.

THE NEW AGE TECHNICIAN

As a *technician*, one who practices the art of technical analysis, I have now more than at any time in the past a greater edge in the marketplace. Through electronic market access and charting software with the power of today's computers, I can take my refined market analysis methods and implement these strategies and apply them to all markets. As long as there is liquidity and a structured environment, and as long as I keep my trading capital intact, follow specific trading rules to manage risk, there will be a bonanza of opportunities in the years ahead. I fully expect the techniques that I am sharing with you in this book to help you discover how to be a consistently profitable trader. This book opens the door to how you can learn to read charts and rely on price rather than on indicators. You will learn what triggers momentum and what to look for in order to spot when a market changes direction. Another important element of this book is that it will help you learn techniques to cut your losses quickly and to stay with the winning trend, to ride a winning tide.

CHAPTER 1

Trading Vehicles, Stock, ETFs, Futures, and Forex

Welcome to *Trading Triggers*. If you are an active trader or a first-time investor looking for a trading method that suits your personality, then you have the right book. Trading for a living is an amazing and yet risky business. There is more to trading than buying and selling. There are often-missed but important issues that many books do not mention, such as not only how to make money in the market but also how to keep it and create a positive cash flow. The purpose of this book is to take you to a new level of trading knowledge by giving detailed explanations of technical tools that will help you develop your own trading system so you can cultivate and extract money from the market, especially those traders who want high alpha (big returns) with reasonable standard deviation (volatility). I will explain some of the most obvious yet simple concepts of how to interpret technical analysis and improve your chart-reading skills so you can make money in the markets.

There are two theories on how markets perform: efficient market theory and random walk theory.

1. *Efficient market theory* lends to the belief that markets are always priced correctly because the current price reflects all factual information. If the markets are efficient, then no fundamental information will give an investor an edge in the market.

2. *Random walk theory* lends to the belief that price movements do not follow any pattern or trend and that past price behavior cannot be used

to predict future price movements. In other words, the markets are completely unpredictable.

I fall in the category of believing that history can and does repeat itself. People can and do make money based on technical analysis, and I am here to help prove it.

IMPORTANCE OF A RULE-BASED APPROACH

You may have heard of Jesse Livermore, who was immortalized by Edwin Lefèvre's book *Reminiscences of a Stock Operator* (G. H. Doran, 1923; Wiley, 2006). Jesse was considered one of the greatest speculators of his day. Many of his principles and ideas are still used. His three key concepts of trading are (1) timing, (2) risk management, and (3) emotional control.

This quote from Richard Smitten's *Trade Like Jesse Livermore* (Wiley, 2005, p. 70) sticks with me because it is as true now as it ever was (keep in mind that Jesse committed suicide in 1940, so this was stated nearly 70 years ago): "All through time, people have basically acted the same way in the stock and commodity markets as a result of greed, fear, ignorance, and hope: that is why the formations and patterns recur on a constant basis. The patterns the traders and technicians observe are simply the reflections of human emotional behavior."

Most traders who are consistently profitable have learned to develop a rule-based approach that doesn't change. They have within their arsenal of trading tools, definitive, recognizable, and frequently reoccurring patterns that can be used to trade by a set of established trading rules. They can clearly define, without guessing or using a vague approach, support and resistance levels and what to do once prices reach those levels. Moreover, they have the ability to clearly define their entry, stop-loss, or risk parameters and their profit objectives in a consistent, repetitious fashion each time they place a trade. This is what I do when trading my own account and what I have taught my son and even my own father. My dad used to think trading commodities was like gambling until I showed him a method. This is the same method that will be disclosed in these pages.

It is important for you to realize that it is the emotional balance that helps keep you on the profitable side of the ledger. You must never anticipate what the market might do, but rather wait for confirmation on your triggers.

Most traders who are profitable are flexible as to the anticipated outcome that may occur on each trade. Successful traders have the mindset to develop the perspective that their trading business is to manage their money rather than to predict the future. Successful traders can emotionally handle losing trades or the negative trades that result from an error or trading equipment malfunction. Remember that the business of trading for a living requires that you establish some kind of structure in a marketplace with countless variables. Why not consider trading by a set of rules? Most traders do not trade by a system; the term "black box" just means that a trader has input a set of trading parameters and automatically executes a trade based on a specific set of criteria—strict rules to automatically trade by.

START TRADING AS A BUSINESS

If you are currently trading for a living or if you are expanding your knowledge to learn how to trade for a living, remember that this is a business. You need to treat it like a business. Therefore, some considerations need to be made, for example, forming a corporation in order to deduct such expenses as your computer equipment, quote feed, DSL (digital subscriber line), office rent, travel to investment conferences, and continued education seminars. What matters most to every trader and investor is creating a positive cash flow. You wouldn't want to finally start learning to make money consistently in the market and find out that you cannot take any expense deductions. You should seek advice from a tax specialist so that you can take advantage of all regular and necessary expenses as business deductions and save thousands of dollars each year.

Let's add up the examples I mentioned: Suppose your quote feed is $200 per month and your DSL is $40 per month. Renting a small one-room office could run $500 to $700 per month. Then there are equipment expenses, such as your desktop computers, a laptop for travel, monitors and printers and ink cartridges and general office supplies to purchase and upgrade from time to time, say $2,000. Attending an investment conference could mean $700 roundtrip airfare, plus $250 per night for hotel and meals. If you have business entertaining expenses and went to at least two conferences per year, you could be talking as little as $5,000 to as much as $25,000 in actual business expenses that can be deducted if you are running trading as a business.

If you are a first-time smaller investor and decide that trading for a living is something you have the financial resources, time, and emotional makeup to do, what business plan do you have in place to protect the money you make in the market? Where will you put your profits as a short-term trader? Some traders have had many problems with this issue; it is similar to the old expression of "Robbing Peter to pay Paul." After all, who wants to make money in a buy-and-hold long-term position strategy only to give it back day trading, and vice versa.

I am going to show you a trading method based on combining candle charts, to help identify shifts in momentum, and pivot point analysis. I will teach you very succinct rules, which is what I have taught to professional traders on the floor of the exchanges and introduced to thousands of private investors, including other leading trading educators who now effectively teach my trading methods. I will walk you through deciding what investment vehicles are available, when and how to decide which investment vehicle would better suit a trader under various market conditions, and how to develop a trading strategy based on the specific trading triggers.

EDUCATION IS THE KEY TO SUCCESS

Traders need and, moreover, have an *obligation* and responsibility to understand as much as possible about how the markets that they trade work and what makes them function. It is vital to your success that you continue to learn not only about the market but also about your trading hardware or computer equipment. For example, if you trade off a laptop, you should know how to disable the tapping feature on the touch pad. After all, who wants to accidentally place the wrong order on line? That has happened to traders because the touch pad is ultrasensative. Simply moving your finger or having your shirt sleeve touch the pad can act as an action click. Traders should know how to set up and troubleshoot office or home Internet connections or at least have a brokerage account that offers assistance in taking over-the-phone orders.

Traders need to learn and comprehend all the features and benefits that charting software packages offer and should know all about the order entry platforms and, more specifically, the brokerage firm rules and procedures for trading. Traders should make sure the brokerage firm has the title of the account set up so if ever there is a situation where you wish to wire money into an account, it matches the name on the bank to your trading account. You don't want an important wire to be rejected. In a situation where you want to either put on more positions or add a second account to trade a great opportunity, how sad it would be for back-office personnel to reject the wire, resulting in a lost opportunity.

A great trader is always looking to learn. One of the best processes to learn is asking a series of questions; evaluating the dynamics of a situation or event; and seeking out how to take advantage of that event within the financial resources, risk factors, and time constraints in place.

The traits that most professional and consistently profitable traders possess are that they follow a trading plan on extensively tested research and limit losses while letting winning positions ride. Winning traders exhibit the qualities of patience and discipline. The techniques that will be taught in this book will help you master those two qualities.

Other traits that winners possess are that they diversify into various trading positions, while committing only 10 to 40 percent of accounts equity in the markets. Successful traders commit their full attention to the market trends and prices, and they act on trading signals immediately.

They also seem to possess the ability to accept winners and embrace losers, and they don't let either of these outcomes generally influence their next trade decision. They stay in the now and react to what the market is currently doing. Winning traders take breaks from trading. Through continued education and the process of asking questions, they gain an edge and stay on top of their competition through diversification or other more advanced trading strategies.

TRADERS NEED TO ASK MORE QUESTIONS

The process of asking questions is what is needed in order to gain more knowledge. The trouble is, most traders do not have enough experience to know what the right questions are. If you apply simple common sense, then you will be on a great start to learn how to identify investing or trading opportunities and find the right strategy to take advantage of those opportunities.

Some questions traders need to ask themselves include, just for starters: How much time do I have to dedicate to the markets? If I enter a day trade, do I have the time to watch this position, or do I have an appointment or meeting scheduled for that day? What are the possible outcomes of what I am about to do, based on what I have control over?

Focus on what it is you want to achieve, write it out, and concentrate on that goal. Think of the consequences or possible outcomes of your actions so you will have a more balanced emotional reaction if the outcome is not as positive as you expected. Ask questions such as:

- Do market conditions warrant increasing or decreasing my position size?
- Are there reports coming out that may impact the market or my position?
- Are my entry and exit targets justified?
- If the market is so bearish, why won't it go down?
- If the market is so bullish, why won't it rally?

Trading without asking questions or without probing leads to trading blindly or without a plan. It opens the door for destructive emotional interference. Another quote from Jesse Livermore helps confirm this: "There is nothing new on Wall Street or in stock speculation. What has happened in the past will happen again and again and again. This is because human nature does not change, and it is human emotion that always gets in the way of human intelligence. Of this I am sure." (Smitten, *Trade Like Jesse Livermore*, p. 167)

That statement was made over 65 years ago and is without a doubt still applicable to this day. Do not let your emotions get in the way of your trading decisions. If you ask the right question before placing a trade, you stand to gain an edge on winning the emotional battle of trading. It is generally those who are afraid of losing through fear itself who stand to lose because that emotion will interfere with rational, well-thought-out trading plans.

Asking yourself the right questions will help you to choose a more apropriate investment vehicle or trading strategy. For example, ask yourself before entering a trade: What are the time expectations for a result to occur? Do I have availability of time to see the trade through? Would short-term day trading or swing trading be possible if I have a regular day time job? In what time zone do I start work? This is relevant because a person living on the West Coast could trade an early morning market such as the Chicago Board of Trade (CBOT) bond contract opening session; however, a person with an early morning job may want to consider foreign currency or forex (Foreign Exchange) trading on the European session starting at night.

In order to know what time demands you need, you should also ask yourself if you have the tolerance for trading a leveraged product and if you have the tolerance for the risks: Should I use a time period stop—if the market does not move or react within a specified time period, should I exit the position? Should I use a conditional stop, such as a "stop-close only" order? Does my order platform take such orders, or do I need to manually watch and then implement such an order? (In intraday trading, the answer is yes, you need to manually watch the close of the time period you are trading in.) Can I afford to place a stop, say, 10 or 20 percent of my overall account value?

You need to be clear and honest with yourself when answering these evaluation questions. Remind yourself by asking: Why am I trading? What are my expectations? (I have met too many people that look at trading as an easy and quick way to make money or to replace their current career.) Based on your trading account size or your risk capital, ask: What returns will I need in order to generate sufficient income? Is my starting equity size or bank roll inclusive of my living expenses? Are my expectations on that return realistic on a constant basis?

These questions are important because they will help you to determine which type of investment vehicle and which type of diversified trading strategies you can incorporate into your trading repertoire.

RISK PER TRADE

A most important yet simple thought process that a trader can start with is learning how to determine how much equity to put into any one trade or position. How much to risk per trade is a concept that many novice traders fail to realize until it is way too late. They end up learning the exact wiring instructions on a regular basis to their brokerage account; the real hard cases end up remembering those instructions by heart. Once you learn and have the confidence to trade a system or follow a trading plan with a set of conditions and specific rules, you still need to have an effective method for risk controls. I would start by considering how much risk per trade I should use by looking at my overall account size, then at the market's volatility and liquidity conditions, and then at a certain percentage of the overall account on a percentage basis. Let me show you what I mean; and when we go over various stop types and methods later in the book, you will be able to better comprehend my meaning. If a person wanting to start a day trading account begins with $10,000 and uses a 10 percent risk factor per trade based on the overall beginning equity size, if the first five trades go bad, then he or she has lost 50 percent of the overall account. Therefore, it is imperative that traders learn different techniques to protect their trading equity. Investors also need to know the number of positions with which they should start in connection to the account size and the point at which they add on to their contract lot or position size. In Chapter 11, I will go over a method to help you determine answers to those questions. Then you will have a better understanding of a proper ratio and the point at which you should start to increase your trading size.

NUMBER ONE TRADING FOCUS—RISK MANAGEMENT

As most trading books will explain, risk management is the key to survival and what trading is really all about. While it may sound like a cliché, the hard truth is that consistently profitable trading, in my opinion, significantly depends on proper risk taking and risk management combined. Winning traders follow a tried-and-tested plan based on rules or on a defined set of criteria. Winning traders recognize the importance of risk management and of money management. As I stated in my first book, the common denominator among losing traders was that most guess and hope and usually say, when asked about placing a stop-loss or taking a profit, "I'll think about it." Always remember that when trading with a set of rules, you will never be 100 percent right. But if you do *not* follow a set of rules, you increase the odds of being 100 percent wrong in your trading. If you manage your trading risks and execute promptly on the trade signal, then you increase the odds that you will be successful. When trading, your mind can play tricks on you. You start to anticipate a buy signal only to act on a false signal. You need to learn when and how an actual signal is generated and what and when you should trigger the action to initiate a trade. When you are trading market signals by a predefined set of rules and a set of criteria, then the mind cannot play tricks on you. When a signal says buy, then buy; when a signal says sell, then sell. It's that simple. Generally speaking, from my experience, if a trader says, "I am tired of this," and decides not to take the signal, that ignored signal is the one that becomes a big winner. If you have traded before, you may relate to that syndrome. For day traders in stock or stock index futures, this usually happens in the last hour of the trading session!

DIVERSIFICATION IS THE KEY TO SUCCESS

This observation was written by Peter L. Bernstein in his book *Against the Gods, The Remarkable Story of Risk* (Wiley, 1996):

> All of the tools we use today in risk management and in the analysis of decisions, from the strict rationality of game theory to the challenges of chaos theory, stem from the mathematical developments that took place between 1654 and 1760 with two exceptions: In 1875 Francis Galton, an amateur mathematician, discovered regression to the mean; and in 1952, Nobel Laureate Harry Markowitz, then a young graduate student at the University of Chicago, demonstrated mathematically why putting all your eggs in one basket is an unacceptably risky strategy and why **diversification** is the nearest an investor or business manager can ever come to a free lunch. That revelation touched off the intellectual movement that revolutionized Wall Street, corporate finance, and business decisions around the world; its effects are still being felt today. (pp. 5–6)

With that notion came the concept of exploiting diversification by means of spreading investment and risk capital in various markets, such as stocks, bonds, real estate, precious metals, and commodities. There are various methods to trade those investment vehicles through the use of real estate investment trust (REIT) mutual funds, exchange traded funds (ETFs), and other derivatives products, like single stock futures, stock index futures, and options. There are simple and complex strategies even more so with the use of options and inter- and intramarket spreading or pair trading opportunities. We will cover some sophisticated strategies in this book as well as basic investment strategies to help you create your own retirement fund.

HABITUAL WINNERS FOLLOW TRADING PLANS

Traders need to consider new techniques that will allow for increased profitability and ways to reduce risks. This book will demonstrate how you can identify *conditional* changes in the markets and how you can utilize my techniques in certain setups and triggers based on an approach to using candle charts and pivot point analysis that may be different from what you have encountered before.

You will learn which leading price indicators are the best to use, plus professional chart-reading techniques and how to apply this knowledge to make trading decisions based on facts rather than on opinions. You would be surprised at how many times I am asked what my "feeling" is on the market. I can feel upset, I can feel warm, I can feel cold; but I just can't feel the market. I can see the price action and can act on a shift in the momentum, and I can determine that the market is currently in an uptrend or a downtrend or in a consolidation phase. I certainly can't feel the market.

I want to walk you through some top chart patterns or setups and triggers so that you can develop a trading plan based on a testable trading system. This will be a method with a complete set of rules that do not arbitrarily change. You will be able to use these concepts in many different markets and in different time frames. This book will go into more specific rules and explanations of setups and triggers than my first book did. Not only was that first project, *The Complete Guide to Technical Trading Tactics: How to Profit Using Pivot Points, Candlesticks, & Other Indicators,* a great introductory book that touched on several trading concepts, but it was the first work that introduced traders to the concept of integrating candlestick charting with pivot point analysis. Some of the principles in that first project will be used here, but this book will cover in greater detail how to apply and use those methods so you can learn to make money with the triggers. I would suggest that you get that book if you have not already done so, as there are many great tips and suggestions described in those pages.

In this book, I want to teach you what to search for when chart reading. I am not going to go into detail on every specific candlestick chart pattern because I generally only use them to help identify where the market closes in relationship to the open or the past price points, such as the high or low points, rather than rely on them to signal a trade based on traditional chart formations.

I believe that, like many things in life, the more you repeat positive actions, the more you will experience and receive positive reactions. In trading, that translates to simply following rules, waiting for signals to transpire, and then acting on those signals, rather than anticipating that signals will form. When signals trigger a buy, then go long; when a signal triggers a sell, then exit the long or go short. As I stated earlier, following a set of rules will not guarantee that you will be 100 percent right in your trading results; but by not following a set of rules, your chances increase that you may be closer to 100 percent wrong in your trading results. One must learn to cut losses and let winning trades ride. It sounds like a cliché to trading veterans; but the fact is that it is so simple, yet it is so hard to do. By accepting this process of learning some simple principles and then following a few sets of rules, which I will go into in this book, you become a better trader; and that may translate into becoming a *more profitable* trader.

One trait I have noticed that most novice traders possess is that they try to overanalyze and overcomplicate matters. In order to help simplify your thinking, remember this: There are only four common denominators that each of us has equal access to—the *open*, the *high*, the *low*, and the *close* of any given market, in any given time frame. There are two other values to measure: *volume* and, for futures traders, *open interest*. However, even these two elements cannot be finalized or completely calculated until the close of each trading session. Therefore, it is important that you realize that the *close* is the single most important aspect when using and applying all forms of technical analysis studies.

So no matter what market or trading vehicle you are trading—whether it is a stock, a futures or commodity market, a stock index, the forex currency markets, or even an exchange traded fund, you need to watch the *close* of the time period in which you are trading to capture a clue in order to initiate a trade, manage the trade, and learn the right exit spot. Always remember that the *close* is the most important element and what matters most to focus on when trading. It is the relationship of the *close* to past price action and to the *high*, the *low*, and the *open* that will help measure or weigh a value of a given market at any given time. Therefore, you can get a more accurate gauge of what to do. In trading terms, the choices you have are to buy, to sell, to spread off, or to do nothing and hold onto your cash. Sometimes not knowing what to do translates into not entering a position. Remember that being in cash or standing on the sidelines is a trade, too.

Once you grasp the understanding that it is the close that shows you what the current market value is, then you should have a clue as what your next trading decision should be. If you learn to act on the close for your trading decisions and on triggers, that information will help stack the odds in your favor that you are going with the current flow or in the right market direction. That includes any time period for which you are trading. That means if you are a day trader using a 5-minute period, you cannot act on an intratime period signal. You need to wait for the five-minute period to conclude before acting on a trigger. The same goes for a 5-minute, a 60-minute, a daily, a weekly, or even a monthly time period.

The clues for which we as traders are looking are what we need to initiate a trading decision and are what I define as a trading *trigger*, which will be explained later in the book. Once you understand how markets work, understand simple charting techniques, and have a fundamental working knowledge of indicators and what dictates increases or decreases in values of a given product at a given time (such as supply and demand factors) and how that is represented on a chart, then you will have gained a better edge in the market and will have stacked the odds of success in your favor.

There is one flaw in any system, and it is generally from the execution side rather than from the construction side of the system. To be specific, most traders who lose while trading a system fail to trade by the signals generated by that system. Either they fail to act once the signal is generated, or they anticipate that a signal will be generated thus acting on a false signal.

It is imperative that once you read this book you learn that you must wait for the actual signal to trigger, and that occurs in most cases by the close of the time period in which you are trading. Even when a system generates a losing trade, it will signal a trigger to get out. You must act on confirmed signals rather than on anticipation of those signals or, more important, on your personal hunches.

Once you have a working knowledge of the markets and the confidence in what the possible outcome of those triggers might be, working with a few setups and signals will allow you to find a trading opportunity; and then you will be able to apply the appropriate strategy. You can diversify trading styles, such as integrating a day trade into a position trade, utilizing an option strategy, or applying the information on various trading vehicles.

I talked about this concept of "finding opportunity, then applying a strategy" in my first book: I called it playing the Monte Hall game, *Let's Make a Deal*. Look behind door number one, and review the risk rewards; then look at the strategy behind door number two, and review the risk and rewards there; and then finally open door number three, and see if that strategy appeals to your analysis of risk and rewards. Remember, you can determine, if an opportunity is longer term in nature, to use an option strategy (such as an outright long call or put); a ratio back spread; or, if the best opportunity exists taking a position in a stock, a stock index future or possibly an ETF or a holding company depositary receipt (HOLDR).

INVESTMENT VEHICLES

There are all types of trading and investment vehicles. Some are slightly more complex than others, and some offer increased leverage, such as futures and even forex currency markets. Some have short life spans due to expirations, such as an option or a futures contract. A trader or an investor needs to examine his or her personality profiles, tolerance for risk, personal time availability to devote to trading, and the time objective or turnover for achieving specific profit objectives. Once those are determined, then he or she needs to choose the right trading vehicle or a mixture of asset classes in order to apply a trading strategy.

Therefore, it is important to have several different types of trading accounts for taking advantage of various investment products and levels of risk, such as long-term retirement versus short-term speculative trading opportunities. A stock account will allow you to trade stocks, stock options, mutual funds, and ETFs.

A futures account will allow you to take advantage of the many opportunities of various commodity markets and options, in addition to day and swing trading the highly liquid stock index futures markets such as the Dow, Standard & Poor's (S&P), Russell 2000, and Nasdaq 100 contracts. Some futures brokerage firms even have access for spot foreign currency trading on their trading platforms. I have been in the futures and trading business since 1978. I trade my own money, I have been a broker, managed a brokerage firm, owned a trading firm, but, most of all, I enjoy trading my own money. In fact, the principles I am sharing in this book are the same techniques that I have taught my family. Remember that my father used to think commodity trading or day trading was like gambling. But at age 71, he started gaining an interest in what I was doing, especially as he saw the fruits of my labors. More important, he witnessed the trading successes my son was also achieving and started to see that the pattern of what I was doing was teachable. In 2002, I had my son start a retirement stock account with what I call a core position of select stocks. One such stock was General Electric, which he purchased at 24.60; another stock I had him purchase was Rambus at 5.62. In both cases, he made out extremely well. In fact, if you know stocks, you may recognize that those prices were darn close to the exact lows in 2003. Let me tell you it was not by chance or luck that I had picked those prices; it was by using the methods I am going to describe in this book.

Incidentally, here is how my son got hooked on day trading: In early 2005, he was watching me on one of my appearances on CNBC. My son is self-employed; he owns cellular phone stores and sells satellite dish systems. He keeps the television on in his stores to show customers the satellite systems. After watching my appearance on CNBC, he left the television on; later that day, he started listening to *Mad Money*—the Jim Crammer show. Anyway, my son started trading his own stock account.

He called me one day to ask my opinion on a particular stock. That's when I found out what he was up to. Now, my son is pretty smart; but there were several things he was not familiar with, for instance, what a stop-loss order was. As you might imagine, I was insanely furious with him for not knowing important yet basic concepts of trading. After I got through yelling at him, his mom (my wife) got hold of him; after that conversation, one of my trading courses was shipped out FedEx, and he quickly studied. He got back on the right track, gained an interest, and learned how to trade by my set of rules and by looking for such trading patterns as a high close doji (HCD) buy signal and a low close doji (LCD) sell signal. Both of these specific setups and triggers are covered in this book. The next course of action was to get him set up with the right markets to day trade and to open the right brokerage account to meet his needs for both his short- and long-term objectives. Now this is what I taught my son, and he has been consistently improving in his trading ever since. That is what my Dad saw, and he found merit in my methods. Therefore, I hope this solidifies your belief that traders can and do make money trading in the markets. Just find the right methods with which you are comfortable, stick to the trading rules (such as waiting for the triggers, rather than anticipating and acting prematurely), find and investment strategy (such as day, swing, or position trading), and then get confident that you are applying the right strategy with the right product (whether it is stocks, futures, options, foreign currencies, or forex markets). You have the potential to become a successful trader once you have these conditions mastered. The next process is finding the right software product and brokerage firm.

I have been in the industry for over a quarter of a century, so I know what to look for in both trading firm and software that suit my needs. I have the experience to know that not all trading companies are equal. The plain truth about it is that some companies are just better than others. Remember the debacle of REFCO? These guys were a behemoth in the futures and spot foreign currency trading business. They had a ton of talented people, some who are ex-employees of mine and some who I consider friends. I never did trade through them. Mainly, I was happy elsewhere. But as the years passed, REFCO just became too big. I like personalized service, and I don't need a company to provide me with daily research. You need to find out what appeals to you and how to make a brokerage firm work for you.

It's not the other way around. Keep in mind that a brokerage firm should be considered an employee—it works for you! I have a rating sheet for my subscribers of my advisory service of the pros and cons of several brokerage firms. If and when you are looking for a brokerage firm and want to see a ratings consensus, just visit www.nationalfutures.com, where I can give you a heads up on the pros and cons of several trading firms and the ones that I have accounts with. You can use it to find out which one fits your trading needs. As I say, some are better than others. Trading expenses such as commissions are important, but dealing with a cheap deep-discount commission brokerage firm that has no backup support does not suit my needs. A solid company that has competitively priced commissions, a loyal support staff, and pleasant customer service is what I look for. I like one that actually answers the phones and takes care of an issue immediately; that is the ideal company to do business with, and there are many of them. That is the information I share on my web site.

FX—FOREX

You may be familiar with or have heard the term *foreign exchange market*, which is known as the spot forex or FX market or foreign currency market. It is an over-the-counter foreign currency market. You can trade foreign currencies against the dollar, which is knows as the *cross*, such as the euro currency versus the U.S. dollar; or you can trade *pairs*, which is two separate foreign currencies traded against each other, such as the euro versus the Japanese yen. It is a 24-hour marketplace in which most companies do not charge commissions; rather, a spread on each side of the bid-and-ask of a trade is taken. Traders like this feature because they feel it is a "pay as you go" cost of doing business.

This book will go into explaining several investment vehicles, such as stocks, futures, options, and forex. I want you to realize that the technical trading patterns, setups, and triggers I will teach and explain in this book are applicable to all of these trading vehicles.

STOCK TRADING OPPORTUNITIES

Stocks offer opportunities to long-term investors based on a company's performance. There are many advantages and disadvantages when trading stocks. Some feel that stocks should be a buy-and-hold investment vehicle, and I agree to some extent. I believe the world and business move in cycles, as does any industry or business sector. Investors need to monitor which sector or industry is hot or running cold, as the dot-com bubble demonstrated. Since we can learn from history and a picture speaks a thousand words, let's go over a few chart examples if you want to know more about the disadvantages of investing in stocks. If you were invested in these companies, had a bad experience, and do not want to be reminded, just flip through these next few pages. If you are new to the investment world and want to know how fast fortunes and retirement accounts were lost, just ask investors who bought Enron, WorldCom, United Airlines, Kmart, and FAO Schwartz just before these companies filed for bankruptcy. And that is just a few of the companies that took major dives. There are those investors that are hanging onto hopes of their stocks coming back to life, companies like Lucent, as shown in Figure 1.1. Lucent Technologies, Inc., engages in the design and delivery of systems, services, and software to communications service providers, governments, and enterprises worldwide. It will take a lot more patience to see this stock come back to life. This stock was going to be the next IBM of the telecommunications world, which goes to prove that you can't believe everything you hear.

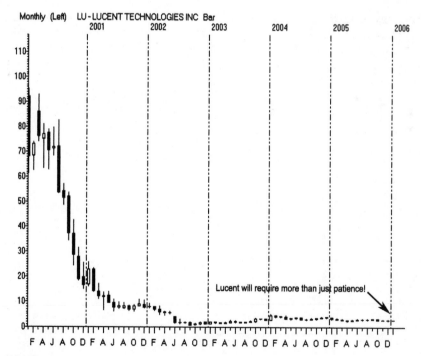

FIGURE 1.1
RealTick graphics used with permission of Townsend Analytics, LTD.

Then there was the new age revolution of fiber optics. Remembers JDS Uniphase? This company provides communications test and measurement solutions and optical products for telecommunications service providers, cable operators, and network equipment manufacturers. The company operates in three segments: Optical Communications, Commercial and Consumer, and Communications Test and Measurement. As Figure 1.2 shows, this stock has just never come back to life.

Then there are some companies that had investors gleaming with joy—that there was never a chance those stocks would drop, but drop they did. However, not all stories have bad endings. Take a look at Rambus, Inc., a company that provides chip interface products and services. Its memory interface products include XDR memory interface, RDRAM memory interface, and DDR controller interface technologies, which provide an interface between memory chips and logic chips. Figure 1.3 shows that there is life and hope for some stocks, this one included.

One more darling from the Internet craze was Red Hat, Inc., which provided a competitive operating system to Microsoft. Red Hat has related

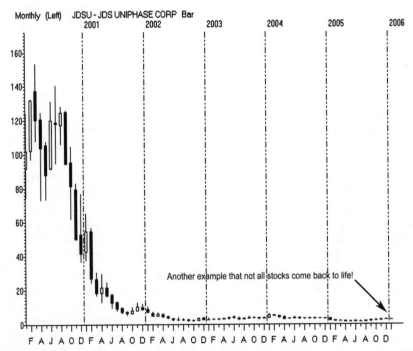

FIGURE 1.2
RealTick graphics used with permission of Townsend Analytics, LTD.

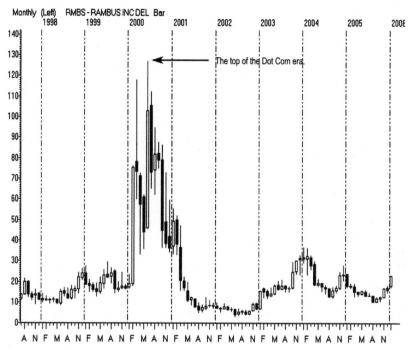

FIGURE 1.3

RealTick graphics used with permission of Townsend Analytics, LTD.

software and services based on open source technology for various enterprises. Its products include Red Hat Enterprise and Linux Red Hat Application Solutions, which include software for managing web content and software development. The Linux systems and storage availability was a sure thing for investors, one of those "can't lose" propositions. As Figure 1.4 shows, that is not how Wall Street saw it in the long run or how it rewarded the stock price. However, there is hope; and as you can see, the stock is springing to life. The examples here illustrate how investors need to watch over their own investments. The markets generally overreact both on rallies and on declines. Sectors and business cycles change; competition can force companies to lower prices, thus resulting in lower profit margins. Business models, consumer spending habits, and the leadership or management of a firm can change. That can have a direct impact on and can change the morale and the business structure of a company. And that is what can affect a company's bottom line.

The dot-com implosion and stock market crash did not wipe out all companies; and, of course, some companies fared better than others. A great example of bringing a company back to life is, without a doubt, Apple Computer, Inc.! This company manufactures, designs, and markets per-

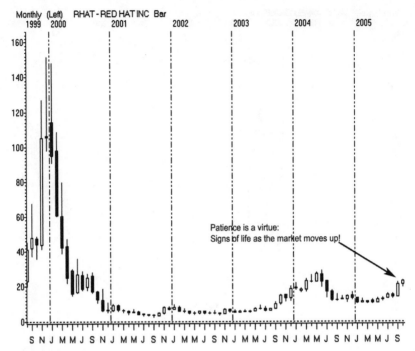

FIGURE 1.4
RealTick graphics used with permission of Townsend Analytics, LTD.

sonal computers and related software, services, peripherals, and network-
ing solutions worldwide. The company's products and services include the
Macintosh line of desktop and notebook computers. It was the introduction
of the iPod portable digital music player, accessories, and services that
helped propel this company into a killer performer and one of the best
comeback stocks from the dot-com and stock market peak in 2001. Steve
Jobs is the cofounder and CEO of Apple; and as I stated a moment ago, it is
leadership and motivation that can help inspire a company to great fortunes, as Figure 1.5 shows.

When you look at a strong performer of a stock in a specific sector,
traders and investors are obviously looking for appropriate risk/reward opportunities to trade that stock. There are many choices and various strategies to employ. This is the selection process of what we do in "finding
opportunities and selecting the right strategy." Once again I call it the "let's
make a deal" game. What we are doing is simply looking for the best strategy that maximizes our level of expected returns while minimizing our
risks. We are looking for the optimal trading strategy. Traders can examine
and weigh what is the most apropriate risk/reward perspective:

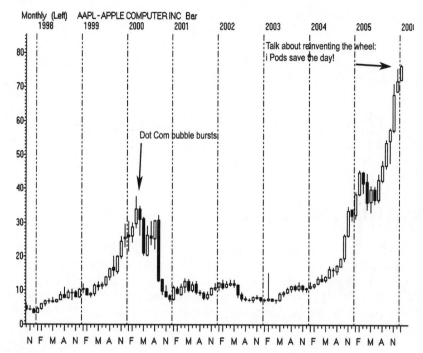

FIGURE 1.5
RealTick graphics used with permission of Townsend Analytics, LTD.

- *Door Number One:* Could be an outright stock purchase with a selective stop-loss.
- *Door Number Two:* Could be utilizing the options market. That can be an exciting and worthwhile exploration of a simple purchase of a call option to utilize leverage or the use of a more complex strategy, such as a bull call spread, or a hedging program, such as a collar strategy. The latter uses the premiums collected from the sale of an out-of-the-money call option to purchase a close-to-the-money put option, which in turn protects the price erosion of an underlying stock position.
- *Door Number Three:* Could be taking a trading opportunity by implementing a spread strategy, which would involve buying one stock and selling short another. This is a sophisticated strategy and one that beginners should study extensively prior to implementing. However, if you enjoy following and understanding who and what the competitor is in a specific sector or industry group, this could be your cup of tea. Selecting the right stocks requires extensive research and a good working knowledge of the fundamentals of that sector or industry. After all, you

are looking for one company to outperform the competitor, so you need to know as much as possible about that business.

Trading decisions and correct stock selection involve more than looking at a chart and a few technical indicators. I believe it helps to look a little deeper in expected earnings forecasts and price-to-earnings (P/E) ratios to see if the stock is expensive or cheap relative to current prices. Calculating P/E ratios is an easy concept; for example, if a stock is trading at $40 per share and has an earnings of $4 per share, the P/E ratio would be the price of the stock divided by the earnings—$40/$4, or 10 times earnings.

SPREAD TRADING TIPS

If you decide to take advantage of a spread trade, you should realize that it is a risky business. You could be on the wrong side of both markets. Since spreading involves selling short one stock and simultaneously buying another stock, if the price goes in the opposite direction of both trades, you can lose on both sides of the trade. Selling short is a hard concept for many traders, both novice and experienced, to grasp. Believe it or not, there are some folks who are not aware that you can sell first without owning the security. Short selling means you are betting that the price of a given product will decline; therefore, you would be selling first without owning the underlying product with the hopes of buying back later at a lower price. Selling short is considered highly speculative for stock traders; the process involves "borrowing" the stock from the brokerage firm, if the firm has that security in inventory. Shorting stock is very similar and should not scare investors. It is a very simple concept; in fact, it is just the opposite for longs. You want to buy low and then sell out later at a higher price. With shorting, you are selling first and buying back later, hopefully at a lower price to generate a profit.

There are certain restrictions; for one, you need to set up a margin account with your brokerage firm. Another restriction carries potential execution risks: Due to Securities and Exchange Commission (SEC) regulations, there is what is known as the "uptick" rule. The uptick rule was established in the 1930s to prevent a bear market raid on a stock. In order to execute a trade, the stock needs to trade at a price higher than the preceding transaction price in the same security. For example, if you wanted to enter a spread by selling Dell Inc. and buying Apple, you would have been anticipating or looking for Apple to outperform Dell's price gains. Or if both stock prices decline, you would want Dell to decline more than Apple. But in order to effectively execute that strategy, you would want to enter the sell side of the spread first because there are no restrictions on entering the long side, just on the short side of the transaction. Let's say you enter the long side first without confirmation that you were filled on the short side; if the market on the position you hold—the long side—goes down and if both markets moved in tandem, you would need an uptick on the short side in order to be in the spread. Imagine if you went long first and the stock dropped. Then when you are finally able to execute the short side, the market has plunged. That would translate into an actual loss. So if you do not get filled first on the short side, the worst that can happen is that you lose a trading opportunity. This is a great example of why traders have the obligation of knowing all there is about the market they trade in. As you can see in Figure 1.6, Dell has moved in the same direction as Apple, but Apple has outperformed as a price leader. The spread opportunity between these two computer manufacturers, long Apple and short Dell, would have generated a tidy profit.

Another example of a spread opportunity within competitors of the same industry or sector would be Best Buy versus Circuit City, as shown in

FIGURE 1.6
RealTick graphics used with permission of Townsend Analytics, LTD.

Figure 1.7. As consumers flocked to retail malls before the holidays to purchase gifts such as Apple's iPods, if you want long Best Buy as the sector leader and short Circuit City, Best Buy stock outperformed Citcuit City stock. As you can see from the chart, after the stock market bubble burst in 2000, Best Buy managed to maintain a positive trend higher. It is the leadership of the company and the consumer loyalty that really have helped to support this company's growth and profitability. One reason is Best Buy continued to sell appliances versus one of their rival competitors and as a result they saw sales rise 7.7 percent from 2004 through 2005. They also had aggressive gains in web sales, and online revenue jumped 40 percent as more customers shopped and redeemed gift cards online for the same time period.

Best Buy's main competitor, Circuit City, decided or needed to cut back and close stores and then discontinued selling appliances to stay afloat. It depended on increasing DVD and CD sales and on electronic products. As the housing boom materialized soon after that decision, Circuit City gave up market share to Best Buy; and no doubt companies such as Home Depot and Sears picked up increased revenues in appliance sales. Therefore, it

FIGURE 1.7
RealTick graphics used with permission of Townsend Analytics, LTD.

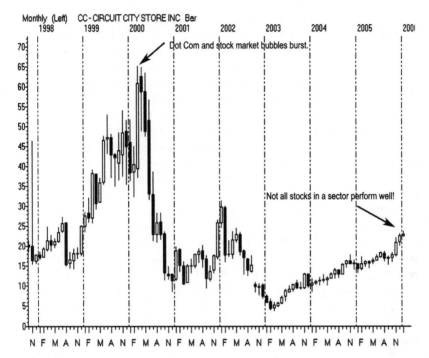

FIGURE 1.8
RealTick graphics used with permission of Townsend Analytics, LTD.

was hard for Circuit City to reenter selling that product line. As you can see in Figure 1.8, Circuit City's stock just had not been a great performer in that sector. The company was founded in 1949, so it has a long history and may survive the competition. However, if consumers start to spend less on home electronic products in 2006 and 2007, this company may have trouble getting its stock price back up to the 2000 high near 65 per share. Circuit City will need consumers to continue to buy and upgrade new televisions, camcorders, and digital cameras to boost revenues. I personally have no intentions of buying another camcorder; I barely use the one I have. As for game software, game hardware, and personal computer software, those are competitive products; so I believe Circuit City will have to do more to survive the next few years of what is being forecast as a consumer electronic sales recession. Therefore, one would need to look closer at these two companies and decide which one has more to gain or which one has more to lose; once a decision is made, this would be a good pairs market for a spreading strategy.

Investors have many trading opportunities with stocks, as you can see from the preceding few pages. There are many ways to analyze a company, from taking a simple look at the P/E ratio to using technical analysis studies. Investors can see which company is the leader in a specific sector and invest with that leader. As you can see in the cases of Apple versus Dell and Best Buy versus Circuit City, holding a diversified portfolio of stocks may help investors see profits or a positive cash flow. Realistically, you can't own shares in every stock. Longer-term investing—you know, the buy-and-hold mentality, sometimes referred to as the Warren Buffett method—helps toward generating big gains in solid companies. But remember that World-Com and even Lucent Technologies were solid companies at one point. So the message here is that investors need not only to be selective in which markets they buy and hold but also to monitor their positions. There is the idea that you can buy stock in a company to which you relate or from which you purchase products . . . companies like Starbucks, as shown in Figure 1.9. This company has solid growth, great coffee; it carries with each 20-ounce cup, named a Vente, a solid jolt of caffeine. That is what keeps me going back, day after day, dropping two dollars per cup for the Starbucks "experience." Starbucks has made stellar gains and is a great moneymaking

FIGURE 1.9

RealTick graphics used with permission of Townsend Analytics, LTD.

stock. It has solid industry leadership, textbook marketing concepts, and, more important, customer loyalty. These are all the qualities to look for when selecting a long-term purchase.

BECOME THE NEXT WARREN BUFFETT

I believe that stocks should be traded as an investment, but there are many ways to capture a profit. I must say for all investors and for every trader, you can start your own mutual fund. It requires discipline not only to open a stock account but also to fund it and add to it every month. If you are a new investor, just reading this book to see if trading for a living is for you, it is imperative that you start somewhere and start with a select stock account first. The discipline is that you should add money in the account every month, like you are paying a bill. If you are under 30, consider it your retirement. You are paying your bills in the future now. That is some of the best advice anyone gave me, and I think it is worthy of passing on to you. Once you gain more experience, you can separate long-term investing from short-term speculative trading, which is one form of diversification. After all, you may see a long period of flat performance in one of your core holdings. Short-term day trading, if you have the time and resources, can be a rewarding experience. Imagine owning Wal-Mart and for literally seven years experiencing a loss to a flat performance. Figure 1.10 illustrates the market's sideways move in one of the world's biggest retail stores.

If you are considering supplementing your investment techniques, one of the many drawbacks of trading stocks for a short-term day trader with a small trading account is that you are limited to how many trades you can make, especially if your account is less than $25,000 and you are not signed up for a margin account. In that case, you are limited to five round-trip buy-and-sell trades per week due to SEC rules. So short-term trading would not be a good consideration for stocks. That is where trading stock index futures and forex markets takes over, as I will explain in the following pages.

There is one high-risk, high-reward method of trading stocks that I have not covered yet: getting in on an initial public offering (IPO) stock. Those investors lucky enough to get in on an IPO like Google (goog), the Chicago Mercantile Exchange (CME), or even the Chicago Board of Trade (CBOT—stock, BOT) were able to double, triple, quadruple, or even better, their initial investment dollars.

The Chicago Board of Trade has been around for over 155 years, and I imagine it will likely continue to be around for another 155 years, with little competition in products traded on its exchange and with the increase in popularity on the electronics metals products, such as gold and silver, plus

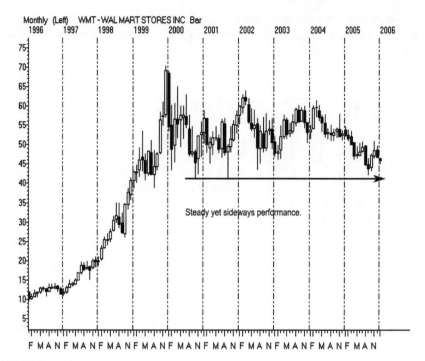

FIGURE 1.10
RealTick graphics used with permission of Townsend Analytics, LTD.

the huge volume of trades generated in the grain markets. And with the action in the U.S. Treasury notes and bonds and Federal (Fed) funds contracts, the CBOT certainly has a positive longer-term outlook for profitable revenue growth. Figure 1.11 shows that the price exploded to nearly as high as 134 but has managed to trade back as low as 86 as of this writing. The BOT stock illustrates that not all IPOs are guaranteed moneymakers; in fact, depending on your entry, these offerings can be hazardous to your financial well-being. The phrase "invest wisely" means "not putting all your eggs in one basket." Find out which is the sector leader, and go with that stock, unless you like the underdog. In this case, the underdog would be BOT compared to CME.

As you can see in Figure 1.11, BOT stock initially shot up from the 80s to a little over 130. At the time I was preparing to write this book, it had not managed to get back over 130 but traded as high as 119. I do feel that once the Treasury reinstates issuing the 30-year Treasury bond, volume will increase, which will translate into more revenue for the exchange. Therefore, the profitability should improve through the next few years. If a drought scare causes the grain complex to go through the roof, you will see

Daily (Right) BOT - CBOT HLDGS INC CL A Bar
2005

FIGURE 1.11
RealTick graphics used with permission of Townsend Analytics, LTD.

this stock price move like a rocket. Many see the Chicago Board of Trade mimicking the Chicago Mercantile Exchange success story. As Figure 1.12 shows, in just three short years, CME stock went from under 40 to close to 400 by late November 2005.

The biggest surprise of the three had to be the gains by Google, as Figure 1.13 shows. After the dot-com implosion in 2001, not many were willing to experiment with any Internet stock. That mentality may be the one reason why this stock had such a move, from a contrarian point of view, that is.

LONG-TERM INVESTING OR SHORT-TERM TRADING

We have briefly covered ways to trade stocks and certain methods to trade leaders of stocks in certain sectors. Investing carries less stress, fewer day-to-day decisions, and less risk than trading does; and with that come fewer rewards. Just as we all have different personalities, there are that many opinions on how to *trade* the markets.

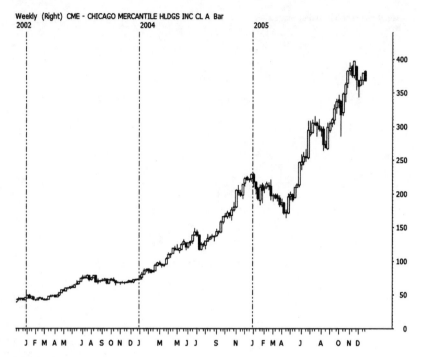

FIGURE 1.12
RealTick graphics used with permission of Townsend Analytics, LTD.

Some of the keys to successful trading are:

- *Diversification.* This not only applies to markets, such as a wide assortment of stocks in a portfolio, but also to trading different strategies and various investment instruments.
- *Risk Management.* Profitable trading also comes from skills acquired from practicing discipline, patience, and risk management techniques that preserve your capital.
- *Behavior or Emotions.* Successful trading means removing the most destructive element, negative emotional feelings that plague investors when trading: fear, greed, and anxiety. Finding the right mixture of investment products and trading styles can teach you to feel secure when trading.

The methods we cover in this book can be applied to the topic of selecting stock and spread trading, as we just covered, and to long-term-position trading, as in the style of trading for which Warren Buffett is famous.

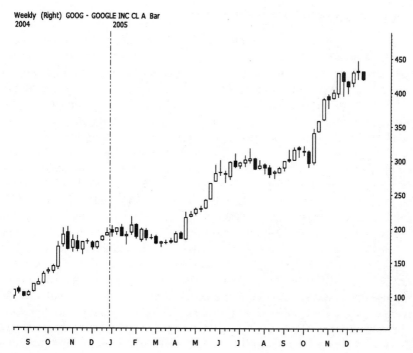

FIGURE 1.13
RealTick graphics used with permission of Townsend Analytics, LTD.

EXCHANGE TRADED FUNDS

Exchange traded funds (ETFs) are listed on different exchanges and are traded on the open market. Choosing this kind of product allows an investor to select the right sector of performance, rather than pinpointing an individual stock. The benefits of trading ETFs compared to a mutual fund are enormous: They allow diversification; they incur more effective transaction costs; there is pricing transparency; and they are tax efficient. After all, it is almost impossible for an individual trader with limited trading resources to effectively track and trade every stock in all sectors of the market. ETFs are index-based investment vehicles and are traded as a share of a single security based on an entire portfolio of stocks. The advantage here is that the trader can mix the benefits of applying technical analysis and fundamental analysis to a combination of stock and index trading.

In the most recent development, ETFs have started to include products related to commodities such as crude oil, gold, and silver; but also they have expanded into the forex arena by launching a euro currency product.

Personalized Mini-Mutual Fund

Instead of agonizing over which stock will outperform in a certain sector, you can use ETFs as an investment vehicle that has certain stocks in a basket as one unit, listed as a sector fund. This allows individual investors to invest in a group of stocks in a sector, rather than relying on a mutual fund to do it for them. Moreover, many mutual funds charge management fees and at times do not fully invest all an investor's cash in the market. Because ETFs trade like a stock, the price of which fluctuates daily, an ETF does not have its net asset value (NAV) calculated every day like a mutual fund. By owning an ETF, you get the diversification of an index fund plus the ability to sell short, buy on margin, and purchase as little as one share.

Another advantage of an ETF is that the expense ratios for most ETFs are lower than that of the average mutual fund. When buying and selling ETFs, you have to pay the same commission to your broker that you'd pay on any regular order. ETFs allow you to sell without the uptick rule, so you can short right away, even after the market is in a strong downtrend. You do not have to wait until the close of the day settlement price as happens in a mutual fund. Another benefit is the tax consequences because of shielding from capital gains due to the fact that ETFs do not change holding like a mutual fund does. So purchasing shares of ETFs is a viable alternative to investing in mutual funds for individual investors. Keep in mind that many of the ETFs available today have access to trading options around the ETF. Therefore, you can develop simple or more complex hedge or spreading strategies tied around an ETF. There are some negatives, such as the three-day settlement restriction and a bid/ask spread just like any other market; but the benefits certainly outweigh the negatives, especially for longer-term swing and position traders.

The Birth of ETFs

The original ETF was offered to the investing public back in 1993 by the American Stock Exchange (go to www.amex.com for more listings) and was known as the SPDRs, which stands for Standard & Poor's Depositary Receipts and corresponds with the price movements of the Standard & Poor's 500.

The more actively traded and by far more popular ETF came with the QQQs, which directly correspond with the Nasdaq 100. Then there are the Diamonds, which move in correlation to the Dow Jones Industrial Average. ETFs have since expanded, and there is now a new breed of investment vehicles to capture opportunities in sectors known as HOLDRs. These trading vehicles are based on certain stocks in a certain sector, known as a basket of diversified stocks in a specific sector.

Just as the examples comparing the U.S. Real Estate Trust (IYR) shown in Figure 1.14 to Toll Brothers, ETFs can offer investors a relationship to overall sector performance that is better than outright exposure in just one stock if you are wrong in your investment decision. As we go forward in the book, I will show you a technical analysis method such as pivot points using a longer-term time frame and how it can help you determine entry and exit targets, such as targeting almost the exact high in Toll Brothers, as well as other stocks.

As you can see in the comparison of the two charts in Figure 1.15, Toll Brothers took a nasty hit while the Real Estate Investment Trust ETF rebounded from the correction.

Looking at a related or similar stock, such as Caterpillar in Figure 1.16, you would assume that if the construction or housing and real estate markets could experience a setback due to the 14 interest rate hikes orchestrated by the Federal Reserve, then a company that manufactures construction and heavy equipment might suffer a significant correction as

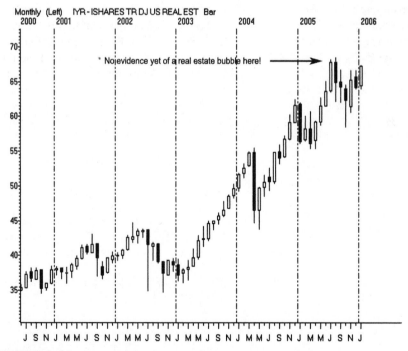

FIGURE 1.14
RealTick graphics used with permission of Townsend Analytics, LTD.

FIGURE 1.15
RealTick graphics used with permission of Townsend Analytics, LTD.

well. However, that was not the case, as the chart illustrates. In fact, it is quite the opposite. So by utilizing an ETF and investing in an overall sector, an investor has a better chance of gaining a better rate of return. By using the technical analysis methods that will be covered in this book, an investor can apply those signals to ETF markets. Keep in mind that options will eventually be available for most ETFs as well. That will offer investors quite an edge as far as hedging or protecting against adverse market moves, too.

Hot Sectors, Hot Stocks

In order to take advantage of a hot sector of the market, such as energy, biotechnology, technology, Internet, brokers, semiconductors, telecom, and cyclical, to name a few, how would an investor identify the best stocks in that sector and then narrow it down to one or two stocks and be right? That is generally the tough part of investing. Trading an ETF or a HOLDR can help remove that difficulty and may help a longer-term investor achieve that goal. Moreover, it can also allow an individual to literally trade like a hedge fund through means of diversified sectors and allow for implement-

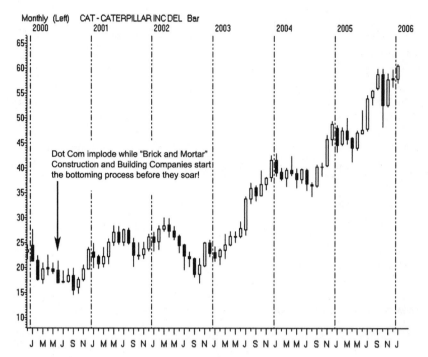

FIGURE 1.16
RealTick graphics used with permission of Townsend Analytics, LTD.

ing simple to sophisticated trading strategies integrating options as stated earlier. With market liquidity and market transparency, traders using ETFs can buy or sell at current market values rather than at assigned market values based on the close, as is the case when investing in mutual funds. In fact, some mutual funds may not be fully vested in stocks at a given time. This means your cash may not be working at 100 percent capacity.

Currency ETFs

This book will also reveal more about the forex markets or foreign currency trading. And on that subject, there was a new ETF that may appeal to those who want to participate in currency investing but have neither the time capacity nor the desire for excessive leverage exposure. Rydex Investments launched the first-ever currency-based exchange-traded product back in December 2005.

The Euro Currency Trust (FXE) is an ETF that tracks the price of the euro, with each share representing about 100 euros plus accrued interest. Shares of the trust, called "Euro Currency shares," trade on the New York

Stock Exchange (NYSE). The ETF has a 0.4 percent annual fee. Investors generally pay commissions to buy and sell ETFs, which trade daily on exchanges as stocks do. Initially, the trust registered 17 million Euro Currency shares, for a total offering price of about $2 billion. Shares of the ETF can be sold short and are eligible for margin, as most ETFs are. Notice the correlation of price movement in the ETF shown in Figure 1.17 with the euro FX currency futures contract shown in Figure 1.18.

Granted there is more liquidity in the price of the euro futures contract; but keep in mind the that the euro ETF was in its third week of trading after its initial launch date. I suspect that by the time this book is published, the volume and liquidity will improve dramatically.

Commodity ETFs

Not all ETFs track the price movement of the underlying derivative market exactly. Take for example the OIH chart shown in Figure 1.19. As you com-

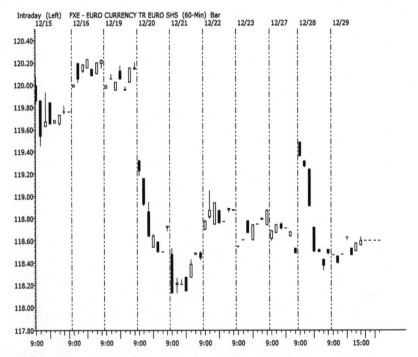

FIGURE 1.17
RealTick graphics used with permission of Townsend Analytics, LTD.

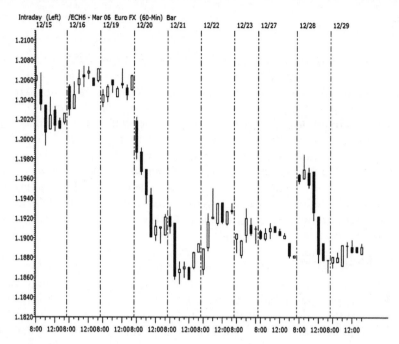

FIGURE 1.18
RealTick graphics used with permission of Townsend Analytics, LTD.

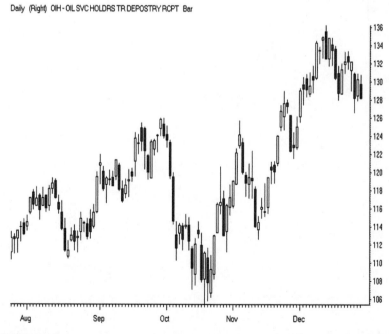

FIGURE 1.19
RealTick graphics used with permission of Townsend Analytics, LTD.

pare moves in the underlying commodity of crude oil, as shown in Figure 1.20, you will see that at times the correlation is not 100 percent exact. In fact, at times the ETF has actually been a leading price indicator of the underlying commodity price move! Now there is an ETF that is more closely correlated to crude oil, such as the United States Oil Fund (USO).

The example in Figure 1.21 is streetTRACKS Gold ETF, traded on the NYSE. It was launched in late 2004; and as of December 2005, when I started writing this book, it was trading roughly 2.1 million shares a day. It has attracted $5.65 billion from investors. Each share of the ETF represents one-tenth of an ounce of gold, which allows mutual funds or private investors to invest in gold without actually owning the metal. It mirrors or tracks the price movement of gold almost exactly, as you can see from Figure 1.21 when compared to the gold futures chart in Figure 1.22.

The objective of the trust is for the value of its shares to reflect at any given time the price of gold owned by the trust at that time, minus the trust's expenses and liabilities. The trust is not actively managed. It receives gold deposited with it in exchange for the creation of baskets of iShares. The trust sells gold as necessary to cover the trust's liabilities, and

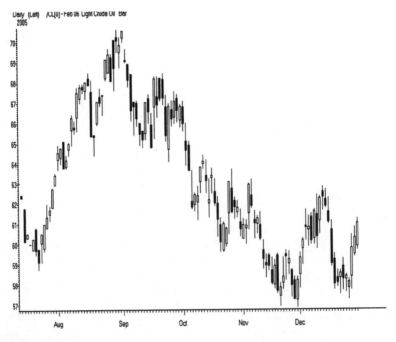

FIGURE 1.20
RealTick graphics used with permission of Townsend Analytics, LTD.

Daily (Right) GLD - STREETTRACKS GOLD TR GOLD SHS Bar
2005

23 26 31S 7 12 15 20 23 28 O 6 11 14 19 24 27 N 4 9 14 17 22 28 D 6 9 14 19 22 28

FIGURE 1.21
RealTick graphics used with permission of Townsend Analytics, LTD.

Daily (Right) /YGG6 - Feb 06 Gold mini CBOT Bar

Aug   Sep   Oct   Nov   Dec

FIGURE 1.22
RealTick graphics used with permission of Townsend Analytics, LTD.

41

it delivers gold in exchange for baskets of iShares surrendered to it for redemption. The trust is not an investment company registered under the Investment Company Act of 1940 nor a commodity pool for purposes of the Commodity Exchange Act. This is traded on the American Stock Exchange (AMEX).

Figure 1.22 shows the CBOT gold minicontract; and as you can see as you compare the two charts, the price movement in the gold ETF shown in Figure 1.21 mirrors almost exactly the price movement in the gold futures contract.

For silver bulls, bears, or spread traders, the newest ETF addition was the AMEX iShares Silver Trust (SLV). It is a fund based on the daily price of one ounce of silver as set by the London Bullion Market Association. Those spread traders buying gold or selling silver now can use ETFs. The key in showing you the various markets as compared to the ETFs is that you realize that once you identify the opportunity, you then can make a good decision on which opportunity best presents itself. While futures offer the leverage, you may want to invest longer term; and an ETF would be right up your alley without having to pick a gold or silver mining stock. If you are bullish on precious metals but don't want to buy the physical metal and if you have the luxury to trade options, then an ETF would be the right choice.

It does not go without saying that an outright stock selection can provide a great return and can at times outperform the sector and even the underlying market. Look at the price move for Newmont Mining in Figure 1.23. This stock took off and never looked back, even when the price of gold and the gold ETF made a price correction. There are times when that can happen. Even if you were to purchase long call options, the most profitable rate of return comes from the leverage of an outright long call option position in a straight up move, such as Newmont experienced. The question is how many times can that trade and, more important, the timing of such an event be replicated.

Another advantage of an ETF is the availability and structured use of iShares. If you are trying to match the most liquid investment vehicle with a specific sector or group of like stocks, this may be the right investment choice. IShares are considered to be like an open-ended mutual fund that reinvests dividends. This investment class is always fully invested in the market; so when the market moves up and you are long, you would fully benefit. These index funds also trade just like stocks. Each fund share represents a proportion of ownership in each stock that makes up the index. As we have briefly discussed, to make the right choice in an investment and choose the right stock, you can utilize fundamental analysis, such as earnings per share and market capitalization, to determine what the potential futures earnings might be. This data can help you determine if the stock is

Daily (Right) NEM-NEWMONT MINING CORP Bar

High Close Doji

FIGURE 1.23
RealTick graphics used with permission of Townsend Analytics, LTD.

ripe as a buying opportunity or if the price is too high or overvalued and should be avoided. Considerations that can never be determined are the hidden demand for a company's product and the way the company is run, to see if the profit margins are high or if operating costs and deep discounts to retailers cut into the company's bottom line. Therefore, it could be prudent to possibly play the sector through an ETF, which effectively would eliminate the issue of selecting the wrong stock or the underperformer of that specific sector.

The Hot Stock

Take, for example, one of the most amazing come-from-behind stories in 2005 and early 2006. Advance Micro Devices (AMD) triumphed, surpassing Intel's price level. It would have taken patience and discipline to stick with this winner; but outperform it did, and what a hot stock it was, as the chart shows in Figure 1.24!

For a specific ETF or iShare that would list AMD and Intel, you would look at the iShares Goldman Sachs Semiconductor (IGW) listing. The top 10

FIGURE 1.24
RealTick graphics used with permission of Townsend Analytics, LTD.

holdings as of 12/31/2005 were Texas Instruments, *Intel*, Motorola, Applied Materials, STMicroelectronics NV, Marvell, Technology Analog Devices, Broadcom, *Advanced Micro Devices*, and Maxim Integrated Products.

Intel was a darling among institutional traders and mutual funds, but it had not performed well, let alone offered enough volatility to day trade or even swing trade a position. There was just not enough movement in this stock, as Figure 1.25 shows.

So how was an investor to make money, and how would one possibly choose to invest in AMD instead of Intel? Actually, once a few simple concepts of identifying market price momentum through candle charts are covered in the next few chapters, you will see how and why to stick around when a market goes into a trending phase. Also, once you learn these techniques, it will be pretty easy to help select the right stock. Another simple investment decision would be to buy the iShares Goldman Sachs Semiconductor ETF! As you can see from Figure 1.26, the semiconductor ETF moved up. It would have been a far better trade simply being outright long AMD from under 15 in March 2005, but the torture of watching Intel go nowhere would have been a reason to buy the semiconductor ETF and

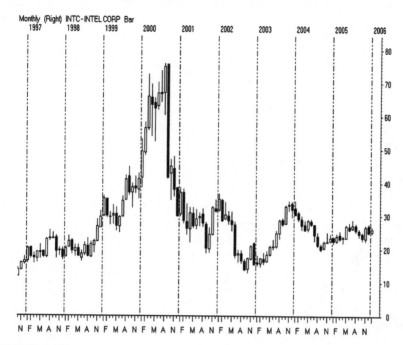

FIGURE 1.25
RealTick graphics used with permission of Townsend Analytics, LTD.

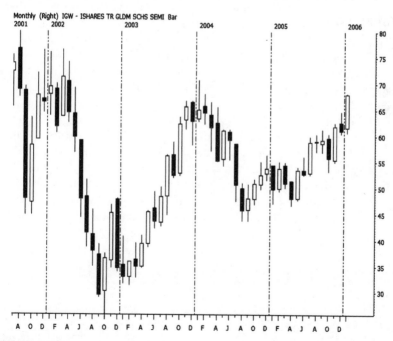

FIGURE 1.26
RealTick graphics used with permission of Townsend Analytics, LTD.

participate in a profit. The key in using these vehicles is for those who like a specific sector and do not have unlimited resources to buy a wide spectrum of stocks. It is also appealing to those who want longer-term trades and who hold a regular day job and cannot day trade for a living, at least not yet.

Once again, the difficulty of choosing the right stock in a competitive industry in a specific sector can be overcome; and it may be more profitable by considering trading an ETF. The previous comparisons of Best Buy and Circuit City, Dell and Apple, and AMD and Intel all are excellent examples of how an investor may have a difficult time anticipating which stock outperforms another in a specific sector. Therefore, for a longer-term stock trader, ETF investment vehicles could be a solution, helping to boost the bottom line, and can be added to his or her investment portfolio.

ETFs and some HOLDRs have the greater advantage of trading put and call options within a prescribed period of time. An investor can even buy calls such as on the pharmaceutical HOLDRs. Here is a tactic that I have used before with some success, especially if there are buy signals on several individual stocks within a sector. Go ahead and purchase, with a reasonable time until expiration, an in-the-money or close-to-the-money call option on the HOLDR itself. The pharmaceutical HOLDRs can be traded based on signals from Abbott, Merck, and Pfizer.

So you can utilize ETFs and their respected relatives and apply several strategies; also you can use intermarket relationships to determine buy or sell signals and devise a trading strategy dependent on those signals. Once you have a good feel for a stock that correlates or links best with an ETF, then you can use a spread or "pairs" trading strategy or even a hedge strategy using options. Deciding what is best for your risk capital making, using an ETF, you no longer need to make a precise pick for a stock in a specific sector.

In conclusion, trading opportunities exist in these investment vehicles for all investors; and best of all, they respond quite well using technical analysis to project support and resistance levels as derived from pivot point analysis and the momentum techniques that certain candle patterns indicate, which are the specific techniques disclosed in this book. This knowledge should give you, the individual investor, quite an edge in the market!

FUTURES MARKETS: LEVERAGE SYSTEM

We will go over several techniques for helping you identify trading opportunities in the futures markets. So far we have gone over using exchange traded funds versus stocks; pairs trading in related stocks; and using commodities for identifying opportunities in ETFs, such as the oil service

HOLDRs (OIH) or the U.S. Oil Fund (USO) versus crude oil futures. The Euro Currency Trust (FXE) is a more direct move for stock traders playing the euro currency futures versus the U.S. dollar. Then there is the street-TRACKS Gold ETF (GLD) compared to the CBOT electronic gold futures contract, or now a trader can use the iShares Silver Trust to trade against the physical silver market.

Stock traders can now apply and take advantage of so many commodity markets; but as I mentioned, the futures market is a great investment vehicle to many savvy and financially well-funded traders. Even smaller-sized traders can benefit from trading the futures market through the *responsible* use of the margin system, otherwise referred to as a "good faith deposit." What is a *futures contract*? It is a legally binding agreement to buy and sell a commodity or financial instrument sometime in the future at a price agreed upon at the time a transaction was made. Contracts are standardized according to delivery points of interest, quality, quantity, and time of accepting or making a delivery. It is estimated that less than 3 percent of all transactions actually result in a delivery. In the case of stock index trading, there is a cash settlement over the value of the contract.

Stock Index Futures

For day or swing traders following the stock market, the futures market offers an advantage over stocks from tax liability perspective. Always check with your accountant; but, generally speaking, profits generated in a futures account are taxed at a rate significantly lower than that for a stock account.

One confusing aspect and perhaps a drawback for many traders switching from equities or even forex to trading futures is that there are so many products with various contract sizes. There is no consistency or constant in tick value fluctuations or dollar value in the price changes. For example, the CBOT mini-Dow contract is $5 times the overall Index. When the Dow was at 10,500, the overall value was 52,500. The margin was set at $2,600, or just under 5 percent. E-mini–S&Ps are 12.50 per tick (four ticks per point). If the point value is $50, the overall value of the contract if the S&P is at 1,200.00 is $60,000. In the currency markets, the euro is 12.50 per tick; the Canadian dollar is 10 per tick; the British pound is 6.25 per point but trades in a minimum two-tick fluctuation. (In my first book [*A Complete Guide to Trading Tactics*, Wiley, 2004], I listed all the commodities and the contract sizes on pages 8 and 9; please refer to that for a comparison. Or you can ask your futures broker to provide the listing of contract specifications.)

The exchanges where the individual futures products are traded set the margin requirements. Generally speaking, an initial margin requirement on a futures product runs anywhere from 2 percent up to 10 percent of a contract's overall value. So now a trader needs to know which exchange the product is traded on, how much risk capital is needed to invest per contract, and how much each point value is. Let's look at the New York Mercantile Exchange's crude oil contract: The contract size is 1,000 gallons; every tick or point fluctuation equals $10. A $1 move per contract is a $1,000 price move. When prices were at $65 per barrel, the contract value was $65,000. The margin requirement was, at one point, nearly $9,000 per contract, almost 14 percent of the overall market value. The extremely high margin requirement reflected the extreme level of volatility and the inherent risk associated with that increased volatility.

The futures markets also have a value for stock traders to make decisions on asset allocations to their stock portfolios. In the agriculture sector, for example, you can study the price direction of soybeans, use traditional technical analysis tactics to determine the strength of a trend, and see if corresponding stocks linked to that market are worth switching or allocating funds toward. In Figure 1.27, we see soybeans making a seasonal harvest bottom at the end of November.

Another advantage futures have is that you can trade signals to diversify in other investments. Anticipating that the market may establish a seasonal bottom, you may want to explore stocks directly linked to the agriculture industry, instead of being exposed to potential risks due to what might appear to be an overleveraged investment vehicle, such as a futures contract. After all, every penny in soybean futures was $50 at the time that I was preparing this book, and the minimum margin requirement was $1,148. That means that on a small 20 cent move, you could lose nearly 95 percent of the initial investment per contract.

There are other considerations you could use, such as an options strategy, to effectively reduce risk exposure, such as going long a futures contract and buying a put option for protection; but in this strategy, you need to time the right option expiration. An alternative strategy would be going long a related market, such as stock in Monsanto shown in Figure 1.28.

Notice that this stock exploded in early November. The best part here is that there were seasonal factors to support a buy signal; and the technical picture shows what I call a "high close doji trigger," which we will disclose in this book. In fact, this is a great example to demonstrate why using a like or related market analysis approach can help you achieve better results in your trading. Cycle and seasonal studies can really help you in selecting stocks. The futures markets can certainly aid in that analytical process. Not only do commodities move in cycles, but the economy and businesses do as well.

There is one man who sticks out above the rest as the premier expert in the field of intermarket relationships—John J. Murphy. He has written

FIGURE 1.27
RealTick graphics used with permission of Townsend Analytics, LTD.

FIGURE 1.28
RealTick graphics used with permission of Townsend Analytics, LTD.

Daily (Right) ADM - ARCHER DANIELS MIDLAND CO Bar

Harvest lows

Hammer

FIGURE 1.29
RealTick graphics used with permission of Townsend Analytics, LTD.

many books on the subject; the latest, titled *Intermarket Analysis: Profiting from Global Market Relationships*, will really help you in your educational journey.

  Let's look at two more agriculture related stocks: One in Figure 1.29 is Archer Daniels Midland, which as you can see did rise but not significantly; however, it did rise in tandem with the soybean market. The other stock is Bunge Limited, shown in Figure 1.30, which mirrored the chart pattern in Figure 1.29 and moved higher at almost exactly the same time that the bottom in the soybean futures was formed.

Tandem Trading Techniques

Intermarket relationships have existed for years. It is very easy to track and look for trade setups in futures from a historical perspective, but timing a trade can be difficult due to the magnitude of the leverage as previously discussed. Don't get me wrong; futures are a very viable investment vehicle. I have made a very lucrative living trading commodities for the past 26 years. I just want you to learn that you can use futures to help make diver-

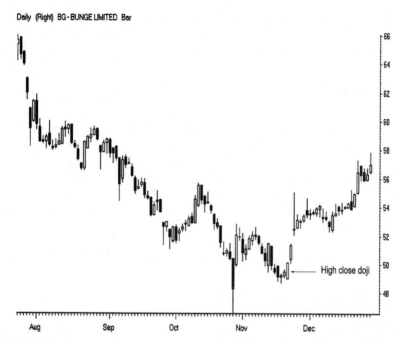

FIGURE 1.30
RealTick graphics used with permission of Townsend Analytics, LTD.

sified investment decisions on a broader scale. The key to making money in the markets is managing risk . . . end of story. Knowing the right strategy and having exposure to other markets and strategies can help you achieve your financial goals. Using similar or like markets or those that trade in tandem, especially markets that have strong relationships, traders can develop trading techniques or strategies by using signals based on one market and applying them to another, such as commodities and stocks or an ETF. Keep in mind that not all relationships work all the time. Look at past market relationships, such as the dollar and gold: Generally when the dollar goes up, gold goes down; but that certainly was not the case in 2005. How about when the Fed raises interest rates? Generally, long-term bond yields rise as well; but that did not occur in 2005 either. In fact, commodities and bond yields usually trend together; and that did not occur in 2005. Federal Reserve chairman Alan Greenspan called the decline in long-term yields a "conundrum."

As we saw commodity prices rise, we saw the Federal Reserve raise rates at a "moderate" pace, acting at 16 consecutive meetings to adjust the Fed funds rate by 0.25 percent each time. This was in response to the perception that inflation was rearing its ugly head. (As of the printing of this book, the Fed was still in rate-hiking mode!) Due to higher energy costs and as reflected in the Producer and Consumer Price Indexes, we had seen a pickup in inflation; and historically, many commodity prices rise besides gold and silver, such as sugar, coffee, and cotton.

The Reuters/Jefferies CRB (Commodity Research Bureau) Index, originally developed in 1957, is one of the most often cited indicators of overall commodity prices, offering investors a broad and reliable benchmark for the performance of the commodity sector. It is traded on the New York Board of Trade and started trading back in 1986. The "RJ/CRB" Index was revised in 2005 to reflect 19 commodity futures prices: aluminum, cocoa, coffee, copper, corn, cotton, crude oil, gold, heating oil, live cattle, lean hogs, natural gas, nickel, orange juice, silver, soybeans, sugar, unleaded gasoline, and wheat.

If you examine the chart of the RJ/CRB Index shown in Figure 1.31, the stratospheric rise is obvious and would indicate that inflation was or will be

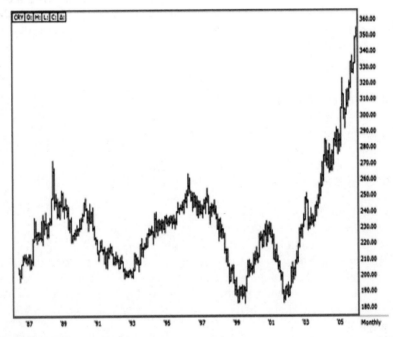

FIGURE 1.31
Used with permission of esignal.com.

trickling down to consumers. Again, price increases in commodities historically signal a rise in inflationary pressures.

Investors and traders can use stocks or ETFs to capitalize on commodity plays; but at times, it pays to diversify and have a commodity account. Not all stocks offer participation in all commodity moves, so it is wise to explore using commodity markets as an investment.

A Case in Point

A fundamental event, besides an increase in demand, that helped create a shortage of supplies in energy and other commodities in 2005 was the weather. Hurricanes Katrina, Rita, and Wilma gave a lift to sugar and orange juice futures while harming certified coffee facilities in New Orleans and, to a lesser extent, Miami. These weather-related events were pure commodity market plays. Let me walk you through one of these 2005 events: The day before Hurricane Wilma passed through Florida, my wife and I had watched the Weather Channel intensely and decided to stick around because all the news reported that the hurricane would be downgraded to a tropical depression by the time it crossed over Naples and exited on the other side of Florida, in Palm Beach. The day before, we had played golf; and it was a splendid day: 83 degrees or so, a light breeze, and not a cloud in the sky. We were planning to leave for Chicago the following Sunday, and we could have easily changed our tickets and left early. Well, at 6 A.M. on October 24, we woke up and discovered that Wilma had gained strength and merged with another storm, named Alpha; and Wilma had turned into a low-grade Category 3 hurricane! All I could think of at the moment my wife turned the TV on was, "I better make some coffee because we are going to lose power." By the time the coffee had finished brewing, click, all the lights went out.

However, we were prepared: The cars had gas, the shutters were up, and we had a generator; so life was not so bad for that week. The morning of the hurricane, CNBC had called to see if I was in Florida and asked me what I thought would happen to the orange juice crop. I did a live interview via my cell phone, reporting on the weather conditions and what might happen to the orange crop. I stated that "we could see at least a 10 percent price gain from the 1.11 level to possibly as high as 1.25, as the storm would pass through sections of Indian River County." It was also that storm that devastated the soon-to-be-harvested sugar cane crop. As it turns out, that was a solid prediction and exactly what played out in the markets. If you had a commodity account, you may have taken up that opportunity in orange juice. In fact, orange juice eventually moved as high as 164 by May 11, 2006.

FUNDAMENTAL EVENTS INFLUENCE PRICE DIRECTION

There is an old saying, "Think like a fundamentalist, but trade like a technician"—a great line that applies when trading commodities or any market for that matter. Here is how that line applies to the hurricane situation. The orange juice crop was slightly damaged; there was a reduction in supplies in the southern growing region in Florida. Prior to the hurricane, prices moved higher in anticipation of a loss of inventory; what was unknown was how much higher. The market traded higher after what appeared to be a significant damaging hurricane.

Fundamentally, the market was vulnerable for any further price shocks. Then, as we approached the traditional seasonal frost scare period in mid-January through February, the market would be more vulnerable to increased volatility. In fact, that was what occurred in 2006, as Figure 1.32

FIGURE 1.32
Used with permission of www.GenesisFT.com.

shows. The fundamental supply/demand report outlook, as shown in the U.S. Department of Agriculture's (USDA's) monthly crop report, did not reveal a major supply/demand imbalance to warrant higher prices. But a frost scare would! The anticipation that crops would suffer from frost damage propped prices sharply higher. The point is that you need to be aware of what fundamental factors influence a market. Markets do not always move when they should on facts presented, but there are circumstances that can and do make markets move! A hurricane in South Florida before harvest time is one such situation.

NOT ALL NEWS AFFECTS MARKETS EQUALLY

Hurricane-related damage in 2005 played a major role in the reduction of supplies to the sugar market more so than it did in orange juice. Also, the fundamental backdrop of the sugar market was more significant than the orange juice market because it has a dual role: Sugar is a food product, and it is used as a biofuel to make methanol. It set record price gains in 2005, especially as energy prices surged. Raw sugar prices more than doubled in 2005, climbing and making new 24-year highs. Brazil, the world's largest producer, uses most of its crop to make fuel because of the high cost of gasoline. With that information, we would expect that after Hurricanes Katrina and Rita impacting the Louisiana crops and then Hurricane Wilma making a direct hit on Florida's crop, prices would take off like a rocket! But don't forget that sugar is produced all over the world and that there are sugar beets and sugar cane. It is almost impossible to measure inventories from all growing regions of the world, and the market knew that after Hurricane Wilma hit. The fundamental event that impacted the orange juice market had a different effect there than it did on the sugar market.

As you examine Figure 1.33, notice that prices actually decline after Hurricane Wilma. It took almost one month for the market to realize that there was a significant loss in Florida's crop, and speculative money pored into the market to take advantage of higher prices. A Trend Traders technical price break signals to get long this market, and substantial profits were made. It may appear that the fundamental and technical outlooks were not in sync; and by late January/early February of 2006, traders started to sense that the market was getting slightly ahead of itself, or overbought. Traders who were long started to liquidate some positions in preparation for the USDA's monthly crop report. If you look closely at Figure 1.33, the very high of the market was formed by a candle pattern named a shooting star. (Chapter 7 focuses on how to spot reversals like this one.) The market did

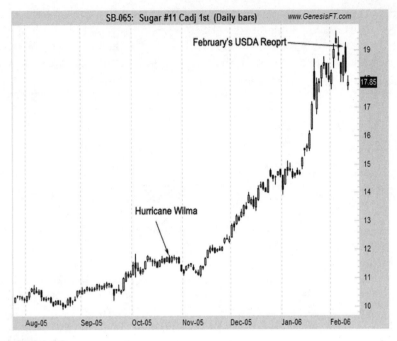

FIGURE 1.33
Used with permission of www.GenesisFT.com.

not behave according to what the fundamentals dictated. Prices rallied in a delayed effect and then continued higher on speculative buying interest.

What I want to illustrate next is how markets do *not* act according to the following:

- What fundamentals dictate.
- Common sense.
- Rational emotional intelligence.

The high was made in the sugar market on February 3 at 19.65, one week earlier than the USDA crop report. Table 1.1 shows the actual government report, the boldface type indicating that total sugar supplies increased from 11,870 to 12,026! But best of all, total usage declined from 10,523 to 10,365! Ending stocks show there are more surplus inventories. Since that report, prices have declined significantly.

Therefore, remember: *Fundamentals do not always jibe with what the charts show. Think like a fundamentalist but trade technically.*

TABLE 1.1

U.S. Sugar Supply and Demand Report 2-9-2006 (1,000 short tons, raw value)

Item	2004/2005 Previous	2004/2005 Feb 9	205/2006 Previous	2005/2006 Feb 9
Beginning stocks	1,897	1,897	1,347	1,347
Production 2/	7,877	7,877	7,593	7,593
Beet sugar	4,611	4,611	4,435	4,458
Cane sugar	3,266	3,266	3,158	3,131
Florida	1,693	1,693	1,455	1,428
Hawaii	258	258	260	260
Louisiana	1,157	1,157	1,263	1,263
Texas	158	158	180	180
Imports	2,096	2,096	2,770	3,090
Total Supply	11,870	**11,870**	11,710	**12,026**
Exports	259	259	175	175
Domestic	10,215	10,215	10,215	10,190
Food	10,046	10,046	10,050	10,050
Other	169	169	165	140
Miscellaneous	49	49	0	0
Total Use	10,523	**10,523**	10,390	**10,365**
Ending Stocks	1,347	**1,347**	1,320	**1,661**
Stocks/Use ratio	12.8	12.8	12.7	16.0

FOLLOW THE MONEY FLOW

Fundamental events are not the only factors that drive prices. We see evidence of increased participation from speculators as reflected by the increase in volume and open interest levels. Most commodity markets, besides orange juice and sugar, showed massive money inflows by hedge funds, pension funds, and individual investors in 2005 as commodities prices rose. The Reuters/Jeffries CRB Index, as shown back in Figure 1.31, is a great illustration of that fact. This trend may continue in 2006 and possibly beyond into 2008. The hurricanes in 2005 affected not only the agricultural markets described here but also the energy markets, as previously mentioned. In 2005, natural gas prices skyrocketed, and unleaded gasoline prices exploded. Many stock analysts may not have been trading commodities directly, but they certainly were watching their price movements and using that data to track their portfolios.

My point is that we have entered a time period in which our civilization and culture are entwined in a very complex financial relationship in which commodity markets play a serious role. Think about this: Ten years ago, we did not trade freely or openly as we do now with China; in fact, China now has its own exchange, the Zhengzhou Commodity Exchange. Then there are India and other parts of Asia; as their commerce and economic growth develop, so will the need for trading.

More and more investors are participating in the markets around the globe, even in Latin America. Markets have become more confusing to trade, and therefore we need to look for opportunities and to keep our defense up to be more risk averse. Using spread trading in the futures markets can help you achieve those goals; the opportunities are endless. Keep in mind the important principles of trading that depend on these elements:

- Prices reflect forces influenced by supply and demand factors.
- Prices represent the collective action of buyers and sellers who are dictating what the current price of a given product is perceived to be at a given time.

Stocks Influenced by Commodities

Now that commodities are moving and have attracted the attention of sophisticated hedge fund and commodity trading advisors, money has been flowing back to this investment industry. Investors use fundamental information such as weather conditions and apply technical analysis techniques to time entries and exits. Corporations, banks, and institutions are using the markets to hedge against losses incurred in the cash markets, for example, the airline industry, where some companies were buying energy futures contracts to lock in prices prior to the big price surge. Smart move! Higher prices in commodities such as crude oil certainly have an influence on the airline stocks. Therefore, tracking commodity prices is important for stock traders.

We will go over specific trading strategies as well as some back-testing results that will substantiate a pretty good method for trading the futures markets. This introduction was designed to show you that there is more to commodity trading than meets the eye and to show you not only how you can utilize price moves in the futures to profit from a futures contract but also how you can apply that knowledge in other areas of investing. In fact, stock traders can greatly benefit from information unique to the commodity markets. One such bit of information is released by the Commodity Futures Trading Commission (CFTC) and is known as the *Commitment of Traders* (COT) *Report*. It is referred to as legal "insider trading" information, which is covered in the next few pages; so read on!

FOREX, THE CURRENCY CASH MACHINE

Foreign exchange currency trading, otherwise known as the *forex* market, offers an investment asset class that is completely different from stocks of futures and offers leverage and virtually unrestricted access 24 hours a day. Forex trades virtually around the clock, from when the Asian market opens on Sunday night until the U.S. markets close on Friday afternoon. One of the attractions from an individual trader's perspective is that there is this constant access to make a trade.

Forex is the simultaneous buying of one currency and selling of another. In other words, currencies are always traded in pairs; in every transaction, a trader is long one currency and short the other. A position is expressed in terms of the first currency in the pair. For example, if you have purchased euro and sold U.S. dollars, it would be stated as a euro/dollar pair.

The foreign exchange market (forex, or FX) is the largest and most liquid financial market in the world, with a volume of over $1.5 trillion daily— more than three times the aggregate amount of the U.S. Equity and Treasury markets combined. This means that a trader can enter or exit the market at will in almost any market condition with minimal execution risk. The forex market is so vast and has so many participants that no single entity, not even a central bank, can control the market price for an extended period of time. Unlike other financial markets, the forex market has no physical location, no central exchange. It operates through an electronic network of banks, corporations, and individuals trading one currency for another. The lack of a physical exchange enables the forex market to operate on a 24-hour basis, spanning from one zone to another, across the major financial centers.

Margin and Leverage

The forex market allows traders to control massive amounts of leverage with minimal margin requirements; some firms offer as much as 100-to-1 leverage. For example, traders can control a $100,000 position with $1,000, or 1 percent. Obviously, leverage can be a powerful tool for currency traders. While it does contribute to the risk of a given position, leverage is necessary in the forex market because the average daily move of a major currency is about 1 percent, while a stock typically sees much more substantial moves.

Leverage can be seen as a free short-term credit allowance, just as it is in the futures markets, allowing traders to purchase an amount of currency exceeding that of their account balance. As a result, traders are exposed to an increased level of both risk and opportunity. Due to the nature of the leverage in the forex markets, positions are normally short-lived. For this reason, entry and exit points are crucial for success and must be based on various technical analysis tools. While fundamental analysis focuses on what *should* happen, technical analysis is based on what *has* or *is happening* at the current time.

Identifying the overall trend, whether it is short-term or long-term, is the most fundamental element of trading with technical analysis. A weekly or monthly chart should be used to identify a longer-term trend, while a daily or intraday chart must be used for examining the shorter-term trend. After determining the direction of the market, it is important to identify the time horizon of potential trades and to apply those strategies to the appropriate trend. Therefore, the techniques covered in this book are highly effective in trading the forex markets.

Technical analysis is the study of historical prices in an attempt to predict future price movements. There are two basic components on which technical analysis is based: prices and volume. By having the proper understanding of how these two components exploit the impact of supply and demand in the marketplace, with a stronger understanding of how indicators work, especially when combining candle charts and pivot analysis, you will soon discover a powerful trading method to incorporate in the forex market.

Long or Short

One of the advantages that the forex market has over equity markets is that there is no uptick rule, as exists in the stock market, if one wants to take advantage of a price decline. Short selling in forex is similar to that in the futures market. By definition, when a trader goes short, he is selling a currency with the expectation that the price will drop, allowing for a profitable offset. If the market moves against the trader's position, he will be forced to buy back the contract at a higher price. The result is a loss on the trade. There is no limit to how high a currency can go, giving short sellers an unlimited loss scenario. Theoretically, a short seller is exposed to more risk than a trader with a long position; however, through the use of stop-loss orders, traders can mitigate their risk regardless of long or short positions. It is imperative that traders are well-disciplined and execute previously planned trades, as opposed to spontaneous trading based on a "feeling that the price will decline."

Benefits for Selling Short

There are obvious benefits to short selling. This aspect of the forex market allows traders to profit from declining markets. The ease of selling contracts before buying them first is in contrast to typical stock trading. Market prices have a tendency to drop faster than they rise, giving short sellers an opportunity to capitalize on this phenomenon. Similarly, prices will often rally gradually with increasing volume. As prices trend toward a peak, trading volume will typically taper off. This is a signal that many short sellers look for to initiate a trade. When a reversal does occur, there will typically be more momentum than there was with the corresponding up move. Volume will increase throughout the sell-off until the prices reach a point at which sellers begin to back off.

Famous Short Plays

There have been quite a few milestone memories from famous currency trades, with both short positions and long. For example, famed financier George Soros "broke" the Bank of England by winning an estimated $10 billion bet that the British pound would lose value! How about Daimler Chrysler, the parent company of Chrysler and Mercedes Benz—reportedly it made more money in the forex markets than it did selling cars! On the negative side, in early 2005, Warren Buffett announced the U.S. dollar was in trouble and stated he was heavily short the U.S. currency. That did not turn out well for him, as the dollar rallied for the most part during all of 2005. What turned the market around? There were many issues—mainly political, geopolitical, and economic developments—that influenced the dollar's value. For starters, many U.S.–based multi-conflomerate corporations were prompted to bring money back into the United States due to the Homeland Investment Act (HIA). The HIA is part of 2004 American Jobs Creation Act and was intended to encourage U.S.–based companies to bring money back home.

The window of opportunity afforded by the HIA prompted companies to increase the pace at which funds are repatriated to the United States. Since companies had only until the end of 2005, many analysts suspected that companies would rush to repatriate foreign profits by year's end and that there would be a high dollar demand to convert foreign currencies. Don't forget, during the middle of 2005, there were riots in France. That contributed to poor market sentiment toward the euro zone, thus giving ground for a flight to safety, and helped foreign investors switch to buying U.S. dollars. The tone was essentially dollar-positive and euro-negative, which is indicative of politics having a negative effect on the euro. Meanwhile, the broader market was also most likely influenced by the high-profile move by Berkshire Hathaway, Inc.'s, Warren Buffett to cut back speculative positions against the U.S. dollar after losing big on it due to surprising dollar strength.

Mr. Buffett had bet that the dollar would continue losing ground, as it did in 2004, as he felt the massive U.S. current-account deficit would be dollar negative. But instead, monetary policy dictated otherwise as the Federal Reserve continued to raise interest rates. That was helping to drive demand as the interest rate differentials widened. In its third-quarter report in 2005, Berkshire Hathaway said it had cut its foreign-currency exposure to $16.5 billion, down from $21.5 billion in June 2005.

As you can see from the dollar Index weekly chart in Figure 1.34, on a year-to-year basis, the dollar did make an outstanding run. However, keep in mind that the dollar was at a high of 120.80 back in 2002; so depending on where Buffett was shorting the dollar, he could still be in a lucrative position. The focus of this story is how shifts in monetary and fiscal policies can and do dictate price swings in the market, as happened in 2005.

Forex trading is considered the juggernaut in the investment world, with more than 3.5 trillion in currency trading taking place per day, according to the Bank for International Settlements. There is more daily volume in the forex market than in all of the U.S. stock markets combined. There is no doubt that that is one reason why foreign currency has become so popular. Other reasons why forex attracts so many individual investors

FIGURE 1.34
Used with permission of esignal.com.

are that the market has liquidity and favorable trading applications, such as the ability to go long or short a position, and that it trends and trades well, based off technical analysis studies.

In the past, currency trading was accessible for speculators through the futures industry when the central marketplace in the banking arena was for the privileged few. This has all changed now, and the competition is fierce. The industry has expanded from what was an exclusive club of proprietary traders and banks to a location where any and all individual traders who want to participate have access in this 24-hour market from their home or office computers or laptops.

The forex markets offer traders free commissions, no exchange fees, on-line access, and plenty of liquidity. Unlike the futures products, the markets are standardized contract values, meaning a full-size position is 100,000 value across the board. The one main element that attracted investors is the commission-free trading. Plus, most forex firms require less capital to initiate a start-up account than a futures account does. In fact, investors can open accounts on their debit and/or credit cards, and the practice of accepting payments online through PayPal exists.

Some firms offer smaller-size flexi accounts, allowing traders to start applying their skills at technical analysis with as little as $500 and trading ultraminiaccounts with leverage. This feature of what is known as miniaccounts allows individual investors to adjust their positions by not having too big a contract value per position; they can add or scale into greater or lesser positions to adjust the level of leverage according to their account size. Smaller-size investors are not excluded from trading; they can participate with minicontracts. What is great about this feature is that a new trader or an experienced trader who is testing a new system can trade the market with real money, rather than simply paper trading, and benefit from the actual experience of working out execution issues and, more important, of seeing how they handle the mental or emotional side of trading. Having real money on the line certainly helps teach people to learn about their emotional makeup. This is one great way to overcome the fear-and-greed syndrome that many traders seem to battle. Another excellent quality that forex miniaccounts have is that traders with low-equity accounts can afford to trade multiple positions without being exposed to excessive risks like full-sized positions for scaling out of positions in order to let a portion of the position ride a profitable position, while capturing profits on a partial exit. We will go over more on that style of trading later.

What Benefits Do Forex Firms Offer?

Besides offering leverage accounts, other benefits that most forex companies offer are free real-time news, charts, and quotes with state-of-the-art order-entry platforms; and some even have automated order-entry features such as one cancels the other and trailing stops. All of these tools and order-entry platforms come at no additional charge to the trader.

These features may sound too good to be true. With all the benefits that the forex market offers, most newcomers want to know what the catch is. There are some slight cost factors that relate to execution; you pay a premium or a higher spread to buy and a higher spread to sell. Also, most forex companies take the other side of your trade; you do not have direct access to the interbank market, as it is called. Since the forex market is decentralized, it is possible that five different companies are showing five different prices all at the same time within a few points (PIPs—percentage in points). Since most forex traders are short-term in nature, meaning they are quick in-and-out players, day trading in the forex markets is beneficial for these traders due to the fact that there are no commissions; but the PIP spreads can and do add up. There lies the catch.

Buy and Sell the Spread

Forex prices, or quotes, include a "bid" and an "ask" similar to other financial products. The *bid* is the price at which a dealer is willing to buy and a trader can sell a currency; and the *ask* is the price at which a dealer is willing to sell and a trader can buy a currency. In forex trading, unlike futures or equities, you have to pay a percentage in price (PIP) spread on entering a trade. The *PIP spread* is the point difference between the bid and the asking price of the spot currency price. This can vary between two and four PIPs on a euro versus U.S. dollar spread. The spread varies on other currency pairs and is usually wider on more exotic cross markets, such as the Canadian dollar versus the Swiss franc.

If you want to hold a position for several days, a rollover process is necessary. In the spot forex market, all trades must be settled within two business days at the close of business at 5 P.M. (EST). The only fee involved here is the interest payment on the position of currency held. At times, depending on the position, a trader can receive an interest payment as well. This is where the term *tomorrow/next* (Tom/Next) applies. It refers to the simultaneous buying and selling of a currency for delivery the following day.

As with futures, forex markets are now regulated to an extent and come under the scrutiny of the self-imposed regulators, such as the National Futures Association after the CFTC Modernization Act passed in 2002; but since there is no centralized marketplace, many forex dealers can and do make their own markets, as discussed earlier.

Why Trade Spot Forex Markets?

Of all financial instruments traded, forex is believed by many professional traders and analysts to be one of the best-suited markets to trade based off technical analysis methods, for a number of reasons. First is its sheer size in trading volume: According to the Bank for International Settlements, average daily turnover in traditional foreign exchange markets amounted to $1.9 trillion in the cash exchange market and another $1.2 trillion per day in the over-the-counter (OTC) foreign exchange and interest rate derivatives market as of April 2005. Second, the rate of growth and the number of market participants in forex trading have grown some 2,000 percent over the past three decades, rising from barely $1 billion per day in 1974 to an estimated $2 trillion by 2005. Third, since the market does not have an official closing time, there is never a backlog or "pool" of client orders parked overnight that may cause a severe reaction to news stories hitting the market at the U.S. Bank opening. This generally reduces the chance for price gaps. Currencies tend to experience longer-lasting trending market conditions than other markets. These trends can last for months or even years, as most central banks do not switch interest rate policies every other day. This makes them ideal markets for trend trading and even breakout systems traders. This might explain why chart pattern analysis works so well in forex trading. With such widespread groups playing the game around the world, crowd behavior plays a large part in currency moves; and it is this crowd behavior that is the foundation for the myriad of technical analysis tools and techniques.

Due in part to its size, forex is less volatile than other markets. Lower volatility equals lower risk. For example, the S&P 500 Index trading range is between 4 percent and 5 percent daily, while the daily volatility range in the euro is around 1 percent.

Trading veterans know that markets are interdependent, with some markets more heavily influenced by certain markets than others. We covered some of these relationships looking at futures and certain stocks and how changes in interest rates can move equity markets as well as the currencies markets. We will learn in coming chapters how to detect hidden yet repeating patterns that occur between these related markets and how forex traders can profit from these patterns.

Which Is Bigger—Stocks or Forex?

Forex is by far the largest market in dollar volume, is less volatile, experiences longer and more accentuated price trends, and does not have trading commissions. Forex is the ideal market for the experienced trader who has paid his or her "trading tuition" in other markets. However, there are no free lunches. Traders must use all the trading tools at their disposal. The better these fundamental and technical tools, the greater is their chance for trading success. While intermarket and other relationships are often complex and difficult to apply effectively, with a little high-tech help, traders and investors can enjoy the benefits of using them without having to scrap their existing trading methods.

Forex versus Futures

The futures market through the International Monetary Market (IMM) of the Chicago Mercantile Exchange has many benefits as well. Some believe there are tighter spreads between the bid and the asking price, plus there is no interest charge or rollover fee every other day. In addition, the futures markets offer options for longer-term traders. There are transactions costs that apply per round turn; but if the brokerage commission exchange, regulatory, and transaction charges are less than the PIP spread in forex, an active speculator would be given a better cost advantage by using the futures markets instead of the forex spot markets.

Let's compare a trade in forex to a trade with a similar-size contract value on the futures exchange, using the example of a euro futures contract on the CME, where it has a contract size of USD 125,000 worth of euros, where each PIP would be 12.50 in value. If the commissions and related fees are on a par with most discount brokerage firms, $20 is your transaction cost per round turn, that is, $10 to buy and $10 to sell out the position. Keep in mind that the contract value is 25 percent higher than a full-size forex position, too. If a day trader in forex does a $100,000 full-lot-size contract and pays three PIPS on every transaction for both the entry and the exit of each position, this trader would be charged $30 per round-turn transaction.

The futures arena also has other interesting features and products; one is the U.S. dollar Index® contract traded on the New York Board of Trade, as was shown in Figure 1.34. That index is computed using a trade-weighted geometric average of six currencies. It virtually trades around the clock—the trading hours are from 7 P.M. to 10 P.M., then from 3 A.M. to 8:05 A.M., and then from 8:05 A.M. to 3 P.M. Unlike the forex, there are daily limits on the price movement with 200 ticks above and below the prior day's settlement, except during the last 30 minutes of any trading session, when no limit applies. Should the price reach the limit and remain within 100 ticks of the limit for 15 minutes, then new limits will be established 200 ticks above and below the previous price limit. Figure 1.35 shows a breakdown of the various currencies and their respective weights on the average. The top four include the euro, which is the heaviest weight at 57.6 percent,

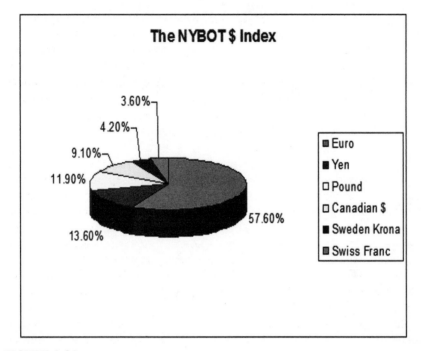

FIGURE 1.35

followed by the Japanese yen at 13.6 percent, then the British pound at 11.90 percent, and the Canadian dollar at 9.10 percent.

FOREX TRADERS BENEFIT FROM FUTURES MARKETS INFO

Forex traders can integrate futures data to help in trading decisions, such as taking a trading signal based on chart patterns in the futures and translating it into a trading trigger signal in a forex market. Because spot FX and futures trade in tandem, the price difference is called the *basis*. Generally, day-to-day, they are geometrically equal (within a few PIPs). Since, as we discussed, forex markets are decentralized, there is not a collective database to measure two distinct studies, such as volume and open interest. These are important tools, so let's review what the basics are and how a forex trader can use this futures information.

Volume is the number of trades for the total contract months of a given future's contract, both long and short combined. For example, the futures foreign currency markets trade on quarterly expirations—the March, June, September, and December contract months. The volume will represent the total for all the trades in each contract month. Most technical analysts believe that volume is an indicator of the strength of a market trend. It is also a relative measure of the dominant behavior of the market. A further explanation is that volume is the measurement of the market's *acceptance* or *rejection* of price at a specific level and time. There are several theories and so-called rules when using volume analysis on price charts: First, if a market is increasing in price and the volume is increasing, the market is said to be in a *bullish* mode and can indicate further price increases. Second, the exact opposite is true for a declining market. If price is declining and volume increases, it is said to be in a *bearish* mode and indicates further price decreases. However, if a substantial daily market price increase or decrease occurs after a long steady uptrend or downtrend, especially on unusually high daily volume, the move is considered to be a "blow-off-top or bottom exhaustion" and can signal a market turning point or a trend reversal. Here are some guidelines to use when using volume analysis.

- *Increasing volume in a rising price environment* signals excessive buying pressure and could lead to substantial advances.
- *Increasing volume while prices are falling* may signal a bear move.
- *Decreasing volume while prices are climbing* may indicate a plateau and can be used to predict a reversal.
- *Decreasing volume with a weaker price environment* shows that fresh sellers are reluctant to enter the market and could be a sign of a future downtrend.
- *Excessive volume while prices are high* indicates that traders are selling into strength and often creates a price ceiling.
- *Excessively low volume while prices are low* indicates that traders are buying on weakness and often creates a floor.

Open interest reveals the total amount of open positions that are outstanding in existence and not offset or delivered upon. Remember that in futures trading, this is a zero-sum game so that for every long there is a short or for every buyer there is a seller. The open interest figure represents the longs or shorts but not the total of both. So when examining open interest, the theory or general guidelines are that when prices rise and open interest increases, this reveals that more new longs have entered the market and more new money is flowing into the market. This reflects why the price increases. Of course, the exact opposite is true on a declining market. Chartists combine both the price movement and the data from volume and open interest to evaluate the "condition" of the market. If there is a price increase on strong volume and open interest increases, then this is a signal that there could be a continued trend advance. Of course, the opposite is true for a bear market when prices decline. Also, if prices increase, volume stays relatively flat or little changed, and open interest declines, then the market condition is weakening. This is considered to be a bearish situation because if open interest is declining and prices are rising, then this shows that shorts are covering by buying back their positions, rather than new longs entering the market. That would give a trader a clue that there is a potential trend reversal coming.

Here is a guide as to how to use this information to identify an opportunity when there is a major top or bottom in the spot forex markets: When observing a continued *long-term* trend in a spot forex currency, if it trades as a futures contract (whether it is in an uptrend or a downtrend), when prices start to fluctuate with wider than normal daily price swings, or ranges, or are in an extremely volatile condition, if it is combined with unusually strong volume and a decline in open interest, this is referred to as a *climaxing market condition*. The market is getting ready to turn or reverse the trend.

In Figure 1.36, the graph is a split chart of the futures euro currency on top with the volume and open interest study in the middle. The spot forex euro currency is on the bottom. Notice that after the peak in prices, the vol-

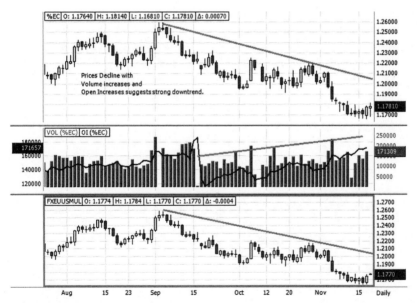

FIGURE 1.36
Used with permission of esignal.com.

ume was increasing, as was the open interest. This was a warning that a trend reversal was forming, rather than a small correction. Therefore, spot forex traders would have a better decision-making process, that selling rallies and looking to take sell signals at resistance would be a more fruitful and profitable course of action.

INSIDER TRADING INFORMATION

There is one more source of information that stock and spot forex currency traders can borrow from the futures industry. It is the Weekly Commodity Futures Trading Commission's Commitment of Traders (COT) report. The CFTC market surveillance staff closely monitors trading activity in the futures markets in order to detect and prevent instances of potential price manipulation. Some consider this "insider trading" information because every week we get to take a look at which investor group is taking which side of a trade. (There are many studies and books written on the subject. In fact, it was covered in my first book on pages 162–165.)

As a futures trader for over 26 years, I have used this information to capture many significant moves in the markets. Figure 1.37 shows that

```
EURO FX - CHICAGO MERCANTILE EXCHANGE                        Code-099741
FUTURES ONLY POSITIONS AS OF 09/20/05                   |
-------------------------------------------------------------| NONREPORTABLE
      NON-COMMERCIAL      |   COMMERCIAL   |    TOTAL    |  POSITIONS
--------------------------|----------------|-------------|------------------
 LONG  | SHORT  |SPREADS |  LONG  | SHORT  |  LONG | SHORT |  LONG  | SHORT
--------------------------------------------------------------------------
(CONTRACTS OF 125,000 EUROS)                    OPEN INTEREST:     118,666
COMMITMENTS
 29,052  30,480     832  52,941  47,456  82,825  78,768  35,841   39,898

CHANGES FROM 09/13/05 (CHANGE IN OPEN INTEREST:   -44,077)
   -269   8,744    -762 -35,756 -54,177 -36,787 -46,195  -7,290    2,118

PERCENT OF OPEN INTEREST FOR EACH CATEGORY OF TRADERS
   24.5    25.7     0.7    44.6    40.0    69.8    66.4    30.2     33.6

NUMBER OF TRADERS IN EACH CATEGORY (TOTAL TRADERS:     95)
     32      29      11      25      20      62      55
```

FIGURE 1.37

there are several categories. The first is the "non-commercial"—all large professional traders or entities, such as a hedge fund, a commodity trading advisor, commodity pool operators, and locals on and off the exchange floors. Any trading entity that hits a reportable position limit (for instance, in the CME currencies, at the end of 2005, the limit was 400 contracts) is reported by the clearing firm to the exchange, which then turns the information over to the CFTC.

The next category is the "commercials"—banks and institutions or multinational conglomerate corporations looking to hedge a cash position. The long and short open interest shown as "nonreportable positions" are derived by subtracting total long and short "reportable positions" from the total open interest. Accordingly, for nonreportable positions, the number of traders involved and the commercial/non-commercial classification of each trader is unknown. This balance of positions is assumed to be the small speculators. If you look at the first column under non-commercials, you will see the breakdown of long positions versus short positions. The next line down shows the changes from the prior week; this is important information because you will be able to see if these guys unloaded some of their positions or added to them from one week to the next. The line under that tells you the percent of longs and shorts that are held. The last line shows how many traders there are that control longs or shorts. The information is gathered as of the close of business every Tuesday by each of the clearing brokerage firms and is turned over to exchange officials, who then report the information to the regulatory body know as the CFTC. This information is released on Friday afternoons at 3:30 P.M. (ET).

It is critical before acting on a decision based on this information to see if there was a major price swing from Tuesday's close to the time the information was released on Friday, because positions may have changed hands. For example, in Figure 1.37, if the British pound was at 1.7400 at 5 P.M. on Tuesday and the price at Friday's close was 1.7000, it will indicate a 400-point move. If the COT showed small speculators net long, I will assume that the speculators were no longer long, as not many small speculators can handle a 400-point loss.

Can traders benefit and make money from this information? The answer is that there is always a chance to make money. The key is to be able to afford to be not too heavily leveraged if the market moves further than anticipated. The COT is like an insider information report. It acts like a true consensus of who literally "owns" the market. A forex trader can use this data to determine in a long-term trend run if market participants are too heavily positioned on one side of the market. It is generally the small speculator who is lefty holding the bag. Let's face it—money moves the market, and the banks and large professional traders are a bit savvier when it comes to their business. After all, one would think a bank has a good idea of what direction interest rates are going to go once a central bank meeting occurs, right?

Suppose the small speculators are showing a nice short position of, say, at least two longs for every one short. If the non-commercials are net long and the commercials are net long, chances are that the small speculators will be wrong. I am looking for imbalances in markets that have been in a trending market condition for quite some time, and therefore I can develop a game plan and start looking for timing clues to enter trades accordingly. Keep in mind that the commercials sometimes are not right; they are not in the market to time market turns. They are hedging their risk exposure in a cash position. Therefore the non-commercials, or professional speculators, in the short term are considered the smart money.

Here are some general guidelines to follow for using the COT Report:

- If non-commercials are net long, commercials are net long, and the nonreportable positions category is net short by at least a two-to-one margin, look at buying opportunities. In other words, go with the pros.
- If non-commercials are net short, commercials are net short, and the nonreportable positions category is net long by at least a two-to-one margin, look at buying opportunities.
- If non-commercials are net long, commercials are net short, and the nonreportable positions category is neutral, meaning not heavily net long or short, look at buying opportunities and stick with the smart money speculating non-commercials.

WHAT EVENTS MOVE THE CURRENCY MARKETS?

Traders need to be aware of several key elements and events that can cause currency values to move. For one, intervention plays a role in the currencies. When the Bank of Japan felt that its export business would suffer at the hand of an overvalued yen, it would intervene and sell yen to buy U.S. dollars. Countries like Canada and Australia, which produce raw commodities, saw a rise in their currency valuations as global demand increased for their goods and as their economies improved as well.

Foreign currency markets are mainly influenced by international trade flows and investment flows, which are the same factors that influence the equity and bond markets:

- Economic and political conditions.
- Interest rates, inflation, and political instability.

These factors have a long-term impact, which makes forex attractive to trade due to the long-term trending conditions established by central bank decisions based on these factors. Forex also offers investors some diversification necessary to protect against adverse movements in the equity and bond markets. Japan is closer to changing its zero-interest rule policy; and when it does, it may attract money back to Japan and boost its currency value

STUDY THE "MACRO" ISSUES

Traders who are new to forex can take comfort in knowing that analyzing and forecasting exchange rate movement rely solely on macroeconomic factors—the "big picture" issues and concepts for which information is readily available and intuitively grasped. Once traders have an understanding of the big picture pertaining to an economic region, they can place trades in the currency market to profit from their analysis. Currency traders who are looking to capture big moves in exchange rate movement definitely should focus on three issues when attempting to assess the value of currencies:

1. *Interest Rates—The Carry-Trade Strategy.* Each foreign currency has a central bank that issues an overnight lending rate. This is a prime gauge of a currency's value. In recent history, low interest rates have resulted in the devaluation of a currency. Many analysts assume this is a function of the carry-trade strategy employed by many hedge funds. This is a trade where one buys and holds currencies in a high-yielding interest rate market, such as the United States, and sells or borrows money from a foreign country where the currency is in a low-yielding interest rate market, such as Japan. There is a significant risk exposure to this investment, which requires large capital or a highly leveraged position from an exchange rate fluctuation.

2. *Unemployment Rate.* The unemployment rate is a strong indicator of a country's economic strength. When unemployment is high, the economy may be weak and, hence, its currency may fall in value. The opposite is true as well. The question that many economists look to answer is what a specific country's full-employment capacity level is. That knowledge will give clues to the peak in productivity and economic output. That knowledge also helps determine a country's capital flows and, therefore, is good information for currency traders to follow for longer-term trend identification.

3. *Geopolitical Events.* Like all markets, the currency market is affected by what is going on in the world. Key political events around the world can have a big impact on a country's economy and on the value of its re-

spective currency. Turmoil, strikes, and terrorist attacks, as we have witnessed in the new millennium, all play havoc with and cause short-term price shocks in the currency markets. Terms such as "flight to safety," as traders move money from one country to another, cause shifts in currency values. These events need to be monitored by forex traders as well.

Forex traders use fundamental analysis as described earlier to identify trading opportunities by analyzing economic information for a longer-term perspective. Short-term traders should also understand what and when reports can cause a shift in currency markets. Knowing what time is best to trade the markets will help you nail down when a potential trade may materialize. As the pie chart in Figure 1.35 showed, the largest percentage value traded against the U.S. dollar was the euro. Therefore, that would represent the European session. The central place of foreign currency dealings is London, where the second-most-active trading volume occurs. Therefore, it is where there are likely to be large range swings in the market, granting day traders an opportunity to profit. The European session runs from 2 A.M. (ET) until 11 A.M. (ET), so a euro currency to U.S. dollar (EU/USD) or euro currency to British pound (EU/BP) or a British pound to U.S. dollar (BP/USD) would be an appropriate pair selection to trade.

The U.S. session opens at 8 A.M. (ET), which overlaps the European session; and these two sessions combined generate the bulk of trading activity. Most major U.S. economic reports are released at 8:30 A.M. (ET); and, as expected, the currency markets generally react off those reports. This offers traders the opportunity to trade off what is normally a violent price spike. Once the U.S. markets close at 5 P.M. (ET), the currency markets are available to trade; but it is not until the Asian session opens at 7 P.M. (ET) that markets will experience potential price swings. The Australian dollar (AUS) and Japanese yen (JY) would be what traders would want to focus on, and the trade opportunities there would be the USD/JY or the USD/AUS or the cross pair trading the JY/AUS. Notice that the Asian markets overlap the European session as well, so a Japanese yen versus euro currency cross (JY/EU) is a popular pair to trade. Here are the time zones a trader wants to focus on when trading spot forex markets.

- European session—2 A.M. (ET) until 11 A.M. (ET).
- U.S. session—8 A.M. (ET) until 5 P.M. (ET).
- Asian session—7 P.M. (ET) until 4 A.M. (ET).

The prime trading periods for day traders are from 12:30 A.M. (ET) until 5:30 A.M. (ET), from 7 A.M. (ET) until 12 P.M. (ET), and from 1:30 P.M. until 5

P.M. (ET). These periods are when peak volumes occur, due to the opening of the European session and economic reporting times in Europe. Then, as the U.S. market opens, you have the window of opportunity to trade off the volatility from the time when U.S. reports are released. In the afternoon of the U.S. session, volume increases as traders rush to balance their positions before the end of the day. These are the select times to trade forex markets (more information can be found at www.fxtriggers.com).

For the most part, day and swing traders use technical analysis to identify opportunities from specific chart patterns that demonstrate frequent reoccurring results. They need to trade in active time periods, trading off trend lines and moving averages, which are a form of trend line analysis that will help in certain market conditions. We will go over a set of moving averages that is different from what is normally written about and that will help identify conditional changes in the market, thereby giving forex traders a better edge. We will also incorporate and show you how to calculate support and resistance levels from mathematical-based models, such as pivot point analysis, and other means, such as Fibonacci corrections and extensions, to identify opportunities and drive trading decisions. These are the methods I will be covering in this book to help you form a trading plan based on specific rules and conditions for trading the forex markets.

CHAPTER 2

Determining Market Condition

Bullish, Bearish, or Neutral

I would say the hardest thing for any trader to do is buy high, especially after seeing a huge run in the market. Buying high is a technique that very successful professional traders use. It is also a contrarian approach. After all, if you feel that the value cannot go any higher, it probably won't, right? This market condition generally tempts traders to sell. That is absolutely the *wrong* thinking! In most bull markets, that thinking falls under the category of "picking tops without cause," "justification," and "trading based off a set of rules or technical reasons"! Do not try to anticipate what the market will do next. Simply go with what the market tells you it is currently doing. In other words, try to avoid concerning yourself with why the market is moving; focus on what is occurring. That is my definition of *staying in the now* and, most important, staying with the trend.

Forget that last week the market may have taken a nosedive or that yesterday the market rallied significantly. Concern yourself with what the market is doing now. Ask yourself where prices are in relation to the current trend. It is up to you to identify the type of trader you are (day trader, swing trader, long-term trader) and the time frame in which you trade (minutes, days, weeks, . . .).

For example, a day trader in the mini–stock index futures or the foreign exchange (forex) markets may only be working with a five-minute time frame. In that case, she could care less what the market did last week or yesterday. A day trader may also want to focus on a 60-minute trend to decide whether she should hold the position for two or more periods. A swing trader, who would hold a position for several days, may want to see what the trend is doing from a weekly time perspective or from a time interval based on the past several days. Longer-term position traders may want to view the trend over several weeks or months. Cracking the code and understanding how to interpret what the market is telling you is what this book is about and what it will hopefully teach you.

As a trader, you should recognize the immediate environment or market condition. Is it up, down, or sideways? After a trend is established, let's say a bullish trend, it should consist of higher highs and higher lows. It is usually a more fruitful situation to buy dips in that environment, as you will you get more out of the trade in price magnitude than you will in selling the rallies. In a bullish environment, buying begets buying. Higher *closing* highs more importantly bring higher highs as momentum and assigned values are justified.

WHAT DEFINES MOMENTUM?

The *close* is the assigned value for any market. The law of physics that states "a body in motion tends to stay in motion until a force or obstacle stops or changes that motion" really applies to this concept, because higher assigned values can and do usually attract more buying and even new buyers. That is what *momentum* is and why it is the key in trading. Think of what an auction is like. There is excitement. People are furiously bidding up the price of an object. It attracts more buyers. Gosh, it even attracts people to bid on items they don't even want. Then as value has peaked, the bidding dries up; and the last person with the highest bid is awarded the item (or stuck buying the high). Trading is essentially the same if you know when it's the right time or price level to enter the market and what signals to look for to exit a trade.

There are all kinds of traders, and each one uses different forms of analysis. What I teach short-term stock, forex, and futures traders is that there is immediate equal access to the four common denominators that each and every trade has to work with, without prejudice and exclusivity: (1) the open, (2) the high, (3) the low, and (4) the close. For stock traders, there is a fifth element: volume. Fugures traders who are longer term or who like to confirm the strength or the weakness of a trend should also be concerned with volume. In futures, unlike in stocks, the volume is not given to the investing public in realtime intraday. Truthfully, that is why the futures and forex markets depend on technical analysis to speed the analytical process to determine a market move on pure price action. After all, it is how we analyze, interpret, and act on the information that makes us different as traders. As for forex, we do not have a means to measure volume as discussed previously. Therefore, it is wise for a forex trader to learn how to borrow information from the futures markets.

WHAT MAKES A SUCCESSFUL TRADER?

The key elements to making money are this: Successful traders *interpret correctly* and *act swiftly*! Successful traders have the courage to act and act promptly. I often ask what are the differences between successful traders and not so successful traders are. I get all kinds of relatively good answers of why traders fail, mainly due to the fact that folks share their own bad experiences with me. The reason I give for success is very simple: Generally, a successful trader does not make a habit of consistently buying the high of a given time period and riding the loss out until it "turns around." Inversely, successful traders do not make a habit of consistently selling the low of a session and riding that loser out. Successful traders have a plan; they follow the market and go with the flow. After all, that is where the saying, "The trend is your friend," came from. So we need to determine the trend. That is where charts come in handy.

As Figure 2.1 shows, there are but three states the market is in: (1) bullish, or uptrend; (2) bearish, or downtrend; and (3) neutral, sideways, or

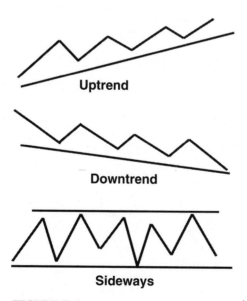

FIGURE 2.1

what is known as a consolidation phase. We can see the current trend or conditional state that the market is in. What we can't see is when and by how much that condition will change. That is one reason why many traders lose—they anticipate or guess which direction the market will go; they trade without a plan or set of rules to enter a trade. If you do believe that the markets are an effective mechanism for reflecting the perceived value on a given product at a given time, then you need to learn how to follow the flow of the market. A chart shows the market in its current condition. Until that condition changes, you need to go with the flow. So what signals should you look for when conditions change? When the market is in an uptrend, a simple signal is once the market ceases to increase its assigned value by establishing not only higher highs and higher lows but, most important, when a market stops making higher closing highs.

As for a market that is in a downtrend, when different events occur—such as lower highs, lower lows, or, more important, lower closing lows—then it is starting to change conditions. If a bearish market or a bullish market changes conditions, it will most likely go into what is called a consolidation or congestion phase. Figure 2.2 shows the market moving from an uptrend to a congestion phase, or sideways pattern. What we need to do then is, first, learn how to anticipate or discover what forecasting tool would help us determine what the potential top of that uptrend would be and, second, understand what clues to look for once it establishes the top to help signal us that the trend may resume or that a reversal of the trend will occur.

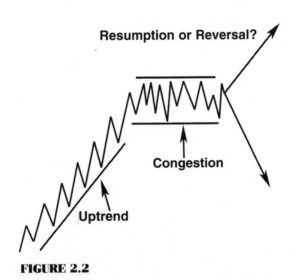

FIGURE 2.2

WHERE'S THE CATCH?

As the market starts to trade higher once, it enters a trend phase. Generally speaking, the market will pause or consolidate before resuming the uptrend. However, there lies the catch and what substantiates the Random Walk theory. Not at all times do markets resume an uptrend from the consolidation phase. False breakouts and reversals do occur. Most bullish chart patterns, such as flags, pennants, rising wedges, and ascending triangles, are just an assortment of classical technical continuation patterns that exist in trends. These work in bar charts and candle charts. The larger patterns tend to give a clue to the next move by forming in the direction of the trend; the smaller corrective patterns, such as flags and triangles, lean away from the trend. Sideways channels that form after a bullish trend have a tendency to support off a past breakout point or an old high.

Figure 2.3 shows weekly chart of Apple Computer; it had an amazing run after it went out of a period of congestion and blasted off to the upside. Notice that after the bullish price direction resumed, prices do not make

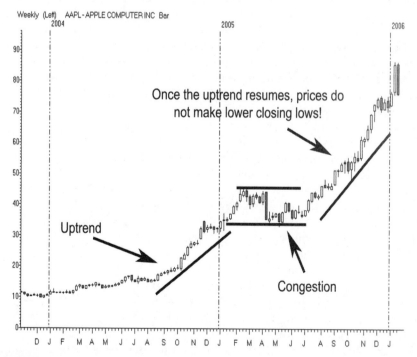

FIGURE 2.3
RealTick graphics used with permission of Townsend Analytics, LTD.

lower closing lows until the second week in December. After that, as you can see, it did move higher at the start of 2006; but the tweezer top formation (equal and opposite) contained the rally, and prices ended back where they started.

FIND THE CLUES!

From a strict chart-reading perspective, finding the clues as to when a trend is nearing completion is a matter of watching the relationship of the close of the time period for which you are trading to past highs and lows. If you study the chart in Figure 2.3, you will see the first leg or run-up in the market from September 2004 until the first lower closing low occurred in March 2005. The market never made a lower closing low during that time period. Once it did, the market entered a consolidation phase. That was the first conditional change. The sequence of higher highs, higher lows, and higher closing highs stopped; and a new conditional change occurred—the market made a lower closing low and closed below the open twice in a row. The chart in Figure 2.4 zooms in on that specific area to help highlight what occurs when a trend pauses or exhausts itself.

As traders, we are searching for information that will give us clues to an advantageous entry spot to go long, whether it is at the beginning stages of a bottom or breaking out of a congestion phase or a sideways channel. Determining the market condition, whether it is bullish, bearish, or neutral, is what will help us in our trading decisions. There are many forms of technical analysis studies to help us achieve that. The best form of trend analysis is the simple trend-line approach; you start with the lowest low point and then draw the line up until the next corrective low point. Figure 2.5 demonstrates the most common way to draw a supporting trend line. After a long hard crash in IBM, a low was made on 4/17/2005 at 71.85 (the Weekly Pivot Point S-1 targeted a low of 72.50). Drawing a line from that low and extending it out to the second reactionary low and extending forward illustrated a rising trend. As the market kept bouncing near that support line (S-1), it advanced higher. Using this form of simple analysis will help you identify the market's condition and, therefore, develop a trading plan or keep you focused to buy breaks.

As for determining a bearish or downward trend, you need to draw a line from a peak, or top, in the market, as shown in Figure 2.6. You have a series of lower highs to draw a resistance trend line. Start with the first peak, extend the line downward to the next high, and then extend the line forward. This will help you remain focused that the market is bearish, and therefore you want to focus on selling opportunities.

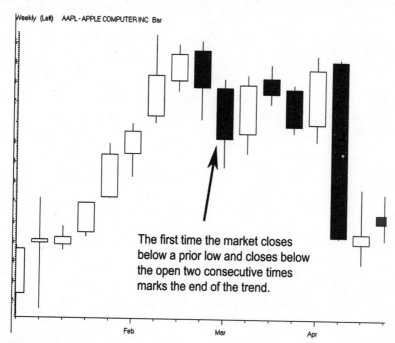

The first time the market closes below a prior low and closes below the open two consecutive times marks the end of the trend.

FIGURE 2.4
RealTick graphics used with permission of Townsend Analytics, LTD.

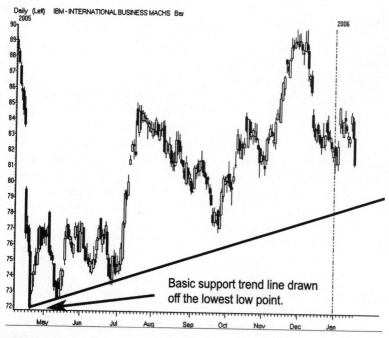

Basic support trend line drawn off the lowest low point.

FIGURE 2.5
RealTick graphics used with permission of Townsend Analytics, LTD.

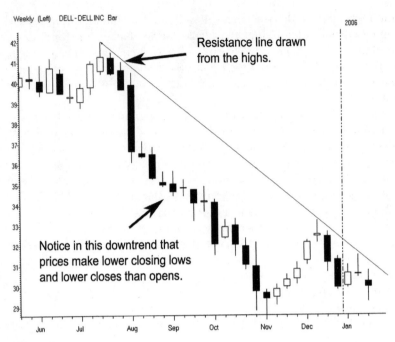

FIGURE 2.6
RealTick graphics used with permission of Townsend Analytics, LTD.

As the trend line is drawn from the top and extended down to the next high, notice that the highs are touching the newly drawn resistance line as the market pushes away from the trend line. Also notice the sequence of events that occur. It is the opposite of what we saw in a bull trend: Prices are making lower highs and lower lows and closing below the opens (as indicated by the dark candles); but more important, prices continually close below the prior time period's low. In addition, the downtrend does not end until late November, when prices reverse these negative conditions. The conditional changes that occur on the way down reverse at that time with higher highs, higher lows, higher closes than opens, and, once again, the most important feature of all, higher closes than a prior period's high.

BE ON GUARD FOR CHANGES

I must reiterate that no one, no matter what, can foresee the future. Therefore, you must be aware that changes can and do occur. You must understand what drives these changes as reflected on the chart patterns. Once you can master identifying what drives price changes or trending market conditions, then you need to learn how and when to execute a trade based on those signals. Then the next phase is to manage the risks of the trade and to learn how to exit the trade to harness the profits accrued in the trade.

I will teach you how to spot these changes and what you can do to protect yourself from giving back profits by scaling out of trades, which will be covered in Chapter 10. First, you need to be aware of the process that markets go through. Prices do go in trend mode as we have covered so far. From a technical standpoint, there are certain clues that candle charts illustrate to show you the true condition of the market. Pivot point analysis will also help guide you as to price targets, either the high or the low or both of a given session. If you have the understanding that markets can either continue the original trend or reverse it on a dime, then you will be able to filter out preconceived emotional opinions rather than "fight the tape," as it is called. You will read that the mind can, will, and does play tricks on you when you are trading. So you need to focus on what the market is showing you at the current moment.

The graph in Figure 2.7 seems a bit harsh—that a market condition

Not all consolidations resume trend!

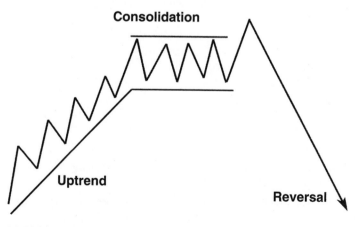

FIGURE 2.7

could be so bullish and yet completely fall apart at the seam after a consolidation period. What can and usually does happen is that a trader gets a preconceived notion that the value of a given market should continue to move in one direction. Most traders will continuously buy breaks after a consolidation period. Granted, that might be a correct notion; but it might not be the correct move, especially when proven wrong by the markets' conditional changes as highlighted by specific candle patterns.

As you can see in Figure 2.8, the 5-minute e-mini–Standard & Poor's (S&P) chart shows how a market moves from bullish (or an uptrend) to the consolidation phase to a complete trend reversal. Drawing a simple trend line would help you identify a breakdown of the support; but the one most important element that signaled a trend reversal was the fact that once the market traded below the consolidation sideways channel support—more specifically, *closed* below that level and remained below the channel support level—you had sufficient evidence to identify that the market's bullish condition had changed.

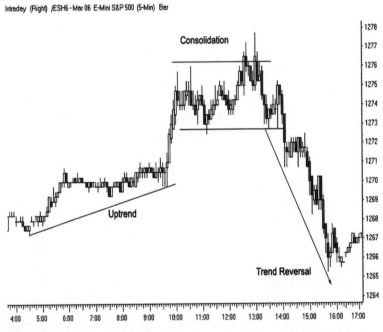

FIGURE 2.8
RealTick graphics used with permission of Townsend Analytics, LTD.

FOREX MARKETS FALL PREY TO REVERSALS

Let's examine a market that is not correlated to stocks, such as the euro currency, to see how this market phenomenon known as a trend reversal occurs. Keep in mind that the markets are a reflection of the cumulative total (or sum) of market participants' perceived value of a given product at a given time. We went over the fact of how massive the spot forex market's liquidity is; not a single entity can manipulate prices. Something or some event must drive traders' opinions of the markets. One such event is a news or economic report, which can change people's opinions on a given market's value.

As we look at the euro currency chart in Figure 2.9, we see the market develop into an uptrend, then consolidate, and then, *bang*, on the drop of a dime, drastically reverse. This is the kind of trading environment in which traders can and do make lots and lots of money. If you know what to look for and if you understand once a market goes from trend to consolidation, you should be aware that the next possible outcome might not be a trend continuation but rather a complete trend reversal. Then you have a better chance of not fighting against the current of the market, otherwise known as the *tape*.

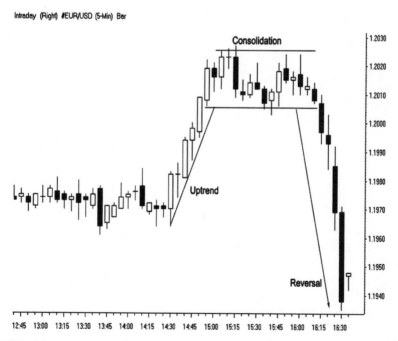

FIGURE 2.9
RealTick graphics used with permission of Townsend Analytics, LTD.

MOVING AVERAGES HELP!

The next method for identifying whether the market is bullish, bearish, or in a consolidation phase is utilizing moving averages. The most familiar one is the benchmark 200-day moving average. Most technicians and short-term traders feel this is a worthless time period, with which I agree for short- to intermediate-term trading.

Remember that the idea in using moving averages is to help determine the true direction of the market. The longer the time period used in a moving average, the less effective it is for shorter-term trading. Keep in mind that a 200-day moving average is over 28 weeks, more than half a year. The Federal Reserve raised rates four times in 2005 in that same time period. That leaves way too much time and, more important, distance between prices and the moving average to generate buy or sell signals.

When using moving averages the general guideline is simple:

- If prices are above the moving average, look to buy pullbacks or to take buy signals, as the market is in a bullish mode or in an uptrend.
- If prices are trading below the moving average, look to sell rallies or to take sell signals, as the market is bearish or in a downtrend.

Another instance in which traders use moving averages in helping their trading is determining what is called "regression to the mean." This is a term many traders hear but really do not understand. It refers to the condition when prices deviate too far from the mean or average. At that tme, prices will *regress*, or return, to the average; or the market will pause or consolidate until the average catches up to the price. You will notice what I call a "gap band" signal. This is what will occur when the prices gap too far away from the moving averages or bands and give a trader an opportunity for a countertrend trade. Another way to describe this is that when a market deviates, or departs, too far from the moving average, it gives an opportunity for a speculator to take advantage of this condition, which generally ends up with prices reaching an unsustainable extreme and then returning back toward the moving averages for a short-term price swing. The question is at what distance or price level do prices deviate, or move too far away, from the moving average before market prices return to the moving average or the market pauses in order for the moving average to catch up to the prices.

As you can see in Figure 2.10, the market trends higher; but at times we see reactions that shift values from one extreme to another. How do we use moving averages effectively? More important, which time frames and which set of conditional settings should we employ to give us a true sense or value of the market? We will cover a different concept using a pivot

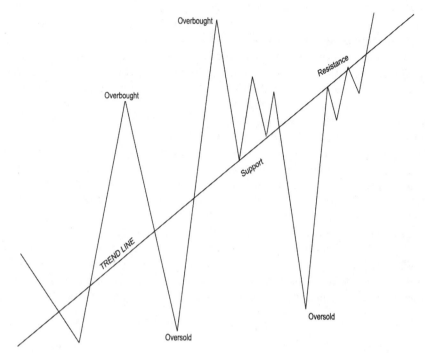

FIGURE 2.10

point method later in the book. Right now, I want to set the foundation be-hind the principle of why we use moving averages to help determine bull-ish, bearish, or neutral market conditions and how to trade these conditions. I try to figure out not why a market moved, but rather where the market is now in relation to specific points of interest, such as past opens highs, lows, and closes.

FILLING IN THE GAP

As you can see in Figure 2.10, the gaps that occur show that prices move too far too fast in one direction, which is a condition known as overbought or oversold. Those moves are unsustainable and thus form what we call overvalued or undervalued in relation to the trend line or moving average. Most market behavior as reflected by the human emotional state goes into extremes. This is even the case in trending markets: They move either too fast or too far in any one direction and then simply pause or correct back above or below the various moving averages, as you will see. The chart in

Figure 2.11 is the spot euro currency. This market has an inverse relationship with the U.S. dollar. As the dollar moved lower, the euro moved higher, and vice versa. Notice that when it separates too far away from the longer-term moving average (M/A), it would return back to test the M/A as a support line or fill the gap, as it is known. Finally, as it breaks below the M/A support in the middle of September, it declines too far too fast and returns back up to test the line, which now acts as a resistance trend line.

In conclusion, trend lines and moving averages help us determine the price direction of a given market at a given time. They can also help us discover when a market is overbought or oversold. In simple terms, when we use moving averages, the more time periods we use, the slower or less sensitive moving averages are to price changes. Prices will trade and close below a moving average in a bearish market condition, or a downtrend; and prices will trade or, more important, close above a moving average in a bullish market condition, or uptrend. Introducing more than one moving average with two different calculated values, such as 10-period and 20-period simple moving averages on a closing basis, will generate buy and sell signals as one value crosses above or below the other. We can compute and change the variables we use as well, such as closes and volatility calcula-

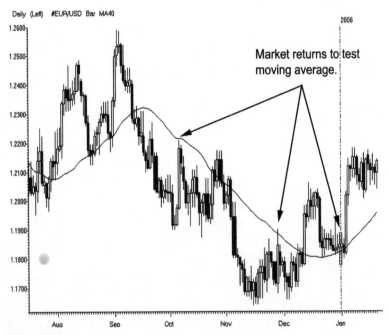

FIGURE 2.11
RealTick graphics used with permission of Townsend Analytics, LTD.

tions. Moving averages help in the development of trading strategies, as we will see in later chapters. There are also variables other than just a simple moving average based on a closing time period that you can use. I will introduce to you a pivot point moving average method in Chapter 6.

Forex, or currency, markets tend to establish longer-term trends, so moving average studies are very popular with these markets. Also, moving average systems can be back-tested; therefore, hypothetical results can be produced for those looking to explore running a hedge fund.

In the next few chapters, we will introduce the pivot point system and incorporate that as one of our moving average values. We will blend this with a series of conditions and introduce various time frames to help us determine:

- Market condition and direction.
- Overbought or oversold conditions.
- Potential turning points or reversal areas.
- A moving average system to determine buy and sell signals.

If you are looking to improve your skills as a trader, then these next few chapters will help. I hope I will inspire you to learn how to develop a predetermined game plan, to act on that plan, and to manage and maintain the profits in the trade and to learn how and when to cut the trade when the market signals to do so.

If you understand the three directions in which a market can go—up, down, or sideways—then you will have an edge on learning how to "read the tape," which should enable you to cut losses and let your winners ride.

CHAPTER 3

How to Read Oscillators to Spot Overbought or Oversold Conditions

In a bullish market environment, prices break out of a previous range and trade higher. Depending on the move, sometimes the market reaches an unsustainable extreme, which we refer to as "overbought." After all, market prices can't go up forever without a pause. The outcome varies when markets reach overbought conditions. They can, as stated, pause or consolidate, correct back down a bit, or completely reverse the entire price advance. Understanding when a market is likely to reach an overbought condition is vital to knowing when to take a profit in a long position, especially after a long uptrend, or when to profit from a countertrend trade opportunity. This is also referred to as a "mean-reverting strategy" or "trading against the trend."

We can measure or profile a market price extreme several ways: One is by looking at past price resistance levels; another is by looking at the strength or weakness of the market's move by using certain technical indicators that measure the current price, relative to previous highs and lows.

Some of my favorite tools that I use to compliment my trading method include predictive analysis based on pivot point studies, as we will see in the following chapters, with a strong emphasis on studying pure price action, as we discussed in Chapter 2, by identifying higher closing highs in an uptrend and lower closing lows in a downtrend.

I look to identify certain chart patterns or a signal that shows a shift in momentum; and then I look for a sequence of events, such as higher closing highs at predetermined support levels or lower closing lows at predetermined resistance levels determined by the aid of pivot points analysis, into which I incorporate various time frames to help me pin down reversal target levels. This method is great for short-term day trading to long-term investing. This method also works when I am looking at a swing trade, which is a trade that may last anywhere from one to three days. For longer-term trading, I use volume studies in the stock and futures markets to help me confirm the strength or weakness of a trend or to gather a clue as to when a major reversal is ready to occur. For spot foreign exchange (forex) currency trading, volume figures are available to use from the futures markets; but because those figures are not available until the end of day, they are not good day trading indicator tools. Therefore, the use of oscillators and indicators help to confirm the condition of the market once I am in a trade or about to make a trade based on an extreme price swing.

Some questions that are often asked when I am giving a seminar or a presentation at a conference are: How many indicators do you suggest using at one time? Do you get analysis paralysis from using too many? The answer is that I use two indicators: stochastics and moving average convergence/divergence (MACD).

Since trending conditions exist for less than 30 to 40 percent of the time, you can anticipate that after a nice trend directional move, the market will move in a consolidation phase, or "whipsaw" as most people call it. In choppy range-bound conditions, stochastics is your friend; in trending market conditions, MACD will give you solid signals.

The myth surrounding MACD is that one of the best indicators out there is not necessarily true. So goes the old adage that there is no holy grail for any single trading indicator or style. This is due to the fact that markets change, as do market conditions and people's perception on a product's given value or anticipated value in any given time. I believe that the stochastic indicator is a more useful tool than the MACD during certain market conditions and for determining various signals, such as divergences or convergences. They both can be used for pinpointing reversals.

It is likely that one will give a faster signal than the other, and vice versa. The one fact is that in trending markets, MACD can be your friend by helping you to stay in a trade longer, thus milking a position for more than you would imagine. This chapter will show several rules and techniques for using both of these indicators.

STOCHASTICS

Stochastics, a range-based oscillator, is also considered a momentum oscillator. George C. Lane is credited with creating the formula. I had the privilege of working for George back in 1980. His indicator is a popular technical tool used to help determine whether a market is overbought, meaning that prices have advanced too far too soon and are due for a downside correction, or oversold, meaning that prices have declined too far too soon and are due for an upside correction. Stochastics is based on a mathematical formula that is used to compare the settlement price of a specific time period to the price range of a specific number of past periods.

The method works based on the premise that in a bull, or up-trending, market, prices will tend to make higher highs and that the settlement price, or close, will usually tend to be in the upper end of that time period's trading range, or at least closer to the high. When the momentum starts to fade, the settlement prices will start to push away from the upper boundaries of the range; and the stochastics indicator will show that the bullish momentum is starting to change. The exact opposite is true for bearish, or down-trending, markets.

There are two lines that are referred to as %K and %D. These are plotted on a horizontal axis for a given time period, and the vertical axis is plotted on a scale from 0 percent to 100 percent. As you will see from the formula, %K will be the faster of the two lines and will change direction because the %D line is a moving average of %K. The unique feature of the stochastics reading is the moving average crossover feature.

Stochastics is a range-based oscillator with readings between 0 percent and 100 percent. The main guidelines reflect the thought that readings over 80 percent indicate that a market condition is overbought and ripe for a downside correction and that readings under 20 percent signal the market is oversold and ripe for a bounce. While that certainly is the case, generally speaking, I look for more clues within the indicator to trigger a trade signal.

The formula to calculate the first component for fast stochastics using a 14-period look back setting for %K is:

$$\%K = c - Ln/Hn - Ln * 100$$

where c = closing price of current period
Ln = lowest low during n period of time
Hn = highest high during n period of time
n = number of periods

The second calculation is the %D (3-period). It is the moving average of %K.

$$\%D = 100(Hn/Ln)$$

where HN = the n period sum of $(c - Ln)$

RULES TO TRADE BY

When using stochastics as a confirming tool, I see the indicator corroborate the timing of a market turn associated with a higher closing high, especially when it is in proximity of a targeted support level based off a pivot point level. These rules will help to make better trading triggers for buy and sell signals.

- When the readings are above 80 percent and %K crosses below the %D line and *both* lines close back down below the 80 percent line, then a "hook" *sell* signal is generated.
- When the readings are below 20, percent, once %K crosses above %D, and once *both* lines close back up above the 20 percent level, then a "hook" *buy* signal is generated.

The market in Figure 3.1 is a 15-minute candle chart on the Chicago Board of Trade (CBOT) mini-Dow contract. The buy signal or trigger is generated once %K and %D both cross over and back above the 20 percent line. It also confirms the first time after the downtrend that the market makes a

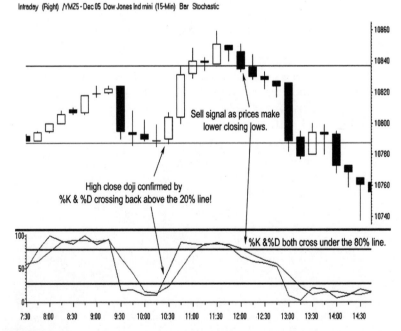

Intraday (Right) /YMZ5 - Dec 05 Dow Jones Ind mini (15-Min) Bar Stochastic

Sell signal as prices make lower closing lows.

High close doji confirmed by %K & %D crossing back above the 20% line!

%K &%D both cross under the 80% line.

FIGURE 3.1
RealTick graphics used with permission of Townsend Analytics, LTD.

higher closing high. We have not yet discussed candle patterns; but for those already familiar with that charting method, you will notice that it is a higher close above the doji high. The trigger to go long is on the close or the next open, once the market makes a higher closing high, which in Figure 3.1 would be at 10810.

When the market trades near the daily projected resistance, as determined by using pivot point analysis, once prices start to make lower closing lows, which is a clue that helps us identify that the uptrend has concluded. That is what generates a sell signal at 10838. That would be a profitable scalp of 28 points at $5 per point, which is $140 on a day trading margin of $500, which is what most futures brokerage firms charge.

STOCHASTICS CONFIRMS THE TURN

Now looking at the sell signal, we would have an opportunity to go short at 10838 as the market pivots and turns, as I say, off the resistance level as the stochastics confirms with a %K and %D hook sell signal once both lines cross and close below the 80 percent line. Follow the flow of the market after that point: lower highs, lower lows, and, more important, lower closing lows all the way down to a low of 10739. That is a 99-point decline or $495 per contract—almost a 100 percent return on your day trading margin. As the market declines, we see the stochastics crossing above and back below its respective values; but never does it cross back and close above the 20 percent line. I am asked at what level do you take profits. I will go over specific target exit levels later; but for right now, the most simplistic answer is at the last trading price near 10758. The reason is that this would have been a day trade; and as you can see from the bottom of the chart, the day is running short on time. Profit objectives can be based not only on price targets but also on time limits.

Figure 3.2 shows a pattern similar to that in Figure 3.1: a higher close above a doji high. Candle chart aficionados may see a variation of a morning doji star pattern. I keep it very simple; I call it an HCD pattern, which stands for a *high close doji*. This pattern has specific rules on entry and exits and will be disclosed in just a bit. For now, please focus your attention on the fast stochastics, as %K and %D both confirm the trigger to go long once both lines cross and close above the 20 percent line. That trigger corresponds on the close of the candle, which was 10756. As the market moves higher, follow the flow again as the momentum builds. The stochastics does not generate a sell signal, as the high was made at 10805. We see a crossover of %K and %D above the 80 percent line, but the stochastics does not close back under that line.

The 20 percent and 80 percent levels in relationship with the %K and

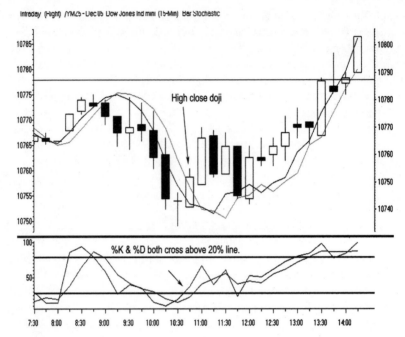

FIGURE 3.2
RealTick graphics used with permission of Townsend Analytics, LTD.

%D values will help confirm your entries and exits in the markets, especially when you follow the trend or market flow as shown by the candle charts. There is a reason why I have focused on the high close doji signal, as we shall soon discover from a back-test study on percentile perspective. But once again, this chapter is to help you better understand the confirming power that stochastics offers.

Markets need volatility in order to move, and we need markets to move in order to trade. We also need to base our trading plans on reliable signals. Not all times do the setups that trigger an entry work as perfectly as in these examples, which is why I have other confirming signals to corroborate timing a trade signal. I also like to see if the methodology works in a diverse group, or noncorrelated markets. Testing for robustness, or how well a system or signal responds in different markets, helps validate the reliability of that signal. The chart in Figure 3.3 is a spot forex euro currency that demonstrates the same setup and trigger that would enter a long position with %K and %D crossing over above the 20 percent line with a con-

FIGURE 3.3
RealTick graphics used with permission of Townsend Analytics, LTD.

firming higher closing high candle pattern. The sell signal also works well as confirmed when %K and %D both cross over and close back below the 80 percent line.

TIPS AND TRICKS TO HELP

There are other tips and tricks associated when using stochastics. There are fast stochastics and slow stochastics. The difference is in how the parameters are set to measure the change in price. This is referred to as a *gauge in sensitivity*. A higher rate of sensitivity will require the number of periods in the calculation to be decreased. This is what "fast" stochastics does. It enables one to generate a faster and a higher frequency of trading signals in a short time period. The previous two examples used the default fast stochastics settings, which help you discover the cycles of tops and bottoms faster than the slow stochastics setting will.

Stochastics Patterns

One other method in which to use the stochastics indicator is trading off a pattern called *bullish convergence*. It is used in identifying market bottoms—where the market price itself makes a lower low from a previous low, but the underlying stochastics pattern makes a higher low. This indicates that the low is a "false bottom" and can resort to a turnaround for a price reversal. Figure 3.4 shows how prices make a secondary low significantly lower from a primary low, which is posted by a low in the stochastics indicator.

The reverse of this signal is a trading pattern called *bearish divergence*. It is used in identifying market tops—where the market price itself makes a higher high from a previous high, but the underlying stochastic pattern makes a lower high. This indicates that the second high is a "weak" high and can resort to a turnaround for a lower price reversal. Figure 3.5 shows

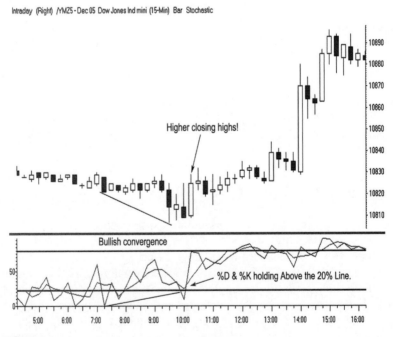

FIGURE 3.4
RealTick graphics used with permission of Townsend Analytics, LTD.

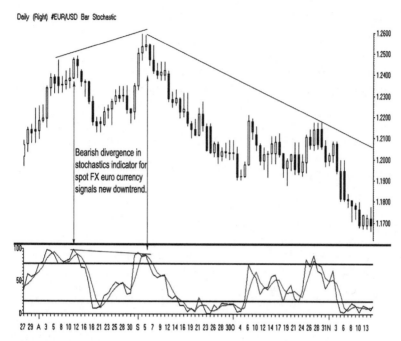

FIGURE 3.5
RealTick graphics used with permission of Townsend Analytics, LTD.

how the market makes a secondary high, but the corresponding high in the stochastics is at a lower level than the price charts' primary high point. This stochastic pattern can alert you to a false breakout. Notice the low close doji (LCD) off the secondary peak; and then as %K and %D both cross over and close back beneath the 80 percent line, a sell trigger is generated. That signal warns of an impending, prolonged downtrend of substantial proportion. Therefore, it is important to monitor for divergence patterns.

Rules to Trade By

The bearish divergence pattern signals that there is an impending price reversal ready to occur in a market. As I mentioned previously, you can anticipate and get ready to place an order to act on the signal; but you should not act until the confirmation of a lower closing low triggers the entry, which would be to act on the close or the next open. Here are four rules to guide you to trading a stochastics divergence pattern:

1. The first peak in prices should correspond with a peak in the %K and %D reading above the 80 percent level.

2. The second peak must correspond to a significant higher secondary price high point.

3. If the secondary stochastics peak is less than or under the 80 percent level, this signals a stronger sell signal.

4. Prices should make a lower closing lower to confirm a trigger to enter a short position. Enter on the close of the first lower closing low or the next open. The protective stop should initially be placed above the high of the secondary high.

Figure 3.6 demonstrates a bearish divergence setup with the rules described. This is a 15-minute candle chart on the CBOT mini-Dow. The secondary high is established at 10940. Both %K and %D make a primary high above the 80 percent line, and the secondary high in price corresponds with %K and %D below the 80 percent level. Once the long dark candle closes below the prior low (in fact, it closes below five prior candles lows), a sell signal is triggered. The initial entry is made on that time period close or on

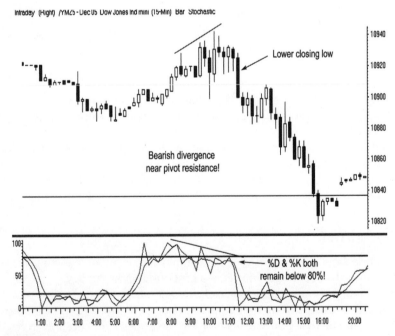

FIGURE 3.6
RealTick graphics used with permission of Townsend Analytics, LTD.

the next open, which in this case is 10897. The stop is placed at 10945, above the high of the secondary peak high. As you can see, the market continues to decline into the close down to 10836, for a 61-point gain had you exited on the close. That equates to a gain of $305 on a day trade margin of $500 per contract. Notice that as the market declines, the stochastics indicator remains below the 20 percent line as the %K and %D cross multiple times but never back above the 20 percent level to trigger a buy signal until after the electronic day session close, which is 4 P.M. (CT).

MACD

In simplest terms, *moving average convergence/divergence* is an indicator that shows when a short-term moving average crosses over a longer-term moving average. Gerald Appel developed this indicator as we know it today, and he developed it for the purpose of stock trading. It is now widely used for short-term trading signals in stocks, futures, and forex markets, as well as for swing and position traders. It is composed of using three exponential moving averages. The initial inputs for the calculations were a 9-period, a 12-period, and a 26-period. The concept behind this indicator is to calculate a value, which is the difference between the two exponential moving averages, which then compares that to the 9-period exponential moving average. What we get is a moving average crossover feature and a zero-line oscillator, and that helps us to identify overbought and oversold market conditions.

I might add that because traders are now more computer savvy than ever before and because many charting software packages such as RealTick allow traders to change or optimize the settings or parameters, it is easy to change, or "tweak," the variables in Appel's original calculations. Traders can increase the time periods in the moving average calculations to generate fewer trade signals and can shorten the time periods to generate more trade signals. Just as is the case for most indicators, the higher the time periods used, the less sensitive the indicator will be to changes in price movements. MACD signals react quickly to changes in the market— that is why a lot of analysts, including myself, use it. It helps clear the picture when moving average crossovers occur. It measures the relative strength between where current prices are as compared to past time frames from a short-term perspective to a longer-term perspective.

The MACD indicator is constructed with two lines: One is the 9-period exponential average (slow line), and the other is the difference between the 12- and 26-period exponential moving averages (fast line). In general, when the fast line crosses above the slow line, a buy signal is generated; the opposite is true for sell signals.

The MACD also has a zero baseline component, called the *histogram*, that is created by subtracting the slower signal line from the MACD line. If the MACD line is above the zero line, prices are usually trending higher. The opposite is true if the MACD is declining below the zero line. The MACD is a lagging indicator; that is, it is based off moving averages. We want to look for the zero-line crossovers to identify market changes and to help confirm trade entries or trigger action to exit a position. As you can see in the e-mini–Standard & Poor's (S&P) chart in Figure 3.7, the MACD readings cross back above the zero line, indicating a confirmed shift in momentum. That zero-line cross helped filter out the bottoming process. A long position would have been initiated at the close of the candle or at the next time period's open at 1267.25, which resulted in an immediate price gain, carrying prices up over 1270.

Clues that identify shifts in momentum as the market moves from one extreme to another or from overbought to oversold to trigger a trading opportunity can be identified with the aid of MACD readings in both the moving average and the histogram component. While profits are higher when

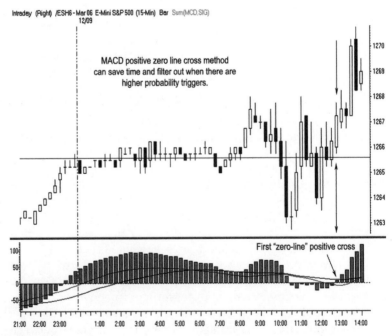

FIGURE 3.7
RealTick graphics used with permission of Townsend Analytics, LTD.

buying the absolute bottom, that is a haphazard guessing game to play. Trading based on a set of rules and using a confirming indicator to identify a change in price direction and then following that price movement are the keys to making money in the markets. Figure 3.8 shows an e-mini–S&P example; the intraday trend is established to be higher by 10 A.M., as the symmetry of higher highs and higher lows exists. The MACD confirms an HCD trigger as the histogram bar crosses above the zero line, initiating a long at 1234.75. Notice that the histogram bars continue to expand higher, confirming that the bullish momentum is accelerating. Identifying a zero-line cross is a powerful tool in confirming entries, and watching the progression of the histogram bars may help you maintain a winning position.

It is not in every single instance that we see the MACD signals work exactly the same as Figure 3.9 demonstrates. The histogram was not under the zero line; therefore, a zero-line cross did not trigger. However, observing that the histogram bars move higher as prices start to advance would certainly help confirm the strength of the uptrend.

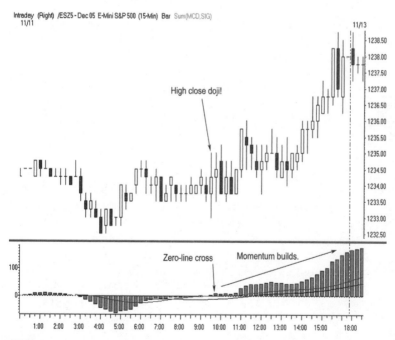

FIGURE 3.8
RealTick graphics used with permission of Townsend Analytics, LTD.

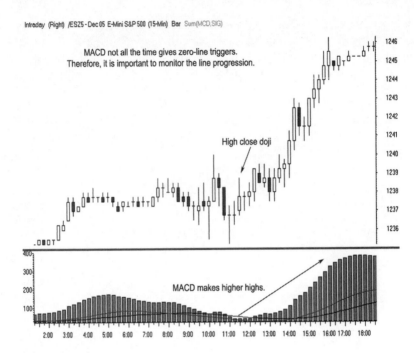

Intraday (Right) /ESZ5 - Dec 05 E-Mini S&P 500 (15-Min) Bar Sum(MCD.SIG)

MACD not all the time gives zero-line triggers.
Therefore, it is important to monitor the line progression.

High close doji

MACD makes higher highs.

FIGURE 3.9
RealTick graphics used with permission of Townsend Analytics, LTD.

RELY ON THE PATTERNS

Another method useful with the MACD indicator, and one that is more reliable for determining a trend reversal, is to identify the pattern called bullish convergence. This is where the market price itself makes a lower low from a previous low, but the underlying MACD pattern makes a higher low, as shown in Figure 3.10. This indicates that the second low is a weak, or "false," bottom and can resort in a turnaround for a sharp price reversal. This is similar to stochastics; however, since it is developed from moving averages, the timing of the shorter-term versus the longer-term moving averages can delay such a signal. There is a high probability that MACD and stochastics work more so than other indicators with this pattern.

As you can see in Figure 3.10, which is a five-minute chart on Intel, the market made a lower low in the next trading session where the MACD histogram makes a higher low. Notice the HCD signal. Then as the price starts to appreciate, the MACD histogram triggers or confirms a long position with a zero-line crossover, and the progressively higher histogram bars con-

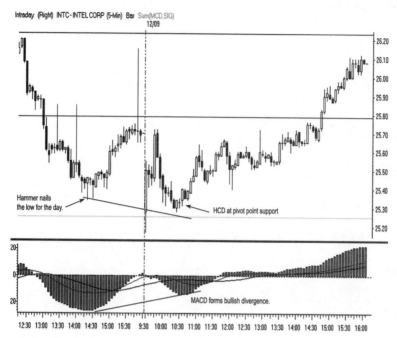

FIGURE 3.10
RealTick graphics used with permission of Townsend Analytics, LTD.

firm the positive momentum right into the close of the day. The MACD is a very useful tool as a confirming indicator once you have entered in a position, especially by following the histogram readings.

The MACD has the same principles as far as a sell signal with what is known as bearish divergence. This is where the market price itself makes a higher high from a previous high, but the underlying MACD crossover lines make a lower high. This indicates that the second high is a "weak" high and can resort to a turnaround for a lower price reversal. In Figure 3.11, a daily chart in the FX spot euro currency, the MACD histogram helps identify both bearish and bullish divergence patterns.

One other useful method in using MACD is to follow as stated the direction of the histogram bars to help *confirm* a turn or a change in trend. Figure 3.12 shows the price advance in the e-mini–S&P as the market closes in on a pivot point resistance level, and the market moves from a bullish condition as prices move higher or in an overbought state and the histogram readings start to expand over 300. As the market price conditions change, as the close is below the open, and as the market makes the first lower closing low, especially near the pivot resistance line, the histogram

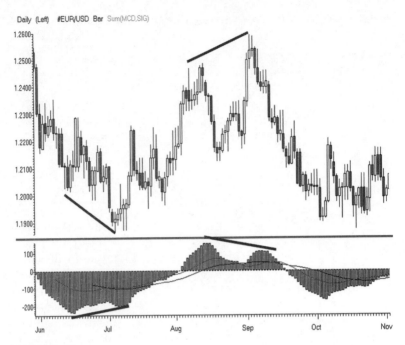

FIGURE 3.11
RealTick graphics used with permission of Townsend Analytics, LTD.

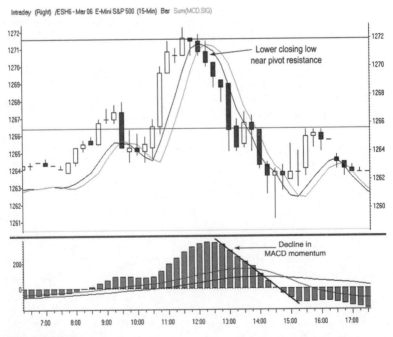

FIGURE 3.12
RealTick graphics used with permission of Townsend Analytics, LTD.

bars start rolling down or making lower highs as well. In a weak or down-trending market, the bars should also be making lower highs; and in this case, they are confirming a sell signal from the change in market condition as well as the moving average crossover as prices trade under the moving average lines. This last example is what we will be going over in later chapters as we combine pivot point analysis with candle patterns.

SUMMARY

In conclusion, all oscillators, indicators, and most moving average studies will give confirmation when a market shifts direction; and knowing these signals will help you identify a trading opportunity. They also will help give you a clue when a market is in an extreme price condition, described as being overbought and oversold. Therefore, as a trader, you need something that gives you a better idea of entering a trade. The next few chapters will reveal ways by which you will learn how to identify shifts in momentum before looking at an indicator as confirmation. Impossible, you say? Well, there are certain patterns such as the high close doji, the jackhammer candle pattern, a low close doji, or the shooting star formation that, when up against a projected pivot support or resistance line, will alert you to a trade entry faster than using these traditional indicators. When I introduce you to the concept of using a pivot point moving average component as was used in Figure 3.12, then you will see how it is possible.

CHAPTER 4

Momentum Changes

How to Spot Divergence or Convergence

The battle to identify when a trend ends or when a trend will start is one of the key elements on which traders make their bread and butter. When a market reaches an unsustainable price extreme either up or down, we want to be able to be prewarned so we can set up our trading account with the right contract sizes and preset the buy or sell order and then wait for the trigger to act. We have the traditional indicators that we went over in Chapter 3 with stochastics and MACD (moving average convergence/divergence), but there is one more measure of data we have that stock traders and longer-term futures traders have been using for over a hundred years. That one bit of data is called *volume*. The one disadvantage that foreign exchange (forex) traders have is that there is no way to measure volume data unless you "borrow" it from the futures markets, as I shared in Chapter 1.

VOLUME IS THE BEST PRICE CONFIRMATION TOOL AND TREND INDICATOR

In Chapter 1, we went over the basic rule structure for volume analysis. But how can we apply that to help confirm market price extremes? This is actually fairly simple, if you know what to look for. That is what this section is designed for. It does not matter what market you are trading, whether it be stocks, futures, or forex. The principles are the same and apply to all three markets. Remember that a good trader has a reason for entering a trade. A *great* trader waits until the signal triggers and then acts on that signal. Just because a market goes up and is "too high" in value does not mean it is going down, at least not until the signals are present. Market price extremes are generally a reflection of high volatility; and with high volatility comes increased market participation or action, and that action is measured or reflected by high volume.

OVERBOUGHT MARKET CONDITION— A DEAD GIVEAWAY

If you drop a boulder off a cliff, it falls at a speed that is much greater than the speed of the boulder being pushed up a hill. That is the analogy of what happens when a bull market or uptrend stretches too far too fast, or is "overbought." So we look for these types of conditions in which to ride the price direction if we are looking to establish a short position or we want to exit a long position before the boulder falls. Using volume analysis in conjunction with indicators is a powerful tool to help you determine whether a market price trend may continue. Look at Figure 4.1. This chart on Amazon

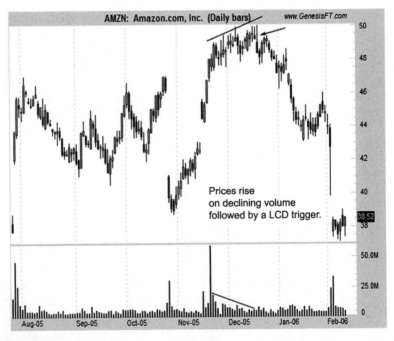

FIGURE 4.1
Used with permission of www.GenesisFT.com.

is a dead giveaway that the price appreciation was unsustainable; as we see, the market moved from a bullish trend to a consolidation phase with higher highs. However the volume levels were declining, giving a direct clue that the price advance was unsustainable. When combined with the low close doji pattern, which we will disclose in Chapter 8, and a shooting star, there was no reason to stay long this market. Notice that as prices started to depreciate, the volume increased, which reflected sellers' active participation, which attracted more selling.

THE "COMEBACK" KID STOCK

In Figure 4.2, we see one of the greatest success stories in 2005 for any company, Apple Computer. It just could do no wrong, except when the price of the stock advanced too far too fast, culminating in an overbought unsustainable price extreme. The fundamentals were quite rosy, as holiday sales were through the roof on iPods and accessories. You want to talk about a

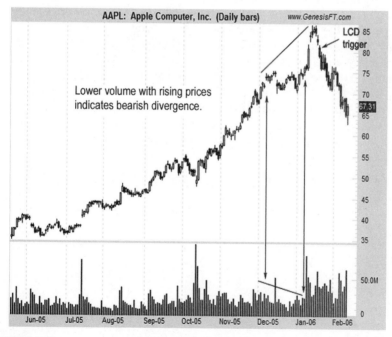

FIGURE 4.2
Used with permission of www.GenesisFT.com.

racket; this company has products on top of products that accessorize the accessories, none of which are inexpensive. What a gold mine! Holiday sales were strong, and the market blasted off. In fact, notice the gap up, then notice the gap down, leaving what we technicians call an island top. (This formation is covered in *Technical Trading Tactics* on page 75.) It also formed the low close doji pattern. It really is the volume that helped confirm the market's overbought condition. As prices broke out of the sideways pattern, from a high near 75 as it went onward to over 85, see the volume decline showing fewer market participants wanting to join the price advance. As the sell-off materialized, like a boulder falling off a cliff, more participants started selling as volume increased, signaling a strong price reversal.

BLOW-OFF TOPS ON VOLUME SPIKES

Volume levels help confirm the true strength of a price move if the market demonstrates a price increase. If volume does not confirm the market's new assigned value, something is wrong and a price reversal is imminent. Volume is also a great indicator of blow-off tops, or what is called an exhaustion rally. Volume spikes or surges can and do indicate price reversals, especially after a price advance on declining volume is preceded by a lack of price follow-through. As we study the chart in Figure 4.3, you see that the huge price advance is accompanied with abnormal or heavier than usual volume. You would anticipate that a breakout to sharply higher levels would occur. The high volatility reflects the increased volume levels; and as the next time frame shows, there is no follow-through to back the price advance. This is a clear sign of a price reversal. The low close doji trigger also seals the deal that this was simply a one-day wonder rally that failed, and a price reversal was to be expected.

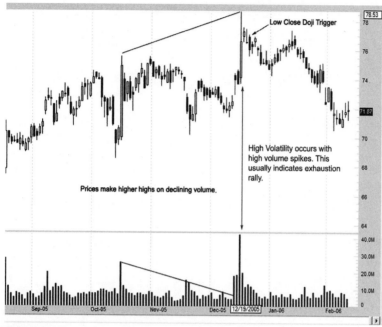

FIGURE 4.3
Used with permission of www.GenesisFT.com.

INTEGRATE VOLUME AND INDICATORS

Volume helps the position trader identify the strength of the trend of the lack of conviction of market participants. Take a look at Toll Brothers in Figure 4.4. This stock took a complete nosedive starting in mid-July. Many thought that the bottom was in and that a rally would take this home builder back to the highs. Not quite so, said the volume! There was a rally attempt, but it was on lower volume. Adding the MACD indicator shows confirmation that a price trend or market rally would not occur. The MACD signaled a negative zero-line cross, and the moving average components crossed as well. The low close doji trigger did not help matters for hopeful bulls either. As the failed rally crumbled, the downtrend resumed and volume started to increase, confirming a bear trend. The MACD indicator continued to back that downtrend, warning traders that lower prices would prevail.

I want to illustrate how you can integrate volume with both MACD and

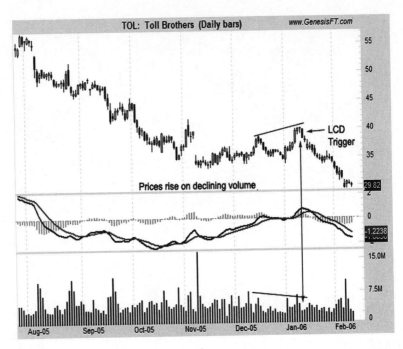

FIGURE 4.4
Used with permission of www.GenesisFT.com.

stochastics so you can see how helpful volume analysis can be to indicate overbought market conditions. Armed with this information, you will have an easier job identifying trading opportunities and a less stressful time choosing a strategy. Figure 4.5 shows Toll Brothers at its peak. It was a media darling. The housing bubble was ready to burst; so when people say they never saw it coming, they just did not know what to look for. The market went into a blow-off phase, which resembles the pattern or condition that Apple Computer was in in Figure 4.2. The volume was declining on higher prices, the MACD had a lower high, and stochastics confirmed the bearish divergence. A low close doji pattern formed at the top (which was within pennies of the monthly pivot resistance number). Once the price reversal occurred, you can see how much volume picked up, confirming the trend reversal. In fact, the average daily volume levels increased as the downtrend materialized.

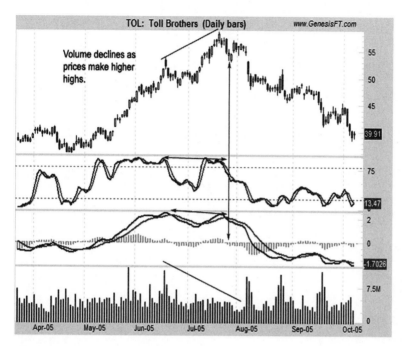

FIGURE 4.5
Used with permission of www.GenesisFT.com.

BULLS TAKE CHARGE

I illustrated the relevance of volume confirming technical indicators and stated the principles that apply to all actively traded markets, including forex or spot currency traders. The opposite signals work for identifying bottoms in all actively traded markets. Let's look at one of my favorite stocks, Starbucks. What an experience! Paying two bucks for a cup of black joe! I'll tell you what, if it hadn't been for my friend Les Zieba (my coffee connection) and Starbucks, this book would most likely never have been finished. Just on my intake of Ventes alone writing this book, I probably added a dollar per share to the value of this stock. In any event, let's look at the chart in Figure 4.6. The stochastics and, more important, the MACD displayed a solid bullish convergence, with corresponding higher lows as prices made lower lows. As the price dipped, forming a hammer, notice how the volume levels declined. As we discussed in Chapter 3, the MACD can trigger a signal later than stochastics can, and here we see that occur. The point is, the volume levels were declining on newer lows, indicating that this market was percolating—ready to reverse higher, full steam ahead!

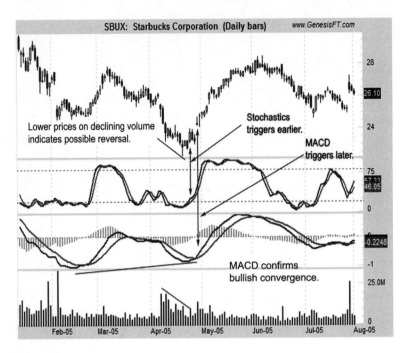

FIGURE 4.6
Used with permission of www.GenesisFT.com.

TRADERS NEED TO ASK MORE QUESTIONS

I always like to ask myself questions about a market or a potential trading opportunity. One such question is, If a market is so bearish, why does it not go down? Figure 4.7 shows Agilent Technologies, a solid company that was one of the many tech darlings that imploded. As we see, the market appears ready to decline and fill the gaping hole called a *gap* between 26 and 28 in August 2005. Notice that the chart pattern makes a lower low formed by a hammer candle. But the market decline was on significantly lower volume. On one hand, one would think the gap would be "filled" as prices trade back near the low end of where the gap was created near 26 per share. But on the other hand, volume and both the MACD and stochastics indicators worked together to indicate otherwise. Prices reversed sharply higher based off the jackhammer pattern (we discuss this very bullish pattern and the rules to trade it in Chapter 8). As the price of this stock traded higher, notice the volume levels moved in the price direction, meaning volume was increasing on increasing prices.

You can identify overbought or oversold conditions based on a variety

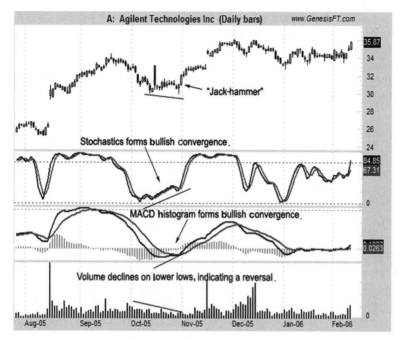

FIGURE 4.7
Used with permission of www.GenesisFT.com.

of methods. Volume studies help me understand what the true strength or weakness of a trend is. When prices are making what can be perceived as a "false high," meaning a higher high, it is accompanied on lower volume levels. When volume levels are not moving parallel with prices, a divergence is occurring. So if prices are moving up, we should see volume moving up. When price is going up and volume is going down, something is wrong and I need to ask myself why. It is at this point that I am aware that something is not internally correct with the market, especially if the fundamentals are wildly bullish. If volume is not confirming the price action, I should take that clue and should start looking for strategies in which to capture a potential trend reversal opportunity, whether it is by liquidating a long or by initiating a short position or by buying a put option or by taking on another option strategy.

The same holds true for the opposite condition: When prices are making a false bottom, we have a bullish convergence or oversold condition. That situation exists and can be spotted as the price direction is not confirmed by volume. If prices are making lower lows, if the market is truly bearish, we should see heavy volume. When volume levels are light and prices are declining, it is a signal that selling pressure is drying up. Then as prices reverse higher to confirm a true turnaround, we should see volume increase as buyers come into the market. This is exactly what happens in Figure 4.7. In addition, using the indicators to help spot these false bottoms will give you added confidence not only to execute a trade but also, more important, *when*.

CHAPTER 5

Pivot Points

Determine Key Price Support and Resistance Areas and the Importance of Confluence

This chapter is the heart and soul of the book. It will explain the methodology of pivot point analysis from "A to Z," or should I say "R-3." This chapter will describe in full detail the principles behind the mathematical calculations and the rationale behind the psychological impact that drives traders to make decisions around these predicted support (S) and resistance (R) levels. I will break this chapter into separate sections to explain how pivot points can be used for short- and longer-term stock trading; how it applies to futures trading, especially when day trading stock index futures; and finally how it applies to the spot foreign exchange (forex) markets. Each investment vehicle has its own nuances, such as trading session hours, time periods in which volume flows change, contract sizes, and decimal point placement so that you know how to correctly calculate the pivot point levels. You need to know the foundation of the methodology of pivot point analysis first, so you will know how to then apply it to the specific markets of interest that you are trading.

The power in using pivot point analysis is that it works in all markets that have established ranges, based on significant volume or a large group of collective participants. After all, the current market price equals the collective action of buyers and sellers. Pivot point analysis is a robust, time-tested, and, best of all, testable form of market analysis; that is, you can back-test to see the accuracy of this trader's tool's predictive analysis. The really unbelievable aspect of pivot point analysis is who uses it. In fact, many traders feel compelled not to learn about it because it seems complicated. I will dispel that myth. Other traders who had read my previous book felt that since I had mentioned futures, rather than equities or forex, pivot analysis did not apply to those specific markets. The truth is that many leading educators in the field of forex and stock trading have either bought my advanced trading course or attended one of my live two-day trading seminars and now share these methods. These are the same techniques I will explain and teach in the following chapters and reveal in the accompanying CD (compact disc).

Remember I explained previously that as a trader you have the right and the obligation to understand everything there is about trading. You need to have a good understanding of game theory. Many traders today use a "black box" method, which is run by algorithm means, that triggers trades automatically. You must understand what goes into building a trading system and how it triggers the automatic reaction when a market price hits at or near a specific level. You are competing not just against fellow traders, but against institutions and major investment groups as well as savvy computer experts, who have a method for removing the emotional element from trading. So what are these levels, and why do we see major reactions or reversals from these mysterious points on the charts?

SUPPORT AND RESISTANCE IN DISGUISE

If a market departs too far from the mean or moving average, there are two sides to consider: one from a profit perspective, and the other from a risk perspective. Institutions and professional traders know this and will have a predetermined price level calculated to either enter or exit a position. In laymen's terms, if a market went too far too fast, it is time to get out and take a profit or to take advantage of an extreme price move by initiating a countertrend trade. So in order to gauge what the standard deviation is, many professional traders use pivot point analysis because it is based on a testable method.

Pivots are disguised price points because they cannot be detected most times using such conventional technical analysis techniques as traditional support and resistance trend lines, Fibonacci levels, and Gann fan angles, and indicators like moving averages and such oscillators as the CCI (commodity channel indicator), stochastics, and the MACD (moving average convergence/divergence) studies. It is imperative that you know how to determine where the pivots are so you are aware at what time and price level the market will most likely change direction. That does not mean to say that at times pivot points coincide or line up near one of these other technical studies. In fact, pivot point levels coincide frequently with Fabonacci extension correction levels, which are referred to as confluence or coincidental factors. I will explain that in more detail as well.

Pivot point analysis is the best "right side" of the chart indicator, as I like to call it, due to its predictive accuracy. It is a mathematical formula, as I understand, originally developed by Henry Wheeler Chase in the 1930s. Chester W. Keltner used part of the formula to develop the Keltner bands as described in his book, *How to Make Money in Commodities* (Keltner Statistical Service, 1961). However, it was really Larry Williams who was credited with repopularizing the analysis in his book *How I Made One Million Dollars Last Year Trading Commodities* (Windsor Books, 1979). Don Lambert, the creator of the commodity channel indicator, uses the pivot point formula that makes the CCI work.

In my first book, *A Complete Guide to Technical Trading Tactics* (Wiley, 2004), I illustrated many trading methods that you can apply using pivot point analysis, including the power of multiple time frames or what is know as confluence of various target levels. This book will highlight those techniques, as well as explain how to incorporate the pivot point as a *moving average* trading system and how to filter out and narrow the field of the respective support and resistance numbers, and will divulge various formulas that are popular today.

MATHEMATICAL CALCULATIONS

Pivot point is a mathematical formula designed to determine the potential range expansion based on a previous time period's data, which include the high, the low, and the close or settlement price. One reason why I believe in using these variables from a given time period's range is that they reflect all market participants' collective perception of value for that time period. In the beginning of the book, I quoted Jesse Livermore: "The patterns the traders and technicians observe are simply the reflections of human emotional behavior" [Richard Suitten, *Trade Like Jesse Livermore* (Wiley, 2005, p. 70)]. The range, which is the high and the low of a given time period, accurately reflects all market participants' exuberant bullishness and pessimistic bearishness for that trading session. The high and the low of a given period are certainly important as they mirror human emotional behavior. Also, the high is a reference point for those who bought out of greed, thinking they were missing an opportunity; they certainly won't forget how much they lost and how the market reacted as it declined from that level. The opposite is true for those who sold the low of a given session out of fear that they would lose more by staying in a long trade; they certainly will respect that price point the next time the market trades back at that level. So the high and the low are important reference points of interest. With that said, pivot point analysis incorporates the three most important elements—the high, the low, and the close—of a given trading session.

THE LEADING INDICATOR

The definition of the *pivot point* is the average of the high, the low, and the closing price. Pivot point analysis is mainly used as support and resistance levels. The pivot point is the heartbeat of the analysis; without it, projected ranges and market condition cannot be determined. It does act as a support or resistance level as well. Pivot point analysis helps as a leading price indicator for traders because it gives traders advanced indication of potential highs or lows or, in some cases, both in a given time period, unlike Fibonacci studies, where there is no predicted time period in which a projected price correction or projection will occur. I want to step up the concept so that you can develop a trading system on some powerful setups and on what triggers a trade. As I disclosed, professional stock, forex, and futures traders have had significant success in utilizing these "hidden lines"; and I think that with a more thorough understanding of the concept, so will you.

As a quick review, one of the main benefits for using pivot point calculations is that they help determine when to enter and when to exit positions. As a trader, you already know you can only book a profit when you exit; and if you don't exit a losing trade quickly, it is hard to maintain, or keep, what you have already made. Pivot points are used to project support and resistance or actual highs and lows of trading sessions. These numbers are derived from a mathematical formula; there are several versions that, for your benefit, I will go into; but keep in mind that I still use the most common method to derive my analysis. Here are the most common formulas:

- **Pivot Point**—the pivot point (P) is the sum of the high (H), the low (L), and the close (C) divided by three.

$$P = (H + L + C)/3$$

- **Resistance Level 2**—R-2 is the pivot point number plus the high and minus the low.

$$R\text{-}2 = P + H - L$$

- **Resistance Level 1**—R-1 is the pivot point number times two minus the low.

$$R\text{-}1 = (P \times 2) - L$$

- **Support Level 1**—S-1 is the pivot point number times two minus the high.

$$S\text{-}1 = (P \times 2) - H$$

- **Support Level 2**—S-2 is the pivot point number minus the high plus the low.

$$S-2 = P - H + L$$

Some analysts are adding a third level to their pivot calculations to help target extreme price swings on what has occurred on such occasions as a price shock news-event-driven market reaction. It seems that I have noticed that the spot forex currency markets tend to experience a double dose of price shocks beause they are exposed to foreign economic developments and U.S. economic developments that pertain to a specific country's currency. This tends to make wide trading ranges. Therefore, a third level of projected support and resistance were calculated

Resistance Level 3—R-3 = H + 2 × (Pivot – Low) or (P – S-1) + R-2

Support Level 3—S-3 = L – 2 × (High – Pivot) or P – (R-2 – S-1)

There are other variations that include adding the opening range, in which case you would simply find the sum of the open, the high, the low, and the close; and then divide it by four to derive the actual pivot point.

$$P = (O + H + L + C) / 4$$

One more variation of that concept—to factor in gaps from adverse price moves from one day to the next—is to take the previous session's high, low, and close, add in the new trading session's open, and then add in those variables and divide by four. In using both open prices, you still calculate the extreme support and resistance levels with the same formulas.

$$P = (\text{new } O + \text{old } H + \text{old } L + \text{old } C) / 4$$

Let's go over what these numbers mean and how price action reacts with these projected target levels. But first, let me state that I personally do not use the R-3 or S-3 levels because I believe in looking at the progressively higher time period's price support or resistance projections. For example, from the daily numbers, I would look at the weekly numbers, and then from the weekly numbers I would look at the monthly numbers. The longer the time frame, the more important or significant the data. Also, it is rare that the daily numbers will trade beyond the extreme R-2 or S-2 numbers; and when the market does, it is generally in a strong trending condition, in which case we have methods to follow the market's flow, which we will cover in the next few chapters. By focusing in on just a few select numbers and learning how to filter out excess information, I eliminate the analysis paralysis from information overload. Do yourself a favor and keep reading because this does get exciting. The following list shows how the numbers would break down by order, what typically occurs, and how the market behaves. Keep in mind that this is a general description. You will learn what to look for at these price points in order to spot reversals so you can become more profitable from trading in the markets.

- *Resistance Level 3*—Extreme bullish market condition generally created by news-driven price shock. This is where a market is at an overbought condition and may offer a day trader a quick reversal scalp trade.
- *Resistance Level 2*—Bullish market price objective or target high number for a trading session. It generally establishes the high of a given time period. The market often sees significant resistance at this price level and will provide an exit target for long positions.
- *Resistance Level 1*—Mild bullish to bearish projected high target number. In low volume or light volatility sessions or in consolidating trading periods, this often acts as the high of a given session. In a bearish market condition, prices will try to come close to this level but most times fail.
- *Pivot Point*—This is the focal price level or the mean that is derived from the collective market data from the prior session's high, low, and close. It is the strongest of the support and resistance numbers. Prices normally trade above or below this area before breaking in one direction or the other. As a general guideline, if the market opens above the primary pivot, be a buyer on dips. If the market opens below this level, look to sell rallies.
- *Support Level 1*—Mild bearish to bullish projected low target number in light volume or low volatility sessions or in consolidating trading periods. Prices tend to reverse at or near this level in bullish market conditions but most times fall short of hitting this number.
- *Support Level 2*—Bearish market price objective or targeted low number. The market often sees significant support at or near this level in a bearish market condition and is a likely target level to cover shorts.
- *Support Level 3*—Extreme bearish market condition generally created by a news-driven price shock. This level will act as the projected target low or support area. This is where a market is at an oversold condition and may offer a day trader a quick reversal scalp trade.

Most of the research and books written on technical analysis cover the topic of trade entry and how to use indicators, oscillators, and moving average studies. Few go over how to target exits. Longer-term traders have read the works done on volume analysis to help determine the strength or the weakness of a trend. There is further information on consensus studies, such as the Commitment of Traders (COT) reports; the VIX, which is a volatility index, is based on calculations using options on the Standard & Poor's (S&P) 500 Stock Index. Plus, the put-to-call ratio helps give investors an idea if a trend is ready to change. None of these studies actually helps a trader with targeting a potential trading range in a given time period. That information will help a trader with setups and triggers on entering a position and, most important, exiting a position. This is where pivot point analysis will help you.

Think for a moment: If most technical tools are lagging indicators and if most traders follow and use these trading indicators to make trading decisions, then it would make sense that most traders get trading signals and execute entering into a position on a lagging basis or well after a move has been established. Then, if the same indicator gives the exit signal too late, perhaps that is what perpetuates habit or the consistency of losing money in the markets, from entering or exiting later, based on lagging indicators.

Then, in order to adjust getting in too late, traders anticipate a market turn; and more times than not, that turns out to be a bad trading decision. Or traders may decide to just "hang in there" a while longer, thinking that the market may just return and give them back the sweet profits that were just accumulated in the trade. That is a syndrome that many traders tell me they fell victim to. By using pivot point support and resistance levels, you can speed up the analytical process on entries; and by employing certain trade management techniques that we will go over in a later chapter, you can effectively help improve your exits. After all, that is one of the most important aspects of trading. A profit is just a paper asset until a position is offset. The offset relies on an exit strategy. Ask yourself this question: How many times have I been in a trade and thought I was doing the correct thing by letting my winners ride, by holding on to the position only to see my paper profits erode and then perhaps turn into a loss? The flip side to this is: How many times have I taken a quick profit, banked the money, and no more than a few moments later watched the market explode dramatically further in the direction of my original position? Just when you say the market can't move any further, that's when it usually does. You need discipline and patience to stay with a trade. These situations will likely happen; but by utilizing pivot points and by watching the market's behavior at or *near* these levels, you will be better prepared to make better trading decisions, especially on exits.

POSSIBLE OUTCOMES WHEN PRICES ARE NEAR PIVOT AREA

You need to stay in the "now," to focus on the current market condition or environment. Keep telling yourself that what happened in the past or perhaps even your last trade is of no concern to the current trade you are in. Remember that each trade will have a different outcome. The patterns we see and the way a market behaves at or near a pivot point support or resistance level will be different. Therefore, the velocity and the magnitude of a price move will vary every time. For example, as shown in Figure 5.1, prices could come close to but not exactly hit the pivot level. That does not mean prices will do that every time. As Figure 5.2 shows, prices can exceed resistance by a small margin; this may invite you to buy a breakout of the resistance level and trap you into buying the high. Then, as Figure 5.3 illustrates, prices can hit the pivot support number exactly, which does happen frequently. But if you program yourself to anticipate, that will be the outcome every time; you will be in for a rude awakening due to the potential that Figure 5.4 represents the occurrence that sometimes prices just come close and consolidate or congest near the pivot point support or resistance levels for a period of time before reacting off those levels. Once again, the market's past performance is not indicative of future results; so we need more information in the thought process to initiate a trade and to exit a trade. The pivot point levels will allow you to set up a particular game plan; therefore, when you apply more layers of analysis, such as candle patterns and a moving average approach of the pivot point, that is where you will improve on your trading decisions, from both your entries and your exits.

Pivot Point Resistance Line

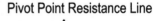

Pivot Point Resistance Line

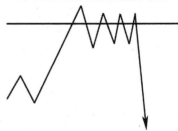

FIGURE 5.1   Prices could come close but not exact.

FIGURE 5.2   Prices exceed resistance.

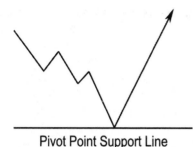

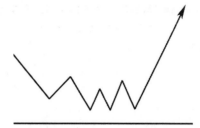

Pivot Point Support Line

Pivot Point Support Line

FIGURE 5.3   Prices can hit exactly at the pivot level.

FIGURE 5.4   Prices congest near support.

DETERMINE THE RANGE

Data should be used for the all session trading markets with the close of business as the settlement price. In the futures markets, I do not use just the U.S. markets' open outcry trading session. Here is why: The night sessions of most markets include the Asian and the European markets; and those participants do trade in U.S. financial markets. If an event took place that caused a market to move and a trade price was recorded, then it is a valid price point and will be put in the history books as a trade occurring. Therefore, I consider that information as accurate from a valid trading session. Most U.S. retail or individual speculators may not be up at 3 A.M. (CT) trading off a market move; but potentially, professional traders are, and therefore the information is considered valid. Gosh, even the exchanges seem to believe it's valid since money moves into and out of an account if a trade is made; so the high or low of that period should be considered.

MULTIPLE TIME FRAME ANALYSIS

Daily, weekly, and monthly time frames can and should be utilized as well. To understand how price moves within the pivots, begin by breaking down the time frames from longer-term to shorter-term. So start with a monthly time frame, for which, as you know, there is a price range, or an established high and low for that given period; so we should be watching these predictive price points as well. Think of this: There are approximately 22 business days, or about four weeks, in every month; and each month, there will be an established range—a high and a low. In a week, there are typically five trading days. Now consider that on one day of one week in one month, a high and a low will be made. It is likely that the high and the low may be made in a minute or within one hour of a given day of a given week of a given month. That is why longer-term time frames, such as monthly or weekly analysis, should be included in your market analysis. It is also the reason why I do not use the R-3 or the S-3 targets. I rely more on the longer-term time frames targeted support and resistance levels. Pivot point analysis relies on data from specific time frames in order to determine support and resistance levels for the next particular trading session. It is prodictive and both time- and price-sensitive information.

The analysis or calculations for the prior day, week, or month may not be applicable two or three sessions later. At the end of each time period, data will need to be recalculated. The exception to this rule is that if there is a time period after a wide-range session that is a smaller range, then I would keep the data from the session with the wider range in mind for another one or two trading periods. For example, using a daily analysis, if Tuesday had a wide trading range and then Wednesday had a small range, I would keep the targeted support and resistance numbers derived from Tuesday in mind for Thursday's session. The same principle applies to a week or a month.

In the world of 24-hour trading, the most popular question I get from those studying and using pivot points is, "What are the times that you derive the high-low-close information from?" There are many different people telling many different stories. Here is what I do and what seems to work best. For starters, just keep things simple and apply some good old-fashioned common sense. If the exchanges and the banking system use a specific time to settle a market, then that is the time that you should consider a close. The exchanges and banks should know—their rules make the money move. I want to follow the money flow.

- *Stock traders* use the settlement price from the close of business at 4 P.M. (ET).
- *Forex traders* should use the 5 P.M. (ET) New York bank settlement close.
- *Futures traders*, in the e-mini–S&P, Nasdaq, and Russell contracts, use the close of 3:15 P.M. (CT). For the Chicago Board of Trade (CBOT) mini-Dow contract, I take the close at 4 P.M. (CT).
- For the *weekly* calculations, take the open from Sunday night's session, and use the close on Friday.
- For the *monthly* calculations, take the open from the first day of the month, and use the close of the last day of the month.

We have established the reasons why we use all sessions for extracting the range, or high and low, and what time periods constitute the closes. We know where and how and when. Now, let me show you what pivot point

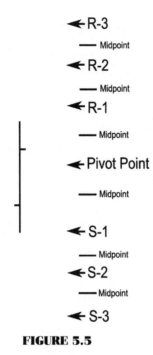

FIGURE 5.5

projected supports and resistance line up to look like. In Figure 5.5, we have a good representation of how the R-3 down to the S-3 levels would line up based on a previous session's high, low, and close data. The hash marks between each level are the midpoint numbers. As you can see, this presents 13 price points to monitor. To most traders, including myself, this is simply information overload. If you include using these 13 levels for each day, week. and month, that would put 39 trading support and resistance numbers on your chart for each trading day. That could cause a trader to possibly go blind or, at the very least, could create analysis paralysis. Granted, you may be right in stating that you picked the top or the bottom of each trading session, but it is impractical or highly unlikely that you can trade off that information. I am not saying that at times it may help having the midpoints or R-3 or S-3 target levels in front of you; I just believe in keeping things simple, and less is better.

FILTER OUT INFORMATION OVERLOAD

I have developed a method to filter out the pivot numbers; this is just one facet that I explain to attendees of my trading seminars and to students.

Keep in mind that this methodology applies to all markets, including stocks, futures, and especially spot foreign currency markets, or forex. This method can work for a short-term application for identifying a potential range for a day, a week, or a month. By having a good idea, well in advance, of what the high or the low for a given time period might be, you are able to use this information to apply the right trading vehicle or strategy, such as whether it is simply selecting an entry level or getting in or selecting a profit objective or getting out of a trade. You could also determine whether to apply an option strategy or when to use an exchange traded fund, as we discussed in Chapter 1.

Predicting Highs and Lows Using the Calculations

What I do to determine the potential range for a given session is to take the R-1 and the S-1 initially for my analysis, especially in low-volume consolidating trading sessions.

I use the actual pivot point for many things; one that is useful is understanding that it can be used as an actual trading number in determining the high or the low of a given time period, especially in strong bull or bear market conditions. In an extremely bullish market condition, the pivot point can become the target low for the trading session. This number represents the true value of a prior session. In an up-trending market, if the market gaps higher above the pivot point, then a retracement back to the pivot will attract buyers. Until that pivot point is broken by prices trading below that level, traders will step in and buy the pullback. The opposite is true in an extremely bearish market condition; the pivot point will act as the target high for the session. If a news-driven event causes the market to gap lower, once traders access the news and discover it is not as bearish as thought, prices may trade back up to test the pivot point; if the market fails to break out above that price level and trades higher, sellers will enter the market and take action, pressing the market lower again.

Filtering the Numbers

Technically speaking, in a bearish market, the highs should be lower and the lows should be lower than those of the preceding time frame. If they are, then I use that information to help me filter out unnecessary data or excessive support and resistance numbers on my charts. I use the actual pivot point up to the R-1 number for resistance, and then I target the S-2 for the potential low or for that time period's trading range.

As you can see in Figure 5.6, if I determine the market is bearish and if

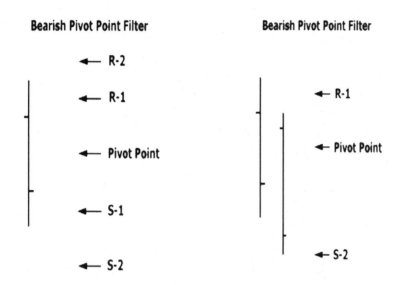

FIGURE 5.6

I understand the relationship of the geometric distance of the resistance and support targets, I can eliminate the R-2 number, since in a bearish environment we should see a lower high. If I am looking for a lower low, then I can eliminate the S-1 support number as well; and now I have reduced the field to just three numbers. If I apply the same methodology on daily, weekly, and monthly charts, instead of 39 numbers, I am now working with just 9 numbers. Once again, I am not using the numbers to place orders ahead of time (even though you could); I use the numbers as a guide. These numbers work so well and often act as a self-fulfilling prophecy because so many institutions and professional traders do use them. Many have different size positions on. Some traders may not wait for the exact number to hit and may start scaling out of positions (as I do); and so should you. With this method, you can use these numbers as exit areas on your trades. As Figure 5.7 depicts, in a bullish market environment, by definition you may agree that the highs should be higher and the lows should be higher than those of the preceding time period. When I have determined that we are in a bullish trend, I target the S-1 up to the pivot point for the low of the session and the R-2 for targeting the high; and that will give me an idea of what the potential trading range will be.

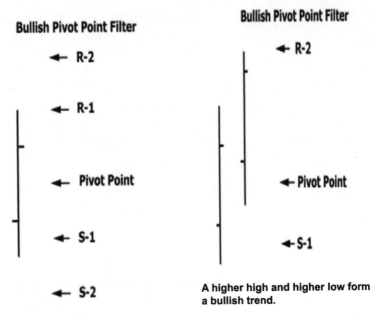

A higher high and higher low form a bullish trend.

FIGURE 5.7

Lining Up the Numbers

When the market goes through the projected daily target numbers, I then use the next time periods for a better gauge or reliability as to the next price objective. That is where the significance of the weekly and the monthly numbers comes into play.

Back in the late 1990s when I owned a brokerage firm, I developed a method to help me line up the pivot point levels as shown in Figure 5.8; I had all my brokers use these numbers, and many still do to this day. The table of information was for the trading session of 1/18/2006.

My method categorizes the pivot point levels to the various market conditions, such as neutral (Target Key) bullish, and bearish. I like to know what the prior time period's range and close were for fast access, so I included that in as well. Since the pivot point is important, I include that on the sheet, as shown in the last column on the right. The third column from the right states Market Direction. That is a moving average of the actual pivot point.

If the pivot point and the close or settlement price are below the market direction number, then the market condition is deemed to be in a bearish mode; and it helps me to line up the R-1 and S-1 numbers as the projected target range for that next session. If you look down the far-left

John L. Person, CTA — 1-18-06

Commodity		Target Key No		Bullish Target		Bearish Target		Market		Previous Range			Pivot
Symbol	Month	Resistance	Support	High	Low	High	Low	Direction		High	Low	Settle	
S&P 500	MARCH	1295.33	1283.58	1301.17	1283.58	1295.33	1277.67	Bearish	1292.03	1295.25	1283.50	1289.50	1289.42
DOW	MARCH	11000.00	10873.00	11066.00	10873.00	11000.00	10812.00	Bearish	10987.67	11005	10878	10934	10939.00
NASDAQ	MARCH	1763.33	1739.83	1775.17	1739.83	1763.33	1728.17	Bearish	1758.00	1763.50	1740.00	1751.50	1751.67
Russell	MARCH	712.90	703.20	717.70	703.20	712.90	698.30	Bearish	710.20	712.80	703.10	708.10	708.00
BONDS	MARCH	115 3/32	114 16/32	115 10/32	114 16/32	115 3/32	114 4/32	Bullish	114 8/32	114 30/32	114 11/32	114 28/32	114 23/32
T-Notes	MARCH	109 31/32	109 21/32	110 2/32	109 21/32	109 31/32	109 14/32	Bullish	109 17/32	109 28/32	109 18/32	109 27/32	109 24/32
Yen-Futures	MARCH	0.8774	0.8670	0.8833	0.8670	0.8774	0.8625	Bearish	0.8788	0.8788	0.8684	0.8715	0.8729
EURO	MARCH	121.80	120.89	122.25	120.89	121.80	120.43	Bullish	121.29	121.79	120.88	121.35	121.34
Crude Oil	MARCH	67.54	65.79	68.15	65.79	67.54	64.65	Bullish	65.03	67	65.25	66.94	66.40
Gold	APRIL	567.10	554.30	575.00	554.30	567.10	549.40	Bullish	556.28	570.1	557.3	559.2	562.20
Silver	MARCH	927.37	895.37	947.43	895.37	927.37	883.43	Bullish	906.08	935.5	903.50	907.3	915.43
Soybeans	MARCH	575.67	568.17	580.08	568.17	575.67	565.08	Bearish	573.36	577.00	569.5	571.25	572.58

FIGURE 5.8
Used with permission of www.nationalfutures.com.

column to where you see "Bonds," you will see that the market direction number classified the market condition as bullish due to the location of the previous settlement and that the pivot point was above the pivot point moving average.

The numbers targeted the high in bonds to be $115^{10}\!/_{32}$ (R-2) and the low to be $114^{16}\!/_{32}$ (S-1). The pivot point was $114^{23}\!/_{32}$.

Since the market closed at $114^{28}\!/_{32}$, there was a strong chance to see $115^{10}\!/_{32}$, as well as a low of $114^{16}\!/_{32}$. Figure 5.9 shows the exact trading session activity on a 15-minute candle chart. If you are a candle chart aficionado, you will have spotted that the high was formed by a shooting star pattern and that the low was made by a bullish engulfing pattern. While the market broke out above the targeted resistance, it certainly did not stay there long. Notice how the price penetrated the low but reversed off the projected low as well. We will use this chart later in the book as we share statistical information on which candle patterns have high frequency of forming tops and bottoms. At this point, just heighten your awareness that there was a doji after the star at top and a doji near the bottom.

This chart also has another component—a moving average method that we will discuss a variation of as well. By using the true value of the

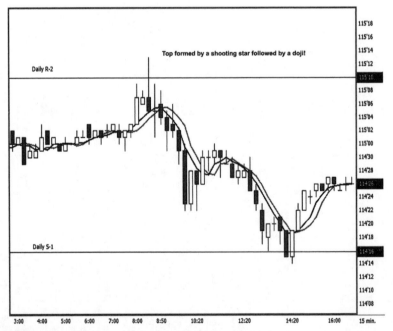

FIGURE 5.9   Bonds trade the predicted pivot range.
Used with permission of esignal.com.

market, which I refer to as the pivot point, we can help determine the market condition and the projected price ranges as well as potential turning points as market conditions change from bullish (uptrend) to bearish (downtrend).

Pivots Combined with Candles

The CBOT mini-Dow is one of several great day trading futures products for selecting trades that connect with pivot and candle patterns as Figure 5.10 shows. Notice how prices do penetrate briefly above the pivot targeted high by forming the shooting star candle. See the market's reaction as the price declines over 70 Dow points (each point is $5 on the mini-Dow). That is a $350.00 move in less than 75 minutes per contract. Since most futures firms carry a $500.00 day trade margin per contract that translates into a healthy return. Now that we know how to line up the numbers, we need to wait for a setup or signal to trigger a short position. The shooting star, the moving average crossover, and the dark candles all confirmed a technical signal to sell.

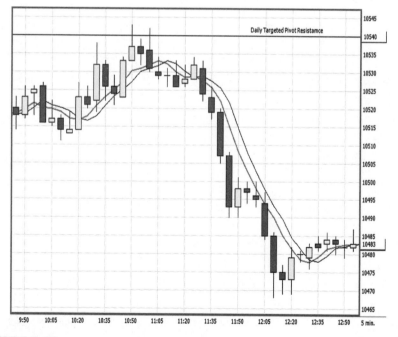

FIGURE 5.10
Used with permission of esignal.com.

The graph in Figure 5.11 represents the e-mini–S&P 500 Stock Index Futures on November 10, 2005; the targeted range was determined to be S-1 and R-2, a bullish market condition. The actual low of the day was formed by a hammer candle pattern (keep notes of what candle patterns form near tops and bottoms, as we will be discussing this in detail in later chapters). A buy signal is triggered with the sequence of higher highs and higher lows but, more important, higher closing highs, as well. The moving average crossover also helps trigger a long buy signal. The market rallies right up within a tick or two of the R-2 number. As a day trader, it is great to have a predetermined exit strategy. In this case, pivot point analysis accommodated you in that respect. Other times, you will need to rely on your timing to exit a trade; for example, as a day trader, once the market is near the close of the business day, you should be offsetting your position. In the example in Figure 5.11, you had a timing and a price element working for you to help target an exit on what was a beautiful trade. The trigger to go long was after the crossover of the moving average one candle after 11:30, as prices established a higher closing high.

This trade would have resulted in a stellar 12.50-point gain from the

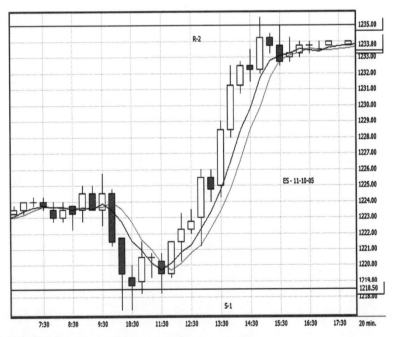

FIGURE 5.11   Bonds trade the predicted pivot range.
Used with permission of esignal.com.

entry of 1221.50 up to the exit, which was 1233. The exit was triggered on the first lower closing low and was confirmed by a close back under the moving averages. On a day trading margin per contract in the e-mini–S&P of $1,000 (brokerage firms vary on *day trading* margins), you picked up 625.00 per position.

The next chart I want to show you in Figure 5.12 is an example of how a market, when targeted to be in a bullish mode, interacts with the series of pivot support and resistance numbers. If there is a bullish bias, then S-1 up to R-2 will be the potential range. Therefore, we are looking to take buy signals at support and have a profit objective in mind near R-2. This is a 15-minute candle chart using the mini–Russell Stock Index futures. Notice that as the market trades near the pivot support of S-1, prices consolidate for almost two hours before triggering the buy signal as a higher closing high and a crossover of the moving averages confirm the trigger to go long at 657.50.

Prices penetrate the R-1 level and come close to the projected S-2 level. As the trading session ends, you still have no reason to exit the position from a technical standpoint except that as a day trader, your time is your exit point. This trade was good for nearly a 9.50-point run, or $950 per contract.

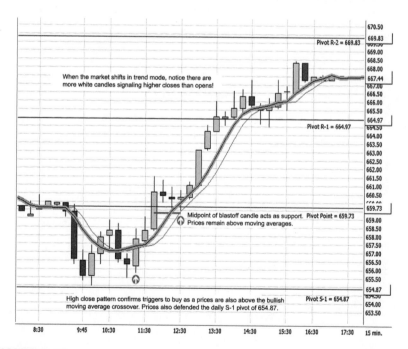

FIGURE 5.12
Used with permission of esignal.com.

Let's look at a spot forex market in Figure 5.13. We are looking at the yen versus the U.S. dollar. The targeted resistance was the R-2; and as you can see, the top was formed by an evening doji star formation, based on a five-minute candle chart. Combining the knowledge of how to determine the right pivot level with practicing the discipline to wait for a signal will certainly help you target and select better trading opportunities. As you can see in this chart, on a $100,000 lot size, you would have realized over a 100-point gain in less than two and a half hours. That translates to $1,000 per lot or contract.

Special note: Big moves do occur in forex during the U.S. nighttime. This trade signal hit at 20:00 hours, or 7 P.M. (ET). So depending on your trading capital and time constraints during regular market hours, the potential opportunities that abound in the spot currency markets may be suitable for you to take advantage of.

FIGURE 5.13
Used with permission of esignal.com.

THE IMPORTANCE OF CONFLUENCE

Time is an essential element in trading. There are many instances when traders are correct in their predictions for a top or a bottom in a market; but they are off in their timing, which results in a loss. Many analysts were calling for a top or for the bubble to burst in the stock market in 1999. In that situation, not demonstrating patience to wait would have resulted in dramatic loss of profit potential or worse, actual losses due to selling short stock too early. How about economists' predictions of a housing bubble back in 2003 and their expectations for a decline in real estate prices? By July 2006 we had started to see prices go back down but not to the severity as was predicted and certainly not at the time that was expected by economists. I can go on and on with examples when prognostications were correct, but timing was really wrong, resulting in a financial loss.

Time and Price

As I stated earlier, pivot point analysis relies on both time and price specifics in its calculations to project future support and resistance levels. By incorporating price data for various time frames, such as daily, weekly, and monthly, the more price areas that coincide with the different time periods, the greater is the likelihood that these price clusters will repel the market's advance in an uptrend or cause prices to reverse in a downtrend. This clustering, or confluence, from more than one time period that convergences with another is an awesome event and can translate into a very lucrative setup. The time frames of numbers that target a specific price level is termed *confluence*; in other words, the more corroborating numbers that target a general area, the greater is the significance of that specific targeted price level. Pivot calculations work to pinpoint almost exact times and prices for trades in various markets and can be used to validate other analysis. Remember this phrase: "There is always strength in numbers!" The more pivot numbers that line up, the greater is the potential for a reaction off those levels. This knowledge, combined with identifying the shift in momentum by identifying and acting on strong triggers, increases the probability of a successful trade.

As an example, Figure 5.14 shows the daily, weekly, and monthly pivot point numbers drawn across the chart; this gives a trader a heads up that the market may reach an unsustainable extreme or oversold market condition. Just by looking at the graph, you can see that the market has been in a prolonged downtrend. Generally, the market may stop its descent at a

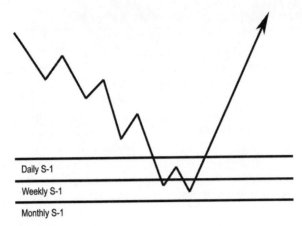

Daily S-1

Weekly S-1

Monthly S-1

FIGURE 5.14

confluence support zone; then you would want to wait for a shift in momentum to trade a potential price reversal. When the market starts to give clues as to a bottom, you can determine a low-risk entry, as a bottom has been defined. What would not be known is how high the market's reaction will be off this target level of support. This is where the candle chart section will play an important role in helping to determine the strength of the trend's reversal.

In Figure 5.15, we have a weekly stock chart on Alcoa. Here we see a confluence of two higher-degree time periods, such as the weekly and monthly support numbers. What is uncanny is that the weekly pivot S-1 target low number was 22.33, with the actual low coming in at 22.28, just pennies below the pivot support number. The monthly number lined up a little higher than that at 22.99, which is a slightly wider margin of error. Remember, when I am trading, I am not looking to catch a falling knife by anticipating a bottom, even though in this example you could have placed a buy order at the weekly number; and as the price moved through your buy order, you may have been filled—and that was a great buy. However, the better course of action, and the more reliable method to trade off this confluence area, was to wait for a confirmed buy signal, such as the high close doji signal (we go over that in Chapter 7). Notice the moving average crossover and that prices confirm a conditional change in the market by closing above the open and closing above both moving average components. The true buy signal was generated at 24.20, and the risk would be using a stop below the low at 22.28.

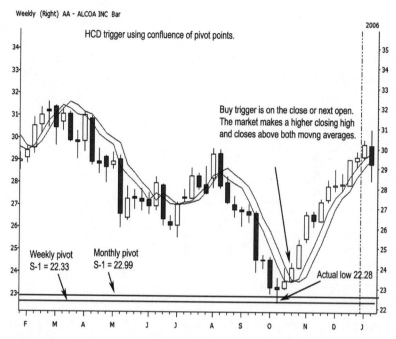

Weekly (Right) AA - ALCOA INC Bar

HCD trigger using confluence of pivot points.

Buy trigger is on the close or next open.
The market makes a higher closing high
and closes above both movng averages.

Weekly pivot
S-1 = 22.33

Monthly pivot
S-1 = 22.99

Actual low 22.28

FIGURE 5.15
RealTick graphics used with permission of Townsend Analytics, LTD.

Volatility Is Good

As long as there is trading volume—liquidity so you can enter and exit positions and price movement, otherwise known as *volatility*—pivot point analysis will work in any market for position traders and short-term day traders. No matter what your choice is for a trading investment vehicle, it makes no sense that you would not want to incorporate this methodology into your trading style. Let's examine the chart in Figure 5.16, which is a daily look at a spot forex euro currency versus the U.S. dollar. The monthly S-2 target low was 116.90, the weekly S-1 lined up in close proximity at 116.58, and the actual low was 116.41. Looking at the market's reaction three days after the low, we see a bullish engulfing pattern. The confluence of pivot support numbers gave one of the best and only predictive support targets. Therefore, it should be noted that the longer-term numbers should be watched carefully for clues not only for trading opportunities to enter positions but also as a warning that the current trend could be exhausted and potentially reverse. At the very least, you may not have wanted to es-

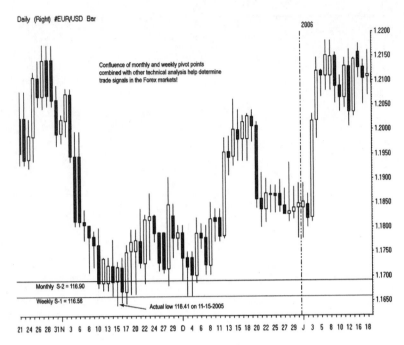

FIGURE 5.16
RealTick graphics used with permission of Townsend Analytics, LTD.

tablish a long position; you certainly would have been alerted not to sell short at the low.

Let's examine the 15-minute candle chart in the 30-year Treasury bonds (T-bonds) shown in Figure 5.17. Once again, the market price scrapes against the lows, and a hammer pattern forms the exact bottom. But notice that the weekly pivot S-1 support target is $112^{14}\!/_{32}$, which coincides with the daily S-1 support target of $112^{20}\!/_{32}$. The actual low was $114^{15}\!/_{32}$! Notice that the market broke the daily support but did not make much of a decline and certainly did not remain below the support for a long period of time. That leads me to this point: There are those who believe that once a support level is violated, you should go with that breakdown momentum and sell short. That may work occasionally, but it needs to be defined in more detail, with a list of special rules and certain criteria in order for that to be an automatic trading rule for me to initiate a trade. I believe that you should look for buy signals at support and for sell signals at or near resistance, especially when there is a confluence of pivot point price targets. It is more fruitful in buying the projected support, as this example shows.

In Figure 5.17, we see a trigger to go long after the high close doji trig-

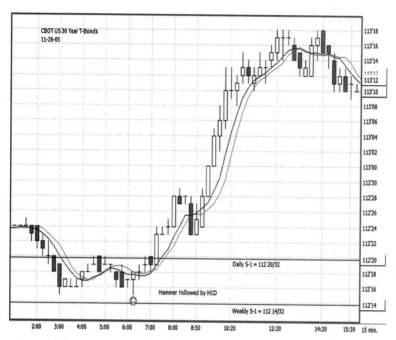

FIGURE 5.17
Used with permission of esignal.com.

ger is made at $112^{18}\!/_{32}$ (notice that the low was also formed by a hammer). As the market goes into trend mode and rallies nearly a full basis point higher, the signal to liquidate occurs once we see prices change conditions. As the candles indicate, prices are closing below each period's open; a lower closing low from a doji top occurs and the moving averages cross; and, finally, the market price closes below both moving averages. That triggers the exit at $113^{14}\!/_{32}$. This was a 28-point (each thirty-second is 31.25 per point) gain for $875.00 profit per position on a day trade.

CONFLUENCES WORK AT TOPS

We have all heard in the field of technical analysis that what works for some patterns or signals is not applicable for all situations. However, the power of pivot point confluences does work at market tops as well as working to indicate bottom reversals, as we just went over. In Figure 5.18, once again the three main time periods that we use are the monthly, the weekly, and the daily. When a congestion of pivot numbers line up, or cluster, near

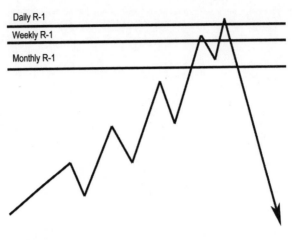

FIGURE 5.18

a specific price zone, this heightens your awareness for possible reversals. It is important to note that if a market has been in a long uptrend, say for more than two months, and if the end of the quarter is near, the market is ripe for a profit-taking correction. Generally speaking, professional trading managed funds receive payment by a performance fee (profits) at the end of a quarter. Since many of these large trading entities use pivot analysis or are aware that others use them, when a confluence of resistance develops, especially near the end of a quarter, look out below. It not only marks a prime price level but also indicates a specific reason why a profit-taking correction can occur at that time period. The same holds true for bottoms. After a long price decline, if the numbers line up and if it is near the end of a quarter, a profit-taking reversal could be in the works. That does not mean to say that the original trend won't resume, but you could take a great countertrend reversal trade. Generally speaking, market sell-offs have more velocity; therefore, spotting resistance confluences can result in very lucrative opportunities, under the right circumstances.

Earlier, I explained the saying "There is always strength in numbers." The concept can be explained further in that there is a strong analytical value found in the number three, not just in trading and technical analysis but also in our universe. As you may be aware, the number three is a Fibonacci number; and when I look at confluences in the three different time periods, "three" represents the three different groups of traders. The daily numbers are used by day traders, the weekly numbers are used by swing traders, and the monthly numbers are used by longer-term position traders and institutions. Even in the Commodity Futures Trading Commision

TABLE 5.1 Japanese Yen Spot Forex

Prior Period	High	Low	Close
Monthly—November	119.95	116.37	119.80
Weekly—12/02/2005	121.24	118.33	120.59
Daily—12/02/2005	121.24	120.19	120.59

(CFTC) COT report, there are three classifications of traders: reportable, commercials, and non-reportable. The number three is a highly correlated number in market analysis. The coincidental factor in pivot pont analyses derives from the fact that one set of numbers from one time frame *generally* has nothing to do with another. If you look at the data for the Japanese yen spot forex data in Table 5.1, you will see that the high and the close of the week coincided with the daily high and close, as that was on a Friday.

Let's look at Figure 5.19 and see how the numbers in the spot forex Japanese yen line up. The market made a tremendous price move from the

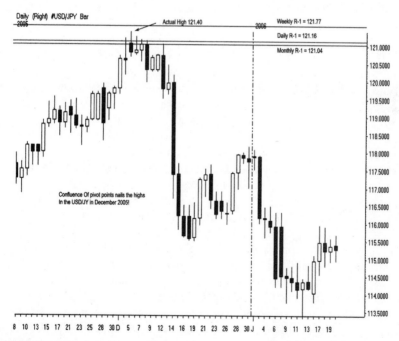

FIGURE 5.19
RealTick graphics used with permission of Townsend Analytics, LTD.

low of 108.76 on September 5, 2005, until the high was made on December 5, 2005, at 121.40.

Let's review before we go further. If you recall in Chapter 1, I stated that forex traders can borrow information from the futures industry. One such piece of data is the CFTC Commitment of Traders report. In essence, this report reveals whose hands "control" the market. *Except* for the yen, all currencies are quoted as the currency versus the U.S. dollar. The yen futures are quoted as the opposite—as the spot forex markets. So spot forex would quote the yen as 117.35; the futures quote would be .8572. What this means is that when the CFTC report shows a net *short* position, traders are in a long position in the spot yen forex markets against the dollar. As the CFTC report showed at the end of the trading session as of 11/29/2005, the funds, or the "non-commercials," were long 22,626 contracts and short 86,626. That is a net short position of 64,000 contracts. Each contract is 1,250,000 worth of yen! The "commercials" were long 154,396 contracts and short 85,604 positions. The small speculators were long 29,368 contracts and short 34,160 positions. This means the banks, or "smart money," established a protective hedge position in the futures, betting that the spot yen would fall in value against the dollar. Keep in mind that the non-commercials are considered professional speculators; they, too, are considered the smart money. The difference is that they are speculating and will not generally take delivery of a futures contract, which is 1,250,000 worth of Japanese yen.

If we examine Figure 5.19 closely, we notice that after a substantial price appreciation in a relatively short period of time, prices hit just past the monthly R-1 of 121.04. Remember that the low on September 5, just three months earlier, was 108.76. So the market made a huge up move, and the banks and institutions or commercials were betting prices would fall. The ends of the year and of the quarter were closing in, and we were hitting up against a confluence of pivot point resistance. The weekly R-1 was 121.77; and on the day the actual price high occurred at 121.40, the daily pivot R-1 was 121.16. When we combine the pivot point resistance levels with a few bearish candle patterns, such as the rickshaw doji that formed the day before the high or the trigger to initiate a sell that occurred on the third day after the target high was made you have a high chance to see a negative market reaction on price reversal. Market tops that align with a cluster, or confluence, of various pivot points can result in tremendous market reversals, as this example shows, especially as they coincide with a major consensus reading toward the end of the quarter.

The power of a sell-off does not necessarily have to occur near the end of a quarter. In equities, end-of-year tax-loss selling prevails; and at the first of the new year, as pension funds are buying stock, others are looking to cash out their profits for tax deferment purposes. As the Chicago Board

FIGURE 5.20
RealTick graphics used with permission of Townsend Analytics, LTD.

of Trade (CBOT) mini-Dow chart in Figure 5.20 shows, the monthly target resistance R-2 was 11105, the weekly R-1 was 11101, and the daily pivot target number was 11076 on 1/11/2006. The exact high was 11086! That top marked a 413-point decline, as the low was 10673 just six trading days later. The power of pivot point confluence from the prevailing three time periods demonstrated that there was significant resistance; and the actions of the three groups of traders may have joined together in identifying that area as a spot to sell. In Table 5.2, we see that the data collected to determine the pivot point resistance levels from the three time frames were all noncorrelated to some degree. The closing, or settlement, prices all had different values, as did the highs and lows of each time frame. The purpose for identifying a confluence zone is to heighten your awareness that a potentially substantial move may be on the horizon and that a bigger reversal reaction may occur, giving a trading opportunity longer than a day trade. Once you identify an opportunity, you can apply a strategy. In this case, you might have been able to make a choice among selling Dow futures, buying put options on the futures, or selling the exchange traded fund (ETF) diamonds.

TABLE 5.2   Pivot Point Confluences for Dow

Prior Period	High	Low	Close
Monthly—December	11007	10728	10744
Weekly—1/06/2006	11014	10720	10998
Daily—1/10/2006	11058	10990	11052

In fact, let's look at the actual chart pattern on that day to see what occurred. In Figure 5.21, the date and time are stamped at the bottom of the graph; and you will see we have a 15-minute candle chart showing that the high was made at the end of the day, formed by a pair of shooting stars followed by a doji.

These candle formations are very ominous signs indicating a bearish tone; but, due to the end of the trading day, it hardly makes for a trading opportunity for a day trader to take a short position. However, the data did give a trader a great opportunity to look at a profit objective from an earlier long position, as the confluence of pivot point resistance levels and the

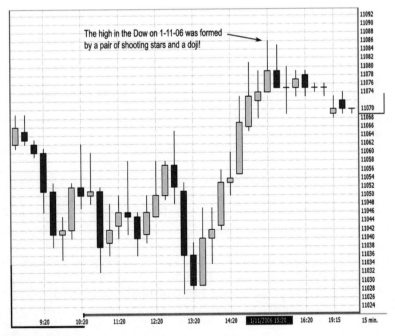

FIGURE 5.21
Used with permission of esignal.com.

Daily (Right) /ESH6 - Mar 06 E-Mini S&P 500 Bar
2005

2006   Actual High on 1-11-06 1301!

Weekly R-1 = 1306

Daily R-2 = 1301.5

Monthly R-2 = 1297.50

Pivot point confluences do indicate
significant taregt resistance levels.

FIGURE 5.22
RealTick graphics used with permission of Townsend Analytics, LTD.

candle patterns confirmed that the bullish momentum was fading. In addition, once the market confirmed a top pattern, the day trader would be able to shift his or her trading plan from buying breaks to taking selling opportunities as the trend conditions changed and there was overhead pivot point resistance.

Looking at Figure 5.22, we see how the pivot points from the three time frames (daily, weekly, and monthly) target the high near the 1300 level. The actual high was 1301.

In Table 5.3, you can see that the three sets of data (high, low, and

TABLE 5.3   Pivot Point Confluences for S&P

Prior Period	High	Low	Close
Monthly—December	1285.00	1251.25	1254.75
Weekly—1/06/2006	1293.00	1251.50	1291.75
Daily—1/10/2006	1296.75	1289.25	1296.00

close) from three different time periods are different values. So the coincidental factor really highlights the importance of pivot point confluences.

In Figure 5.23, the confluence of pivot points in the CBOT 30-year bonds shows a setup similar in resistance levels to both the S&P and the Dow in the examples in Figures 5.20 and 5.22 from the daily chart perspective. In fact, in this case, the bonds peaked nearly at the same time as the equity markets. This is a great point to bring up now; we will see periods in the market where intercommodity or intermarket relationships change. Stock and bond prices go in phases of parallel price moves, and then there are periods in time where they decouple. Generally speaking, when interest rates decline, bonds and stocks move higher. Then there are times when stocks move sharply lower and bond prices move higher because they offer security, which is known as a "flight to quality." And then there was 2005, when interest rates were rising and stocks and bonds moved in sync. Knowing when these changes in market relationships occur is helpful; however, it is best at times to trade the markets independently of each other. This is where identifying pivot point confluences based on two or three time

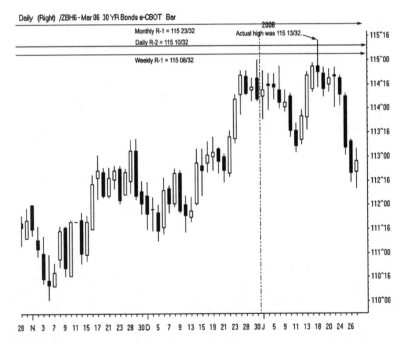

FIGURE 5.23
RealTick graphics used with permission of Townsend Analytics, LTD.

TABLE 5.4 Pivot Point Confluences for Bonds

Prior Period	High	Low	Close
Monthly—December	115	$111\frac{5}{32}$	$114\frac{6}{32}$
Weekly—1/13/2006	$114\frac{25}{32}$	$113\frac{5}{32}$	$114\frac{25}{32}$
Daily—1/17/2006	$114\frac{19}{32}$	$114\frac{1}{32}$	$114\frac{25}{32}$

frames will help you as a trader because you have predetermined price targets figured out in advance.

As Figure 5.23 shows, the daily and weekly numbers were more accurate in determining the top. The monthly number was slightly higher by $\frac{10}{32}$, a small margin of error. The important element to remember here is that we are not looking to pick an exact top; rather, we are looking for a reason and an area that offers a high degree of accuracy in helping to pinpoint a top or a bottom and then looking for a secondary signal to trigger, or initiate, a trade. The importance and coincidental factor in the theory of confluences is once again that the numbers derived from the various time frames are generally noncorrelated. Table 5.4 shows that the high in December was from a different time period and had an assigned value different from the weekly or daily number; and the same holds true for the low and the closing values.

The relationship that exists between geopolitical issues and economic conditions (such as inflation, interest rates, foreign currencies, and gold) from a historic perspective has been easy to track. In general terms, at times when the dollar goes up in value, gold prices decline. When interest rates climb, lease rates are more expensive, therefore putting downward pressure on gold. Gold prices also move higher as investors buy gold as a safe haven investment, as it acts as cash as well in times when doubt exists over the stability of a country's economic condition or when currency values change, as happened in the middle of 2005 when dissention among euro zone countries existed and riots due to political instability in France developed.

By late 2005, the dollar rallied as interest rates climbed, widening the interest rate differentials between the United States and foreign countries. Gold rallied sharply higher on these events, from the low on February 8, 2005, at 410 per ounce. By the end of 2005, gold had made a high of 540 per ounce. By January 20, 2006, gold continued its ascent by making a high at 568.50 in the February futures contract.

The market had made a sharp rally, but the confluence of resistance numbers held the market back, as shown in the 15-minute chart in Figure 5.24. In this chart, you will see the bearish engulfing pattern form as the

FIGURE 5.24
Used with permission of esignal.com.

market makes a violent reversal. Longer-term prices did recover and moved even higher as of the writing of this book. The point is that by using pivot points combined with candle patterns, you can time your entries and exits in the market for a better price point. That is an outstanding advantage from a risk-reward perspective.

In this example, prices did stall over time before continuing higher. However, the weekly and monthly resistance targets kept prices in a consolidating pattern, as you can see from the daily chart in Figure 5.25. It is interesting to note that the exact high was formed by a shooting star pattern. The value in using and identifying these confluence levels is that a trader/analyst/investor is given both elements for successful trading: price objectives combined with a specific time period. It is up to the trader to manage a trade or to identify the magnitude of the reversal. Not all outcomes are the same, but the markets do react off these numbers; so that is why we are looking to combine pivot point analysis with another dimension of market analysis.

The second part of the trading equation using pivot points is combining the idea of how to filter the numbers to help identify which support or resistance numbers to use to determine market condition. Remember we cov-

High made on 1-20-06 was 568.5.
The top was formed by a shooting star.

FIGURE 5.25
Used with permission of esignal.com.

ered the fact that in a bearish market condition, the actual pivot point would act as resistance. Confluence, or the cluster of support or resistance numbers, also works within a specific time period. For example, when the actual pivot point lines up at or near the market direction number or moving average of the pivot point and a resistance target number, we should study that specific price zone for signals that indicate a shift in momentum. This is the part where we need to comprehend what the charts and price action are revealing.

Candle patterns do just that in a clear visual manner. As you look at Figure 5.26, you will see that the exact high of the trading session on 1/20/2006 was formed by a doji. A confluence existed with the lining up of the daily pivot point, the market direction numbers, and the R-1. The market never even had the strength to test the resistance levels. By the end of the day, the Dow fell another 100-plus points from the last price you see on this chart—the low was 10673 that day. Once the low close doji signal occurred and the shift in momentum occurred by making lower closing lows, a sharp sell-off developed.

The September 2004 *Active Trade Magazine* published an article I wrote and made it a cover story. It was on the power of pivot point conflu-

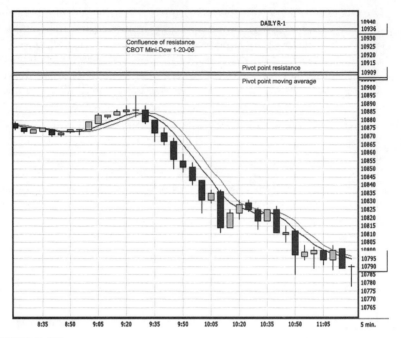

FIGURE 5.26
Used with permission of esignal.com.

ence and how calculating pivot points on more than one time frame can help identify certain price levels that are likely to repel prices. The article (p. 68) was titled "Pivot Points and Right Side Chart Analysis." You may have read that article or seen the issue—it was the one with President Bush and Senator Kerry on the cover. The article's focus was on not only entry prices and risk management, but also profit objectives and how to trade around the support and resistance numbers. What was most interesting about that article was the fact that the confluence of daily, weekly, and monthly numbers lined up near 1160 (see Table 5.5) and the exact high for March 5, 2004, was 1163.50.

TABLE 5.5 Confluence

Time Frame	Confluence Number
Monthly R-1	1161.50
Weekly R-2	1162.00
Daily R-2	1159.25

The average price level derived from the confluence numbers was 1161.00. The high for the year took less than 15 minutes to form and was made by a doji and a shooting star on a 5-minute chart, as Figure 5.27 shows. That high held for 11 months, until after the November elections. The point to this example is that the power of confluence worked to repel prices. The outcome can be different each time, meaning we don't know what the percentage of retracement of price reversal will be. The general idea, however, is that as a trader you should respect the notion that the market will at least pause and more than likely generate a significant trading opportunity.

The particular setup that initiated a sell signal was my signature low close doji trigger, one of the patterns on which we go into detail in the next few chapters! This pattern and the high close doji at or near pivot point support targets are the highest probability trade signals I use.

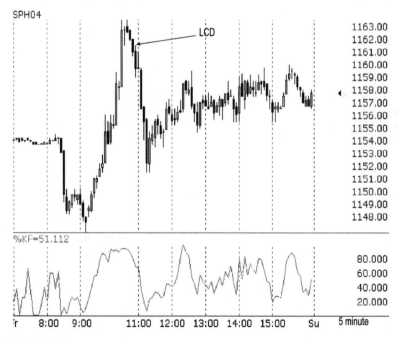

FIGURE 5.27
Used with permission of esignal.com.

SUMMARY

Remember that pivot point support and resistance levels are a great gauge of what a potential turning point or a predicted range in a given time period will be. The more time periods or confluence of target numbers that line up, the higher is the probability that a strong market reaction will occur. Therefore, it is important to raise your attention when prices reach these predicted price support and resistance numbers. If you apply proper risk and trade management techniques, as will be covered in the next few chapters, you should see a tremendous turnaround in your trading performance.

CHAPTER 6

Pivot Point Moving Average System

The moving average is one of the most widely utilized indicators in technical analysis because the moving average is easily identifiable and easy to back-test. Many automated trading systems use moving averages or some derivative of a moving average to generate buy and sell signals. Moving averages are considered classic indicators and are very popular with traders today. Most technicians view the moving average as a way to signal a change in the direction of the trend, as well as a way to smooth out the volatility of the market. In Chapter 2, we covered a key component in understanding the concept of *trend*, which in essence gives you the ability to understand the concept of *momentum*. Remember this: "In a bullish environment, buying begets buying." Higher closing highs bring higher highs as momentum and assigned values (the closes) are justified. The law of physics that states that "a body in motion tends to stay in motion until a force or obstacle stops or changes that motion" applies in this scenario because higher assigned values can induce more buying from existing buyers and can attract new buyers. Once again, the opposite is true of a bearish market: Lower closing lows bring lower lows as momentum and assigned values are justified. The lower assigned values induce more selling by existing sellers and can attract new sellers into the market.

When prices have appreciated and all buyers have exhausted their resources to add more long positions in a bull market, prices have reached what is known as *absolute value*. Prices will more than likely consolidate for a period of time before they change direction and reverse lower in value. The opposite is true in a downtrending market. An important component to remember is that price action typically moves from trend phase to congestion and can either continue with the original trend or reverse the trend. Momentum and the psychology of the perception of the value of a given market in a given time period are what will move prices from a consolidation, or congestion phase, back to a trending condition.

DETERMINING TREND DIRECTION

Simply put, one way to determine the trend is by drawing trend lines. In an uptrend, we should see a sequence of higher highs and higher lows, so we would draw a line against the lows and extend it outward to forecast a support level sometime in the future. In a downtrend, as the sequence of events shows lower highs and lower lows, we would draw a line against the top of the highs and extend it outward to help forecast a resistance point in the future.

Another method used in determining trend line support and resistance is through the use of moving averages. The most popular method of using a moving average is to average the *closing prices* (sometimes referred to as the *settlement prices*) of a defined number of sessions. The moving average is a lagging indicator. The purpose of the moving average is to indicate the beginning and the ending of a trend. Since the moving average follows the market, the signals it generates occur after the trend has already changed. It is argued that most traders (or about 70 percent) lose their money in the markets. If the reason is that most traders focus on moving average values that are predetermined by default settings in their charting software packages or if they use the media's favorite 200-day moving average, it's no wonder that people lose. The majority are following the same indicator.

BEAT THE STREET

As Yogi said, "If you want to do better than the average bear, then you have to think better than the average bear!" If you want to beat the Street, then you need to think better than the Street—use a different set of values or understand how signals are generated. You do not want to follow and trade off what everyone else is looking at; so when it comes to moving averages, you want to look at a different set of conditions and time periods. Think for a minute: If lots of traders are watching for trade signals on 10, 20, and 50 periods and if the statement holds true that the majority of traders lose, then why do you want to trade based off signals on those moving averages? It might serve you well to watch these indicators so you can see where others get in or out of trades, but certainly not to follow those, which would be the same as succumbing to crowd mentality. Some traders and technical analysts use various ways to calculate moving averages, such as the simple, the weighted, and the exponential. I prefer the simple moving average and a different set of values for my moving average, namely the pivot point.

THE SIMPLE MOVING AVERAGE

The simple moving average (the arithmetic mean) is the most popular moving average used in technical analysis. The *simple moving average* is the sum of the closing prices over a period of sessions divided by the number of sessions. For example, a 10-day moving average would be the sum of the past 10 days' closing prices divided by 10. Each new day would drop the first day's closing price and add the *new* day's closing price. As new data is added to the calculation, old data is removed. By averaging the price data, a smoother line is produced, and the trend is much easier to recognize. The disadvantage of the simple moving average is that it only takes into account the time period of the sessions covered in the calculation and that it gives equal weight to each day's price.

In Chapters 4 and 5, we covered the pivot point formulas and the significance of pivot points as support and resistance. As you will recall, the pivot point calculation provides the mean (average) for the session's trading range, or high, low, and close: $(H + L + C)/3$.

This moving average section discusses how the moving average helps clarify the market's price flow by extending price analysis over a certain period of time. In this manner, moving averages can accentuate when a market enters an extreme condition by how far it departs from the mean. Price action either will move toward the moving average or will return to the moving average to retest that level.

The "Market Direction" number that was shown in the Excel sheet in Figure 5.8 is a combination of the use of price session information (pivot point number) over a period of time (moving average). The market direction number utilizes cumulative data from the high, the low, and the close for a session. This information provides a clear picture of the "average true price" for that time period. The market direction number is then calculated by taking the average pivot number from the past three periods. Any time frame can be utilized to calculate the number. However, the longer the time frame, the more significance the number will hold. To calculate the market direction number, add three pivot points from the same session, and divide the sum by three. The purpose of using the pivot point in the moving average calculation is that the pivot point will show the continuance of the trend.

$$\text{Market Direction} = \frac{\text{Pivot} + \text{Pivot} + \text{Pivot}}{3}$$

As stated previously, the market direction number, which is a three-period pivot point moving average, can act as a support number in bullish conditions and has a high degree of importance when one of the pivot point calculations for the current session coincides with or is near that number. The market direction number holds true as a resistance number in a bear market condition. If another number coincides with the market direction number, such as the actual pivot point or an R-1 (resistance level one) number, then it would serve as the target high number for that specific time period. Another way of using the three-period pivot point moving average is as a point of reference or fair value. For example, when the market price departs, or deviates, too far from the mean, then you can use the extreme resistance or support number, such as R-2 or S-2 (support level two), or the farthest target number of that direction, as a potential turning point. When various time frames are incorporated into the analysis (daily, weekly, and monthly), there is more certainty that the target price level can generate the anticipated reaction. If the market gaps too far from the daily pivot point moving average, use the monthly and/or weekly target support and resistance numbers to help identify a targeted reversal support or resistance point. Figure 6.1 shows a spot foreign exchange (forex) British pound daily chart with the three-period pivot point moving average overlaid on top of prices. Notice that as the market changes conditions from bearish (downtrend) to bullish (uptrend), prices bounce off the moving average as a support line and then trade off the moving average as it acts as a ceiling of resistance. If you notice the price action from November 15 to November 25, you will see that the market entered a consolidating phase as prices moved above and below the moving average. The moving average went virtually in a flat line with a bias to an *upside* slope. This was hinting that prices were getting ready to change direction. When you watch the moving average in relation to the underlying price action, sometimes you can get clues as to the true market price direction using the pivot point moving average. Due to the weighting of the high, low, and close combined, the moving average factors in the typical price of that time period, thus giving a better gauge of market value. If the close is closer to the high, the average will be at a higher assigned value. Using the three-period pivot point will help you filter out much of the market noise and will give you a truer sense of the market's fair value within the price range of the past three trading periods.

At times, the *slope*, or angle, of the moving average can give you a clue as to the market's true strength or weakness, especially when combined

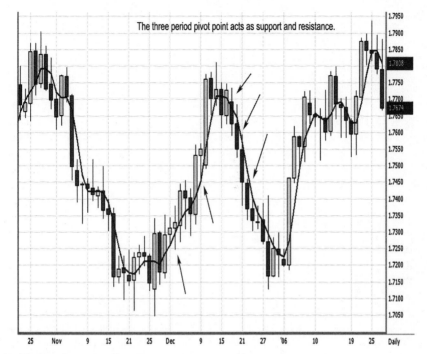

FIGURE 6.1
Used with permission of esignal.com.

with candlestick charting. The slope helps filter out the noise, and you can see if the market's value is progressively appreciating or depreciating. When a market goes from the trending phase into the consolidation phase, it is the slope of the pivot point moving average that can help you identify the potential price direction the market makes next from the consolidating phase, such as if the market will make a continuation or a trend reversal move. For added clarity, when combined with identifying a high-probability bottom or top-forming candle, you have added confirmation of a potential move.

In Figure 6.2, the graph shows a representation of a pivot point moving average in a declining trend phase. Then as prices consolidate as the pivot point average measures the typical price rather than the close, we can determine what the true market value is and which way prices tend to be moving. Markets sometimes demonstrate extreme volatility at turning points, and the moving average approach can help filter out the noise inflicted by wide price swings. These swings often lead to confusion or worse—traders getting whipsawed, causing loss in trading equity.

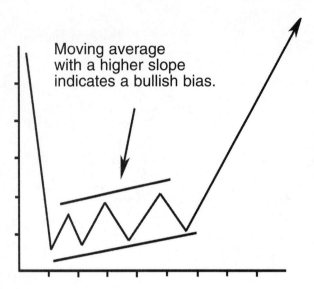

Moving average
with a higher slope
indicates a bullish bias.

FIGURE 6.2

As the moving average slopes up, it indicates that the market values are also tending to trade higher. Eventually, we see a trend reversal, which is what the direction of the moving average indicated.

In Figure 6.3, let's look at a five-minute chart on the Chicago Board of Trade (CBOT) mini-Dow contract. Just to clarify, the minimum tick fluctuation is a one-point move, and every point is worth $5. So the overall contract value is $5 times the index. If the Dow is at 10500, the contract value is $52,500. This may not make sense now, but as you read the book further, you will understand what the low close doji sell signal is about and what the specific rules are for entering on this pattern. For purposes of illustrating what phase a market goes in and how the pivot point moving average can help you follow a market, let's look at the sequence of events:

- The market develops into a downtrend.
- At the bottom, a bullish reversal candle pattern forms.
- Prices start trading wildly, but the moving averages (M/As) are sloping higher.
- The market reverses and then goes into a sideways channel or consolidating phase. (If you examine the pivot point moving averages, you will see they were pointing higher while prices were in the congestion phase.)
- Prices finally break out and continue the uptrend.

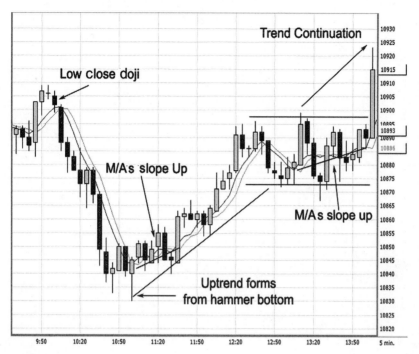

FIGURE 6.3
Used with permission of esignal.com.

This chart was from 2/10/2006; prices went on to trade that day as high as 10963. The moving averages did alert you to the internal strength, and the price direction did continue higher—a pretty good method for getting a clue to the market's next move.

In Figure 6.4, we have the CBOT mini-Dow contract, which shows that the market was coming out of the congestion, or consolidation, period in late October. The three-period pivot point moving average was also flatlining with an upward slope in the direction of the moving average. Once the market made a break for it by establishing the uptrend, the average helped identify the trending condition. As the chart illustrates, the pivot point moving average actually hugs the market's lows when in an uptrend and the highs in a downtrend. It also helps to identify the conditional changes when the market makes reversals.

This moving average approach works just as well for active day trading markets, such as the e-mini–Standard & Poor's (S&P) shown in the 5-minute chart in Figure 6.5, as it does for swing or position traders. This method can help active day traders to see and to confirm changes in price conditions, such as when the market is in a consolidating period to trend-

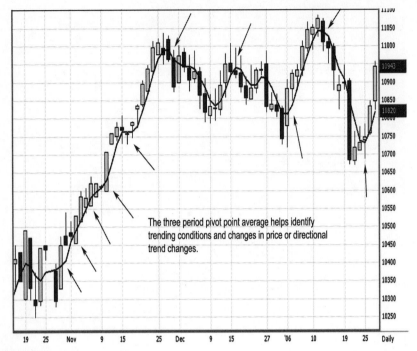

The three period pivot point average helps identify trending conditions and changes in price or directional trend changes.

FIGURE 6.4
Used with permission of esignal.com.

ing mode. Notice how the moving average acts as a support once the market starts the breakout in the uptrend.

The three-period pivot point moving average works as a tool to confirm triggers and exits by price action closing above or below the moving average pivot line. In Figure 6.6, we have a 15-minute chart on the spot forex Japanese yen currency. As the market forms a bottom at 9:00 A.M., notice how the moving average shows a cup formation and that the price of the market closes above the moving average. This gives us a clue that the market is starting to change from a bearish trend condition to a consolidating phase and that the market is starting to move into a reversal of the current trending condition. As the market starts to establish higher highs and higher lows, it also is closing above prior highs and, most important, closing above the three-period pivot point moving average. Now the average starts to act as a support target until prices reach the top, and the moving average starts to flatline again as prices go into another consolidating phase. The Japanese yen chart provides a good example of a high close hammer trigger, confirmed by the price closing above the moving average pivot line.

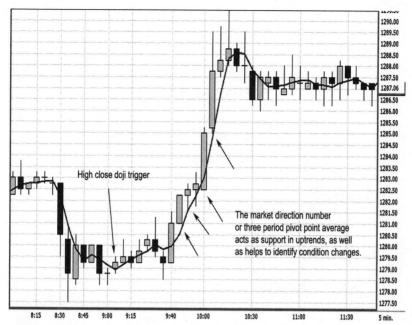

High close doji trigger

The market direction number or three period pivot point average acts as support in uptrends, as well as helps to identify condition changes.

FIGURE 6.5
Used with permission of esignal.com.

TRADING TRIGGER STRATEGY

- *After a Downtrend.* If the price closes above the moving average (M/A) and above the prior time period's highs, with a sequence of higher highs and higher lows, enter a long position, as the uptrend is now confirmed. You will want the moving average to have formed a flat line or a higher-sloping angle. Place a stop below the lowest low point.

  Closing Price > M/A = Go long or exit shorts

- *After an Uptrend.* If the price closes below the moving average and below the prior time period's lows, with a sequence of lower highs and lower lows, enter a short position, as the downtrend is now confirmed. You will want the moving average to have formed a flat line or a lower-sloping angle. Place a stop above the highest high point.

  Closing Price < M/A = Go short or exit longs

  When trading based off the market direction number or three-period pivot point moving average, there is no need to wait for the value of the

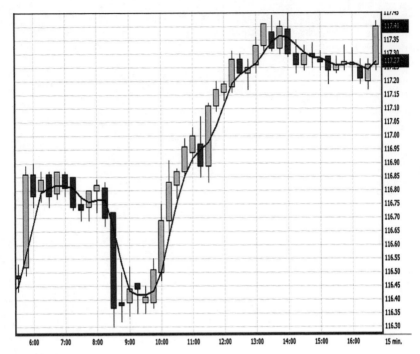

FIGURE 6.6
Used with permission of esignal.com.

moving average to start rising or falling to determine the trigger to enter the market. A close above the moving average will trigger a long position, and a close below the moving average will trigger a short position. However, you want to see the moving average values follow the direction of the price move in the desired trade.

CONDITIONAL OPTIMIZED MOVING AVERAGE SYSTEM

The *Conditional Optimized Moving Average System*™ (COMAS) incorporates the pivot point moving average approach with another variable. This method combines two moving averages. The resulting system provides a powerful crossover trigger to enter the market as well as an indicator of the move's strength with the slope and the difference, or separation, of the moving average lines.

A crossover provides both the entry and the exit signals, in addition to a set of rules or conditions. This system works on any time frame, five minutes and greater, and in any high-volume market. It is an excellent short-term trading method for highly liquid markets such as forex, for certain futures markets, and for stocks that have ample trading volume. One *variation* of what I use in my trading library with the Genesis Software and teach in our Trading Triggers University is the one-period pivot point with the three-period moving average of the pivot point. There are other combinations you can use, such as a five-period pivot point moving average of the pivot point with a two-period simple moving average of a close. I test various time periods and variables for my parameter settings because of the various conditions each market has. After all, bonds move differently than the e-mini–Standard & Poor's (S&P) 500, the mini-Dow, the Russell, or the Nadsdaq does. You may agree that forex currencies move differently than individual stocks. The bottom line is this: I use the two moving average values to help me identify a shift in momentum of the market; and then as the conditions change, such as a close above or below the values of both moving averages, I use the pivot point filtering method to help me identify a potential profit target.

For the purposes of this book, let me show you how to integrate the pivot point with the three-period moving average of the pivot point. In Chapter 5, I disclosed how to filter the pivot support and resistance levels by labeling the market condition as neutral, bullish, or bearish. You can also chart and track the conditional change of the market by plotting the directional change in the two moving average settings. Figure 6.7 shows both moving average values declining; but as the pivot point crosses above the three-period moving averages, it alerts us that the internal market condition is changing to bullish. Once both moving averages start to point up and the pivot point is above the three-period pivot point average the market condition confirms we are in a bullish trend. As a general rule, a trader would look to buy from an area of support in a market that is trending upward (buy pullbacks).

Figure 6.8 shows a five-minute chart on the e-mini–S&P 500 futures. In the preopen outcry session around 8:00 A.M. (yes, you can trade preopen outcry session), notice that the market is trading sideways and that the moving average values are as well. Then by 8:30 A.M., the market turns lower and goes into a congestion phase trading sideways until 9:45 A.M. The tall white candle closes above both moving average values and above the prior time period's high (which was a hammer pattern). As the market starts to move in a bullish trend mode, focus on the action of the moving averages in relation to prices. The pivot point is above the three-period moving average pivot point; and there are higher highs, higher lows, and higher closing values above both moving averages and past highs. This series of conditions continued until after the top was formed by a shooting star at 10:15 A.M. The trigger to go long occurred after the breakout of the sideways

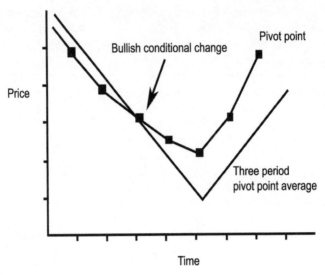

FIGURE 6.7

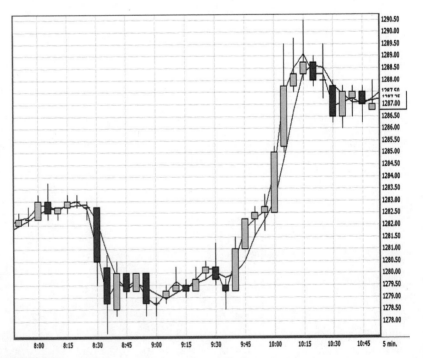

FIGURE 6.8
Used with permission of esignal.com.

range at 1282.25 and after the trigger to exit the trade was initiated at 1288. This was a 5.75-point gain per contract. The focus is that prices traded above both moving average values and that the three-period pivot point moving average acted as support all the way up. Both moving averages were moving in tandem with each other, and the slope of both averages was pointing in the direction of the trend.

TRADING TIPS

This is an important point, so let me reiterate—What helps indicate the strength of a trend when you use two or more sets of values for your moving averages are:

- The slopes of the moving averages are both pointing in the direction of the trend.
- The moving averages have a good degree of separation or are equidistant from each other, which indicates a steady trending condition.
- The moving averages are trending in tangent or are parallel with each other, rather than one significantly outpacing the other.
- If the shorter-term moving average separates or moves too far away from the longer-term moving average, then there is a potential for an overbought condition. Traders should start looking to liquidate half of their positions.
- When a crossover occurs, traders should liquidate the entire position

We have not yet covered candle patterns, an integrating component of this trading method. Most traders have a basic understanding of candle patterns, and I do go over the more frequent and recurring ones. By now you may have seen dojis, shooting stars at tops, and hammers at bottoms in this first section of the book. There is a good reason for that, which we will cover. Right now, let's focus on the moving average components.

Figure 6.9 is a 5-minute chart on the CBOT mini-Dow looking at the same time period as the e-mini–S&P in Figure 6.8. Notice the coincidence factor as both markets form similar patterns at the same precise moment. I bring up this point because it is important that as a day trader you follow like or similar markets to see if there is confirmation throughout the sector. Besides, if one market rallies, it is likely that the other market will rally as well. All 30 stocks in the Dow are traded in the S&P 500. Therefore, they can be considered *like*, or markets that will trade in tandem with each other. One market may develop a specific pattern that is more pronounced than a pattern in the other market, and you can trade one market based on

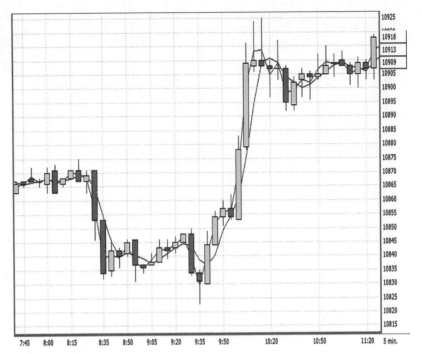

FIGURE 6.9
Used with permission of esignal.com.

a signal from the other. Notice in Figure 6.9 that the Dow made a lower low on that day and was formed by what I call the jackhammer pattern, which I will cover later.

Watch the relationship of the moving averages. Once the long white candle formed after the hammer, which is the candle that made the lowest low point in the market, the tall white candle closed above both moving average values and above the hammer candle's high. As prices started to move in a bullish trend, focus on the action of the moving averages in relation to prices. The pivot point is above the three-period moving average pivot point; prices form a sequence of higher highs, higher lows, and higher closing values above both moving averages and the prior time period's highs. This series of conditions continued until after the top was formed by a shooting star around 10:15 A.M. in conjunction with the mini-S&P. The trigger to enter a long occurred at 10845 until the first lower closing low, or conditional change, occurred when prices closed below prior sessions' lows and below the moving averages at 10895—a nice clean 50-point trade in the mini-Dow, or $250 per contract in less than 50 minutes.

In Figure 6.10, let's go over what the 15-minute chart on the spot forex

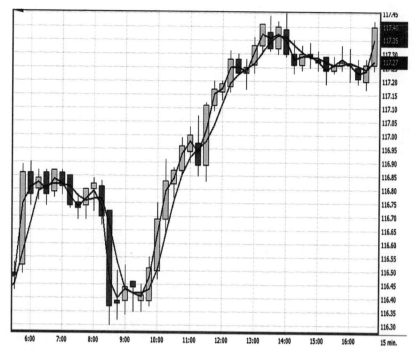

FIGURE 6.10
Used with permission of esignal.com.

yen looks like with the COMAS method. If you look at the candle before 10 A.M., you will see the moving average values actually crossed over first, before the long white candle formed after 10 A.M. This gives an early warning and indicates that there is a bullish bias. Keep in mind that it happened before the price action confirmed a bullish trend with the sequence of higher highs, higher lows, and higher closing highs. This feature allows you to have an early warning system in place that helps spot directional trend changes. Look at Figure 6.11 with the daily chart on the spot forex British pound. As you can see, the moving average crossover that occured on November 25 foretold of the bullish trend reversal that carries the market from the 1.71 level all the way up to the 1.77 area. In that trend run, you will see how the moving averages both lined up and acted as support. By the time December 15 rolled around, see how the moving averages cross back down, giving you an early warning that the trend was in jeopardy; and sure enough, a bearish reversal occurred. From the peak made in December, we see that the market declined, which triggered a sell signal when the pivot point crossed beneath the three-period moving average. That not only indicated a major bearish reversal but also showed that the three-period pivot

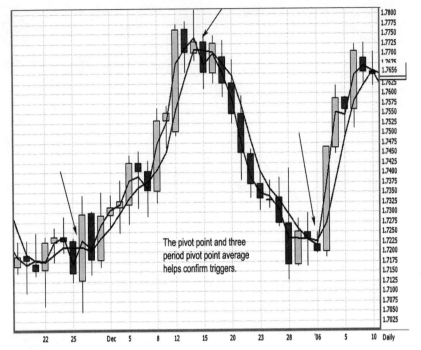

The pivot point and three period pivot point average helps confirm triggers.

FIGURE 6.11
Used with permission of esignal.com.

point acted as a resistance line all the way down as prices kept in the bearish sequence of lower highs, lower lows, and lower closing lows. There is one more element to that sequence, which is that a dark candle represents the market closes below each time period's open. Keep that in mind when we go over candle patterns in Chapter 7.

As illustrated in Figure 6.12, the COMAS method can work in helping to determine changes in market conditions from a consolidating phase to a bullish uptrending phase and then back to a downtrending, or bearish, condition phase. This graph illustrates a bearish conditional change in the market once the pivot point crosses beneath the three-period moving average pivot point. Once you have identified that a bearish condition exists, then you can trigger a short position. As a general rule, a trader should look to *sell* from an area of *resistance* in a market that is trending to the downside; that is, sell rallies. A trader wll see more profits in selling rallies than in buying breaks in declining or bearish trending markets.

In trading, as in life, timing is everything. There is nothing more frustrating to a trader than to correctly analyze the market, correctly predict the direction of the trend, get stopped out due to a premature entry, and

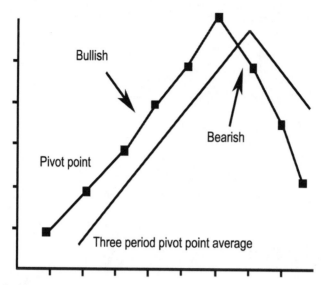

FIGURE 6.12

then watch the market move in the originally predicted direction. As we all determine early in our trading careers, being correct about the direction of the trend is not enough. We must also be able to anticipate when the market is setting up to trigger an appropriate entry into the market. The pivot point combined with a moving average of the pivot point is one method that can help you successfully identify when a conditional change may occur in the market.

Let's look at Figure 6.13, which is a 15-minute chart on the spot forex British pound. Notice the period after the long white candle at approximately 9:00 A.M.—prices go in a sideways mode or consolidation phase. The moving averages also flatline with a bias toward a downward slope. The crossover occurs, followed by a lower closing low, a lower high, and a lower low; and the close is below the open. In addition, the price is closing beneath both moving averages; and, most important, the three-period pivot point moving average acts as resistance, all the way down, until the market moves into a consolidating phase.

The concept of incorporating pivot point analysis with a moving average approach will give you a testable, mechanical, systematic approach to trading. In order to execute a trade, you need to have specific elements occur. Knowledge of these elements will arm you with critical information that can help provide you with protection from overtrading and from suffering from emotional pitfalls.

FIGURE 6.13
Used with permission of esignal.com.

1. In order to execute a trade, you need to see a change in market direction and commitment from the market to illustrate a change in market direction by closing above or below the moving averages.

2. You need to follow some simple rules, such as take buy signals at support and take sell signals at resistance.

The importance of this trading method is that you must be able to apply the techniques on a consistent basis that allows you to make decisions in a mechanical and nonemotional way. A common mistake that traders make is that they do not test a strategy to make a logical determination about whether the strategy is viable for their trading style. Many traders adopt a new strategy, trade with it immediately, and start tweaking different components of the strategy. Then they decide that there is no merit to the strategy, since it is not profitable, and begin looking for a different strategy. A much better approach is to establish a defined set of trading rules and test those rules until an outcome is determined based on a reasonable number of trades. *Patience* to wait for triggers and not act on the anticipation of an outcome and *discipline* to follow through with that trigger are a must if you are to be successful. These character traits can be learned and developed by implementing this methodology. It is what I teach students and other highly successful professional traders.

When the price target has been met and the trigger has presented itself, enter the trade without hesitation. Do not think about the entry; this is a mechanical process. You have already done your homework, and you have satisfied your criteria. Your system is in place, and this is part of the system. If you do not place the trade when the trigger executes and confirms, you are not trading according to your plan. Successful traders have the courage to act and act promptly. It is important to recognize the immediate environment or market condition. Is it up, down, or sideways? After a trend is established, let's say a bullish trend, it should consist of higher highs and higher lows; each period should close above the open, and we should see higher closing highs. The pivot point moving average should help verify this condition. In a bearish trend, we would want to see lower highs and lower lows; each period should close below the open of each period. Under these circumstances, the pivot point moving average should confirm this market condition as well.

Traders need to identify themselves, which will help them know the time frame to follow in a trending market. Are you a day trader? Are you a swing trader who may be in a position that lasts two to five days? Or are you a position trader? Once you acknowledge what your time objective is, you can narrow down your goals and your expectations for the trade. For example, when I am day trading, I will generally be able to identify what the average range for a day is; I will expect that if I miss 20 percent of the bottom and 20 percent of the top, while waiting for a moving average crossover signal, then I can expect to only capture 60 percent of the average daily range. Perhaps this can be achieved only once or twice a day.

HOW DO I START?

First, I need to structure my computer and my charts to a format that is conducive to day trading. For stock index contracts, I watch two "like" or "tandem" markets in two time periods. These are the CBOT mini-Dow and the e-mini–S&P. Lately, due to client requests, I have been alerted to trading the Russell 2000 and the German stock index *Deutscher Aktien* Index, known as the DAX. The DAX, an index portfolio of 30 German blue-chip stocks, opens at 3 A.M. (ET) and closes at 11 A.M. (ET). (On a side note, as of October 2006, the DAX, based in Frankfurt, Germany, will start accepting non-German companies. In order to qualify for the Index, foreign companies must conduct their operations in Germany.) The DAX 30 actually tracks close to moves in the S&P 500 futures. In spot forex, I use the euro and a like market, such as the British pound and the yen.

For day trading, I use the 5- and 15-minute time periods. All of my chart screens look the same: The 5-minute e-mini–S&P and the mini-Dow are on the top, and the 15-minute S&P and mini-Dow are on the bottom. All my chart pages are set up this way; therefore, all chart pages are synchronized so that I do not watch different time periods when switching from one screen to another—I have a uniform setting.

- I find the most reliable day trade signals are confirmed in the 15-minute time frame and triggered in the 5-minute time period as well.
- When both time frames are in sync with each other and when like markets have similar signals, this generates a higher probability trigger.

As I stated earlier, the parameters I use in this book are a variation of what is programmed in my proprietary library with Genesis Software. This is a system that generates buy and sell signals based on the principles we have gone over in the book so far. More information on this software can be found on my web site at www.nationalfutures.com

Figure 6.14 illustrates how I line up the e-mini–S&P with the mini-Dow side by side with the corresponding time periods of 5 minutes at the top and 15 minutes at the bottom. Stock and forex charts are lined up the same way.

The greatest feature with this software is that it highlights a sell signal with a red triangle pointing down, and it signals a buy trigger with a green triangle pointing up. These coincide against resistance levels to sell and support levels to buy. As you can see, the sell signals when aligned against the pivot point resistance numbers offer a fantastic visual confirmation based on my predefined strategies; therefore, it will help eliminate the emotional element and impatience of acting on anticipation rather than on a true signal.

All the signals and methods covered in this book can be applied with most charting packages. In fact, 26 years ago, I was calculating the pivot point support and resistance numbers with a handheld calculator. The pivot point calculator is available on my web site. In addition, this book comes with a CD (compact disc) that has a pivot point calculator as well. All that needs to be done is to input the data for the high, the low, and the close; and the R-2 down to the S-2 numbers will be calculated for you. It is very easy to use; all you need are the prices for stocks, futures, or forex markets for any time frame. Figure 6.15 shows the monthly price range for Dell Inc., which I will use to demonstrate how powerful this method of market analysis is when combined with certain candlestick patterns.

Figure 6.16 is Dell with the monthly and weekly pivot support targets indicating a possible bottom. Using the higher time frames, such as the monthly figures, alerted me to a major bottom. All I then needed to do was

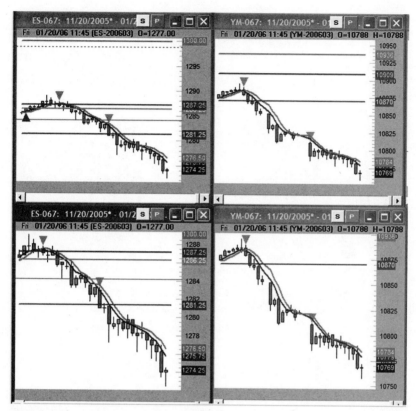

FIGURE 6.14
Used with permission of www.GenesisFT.com.

to look and wait for the reversal trigger, which came when the market made a high close doji pattern.

The next few chapters will really bring home the message of the value of incorporating pivot points and candlestick patterns. Using the pivot point as a moving average in addition to using the pivot point calculations to identify target ranges will certainly make you a more prepared trader.

This method has captured the attention of many experts who are now using it; and its accuracy at predicting turning points in the market constantly amazes me. Believe me, many people are fascinated by this concept. In December 2002, *Futures Magazine* first published an article I wrote on the subject, "Combining Cycles and Pivot Points to Predict Market Values" (p. 38), and has published several other articles of mine. Perry Kaufman, the famous technician and author, in the fourth edition of his nearly 1,200-page

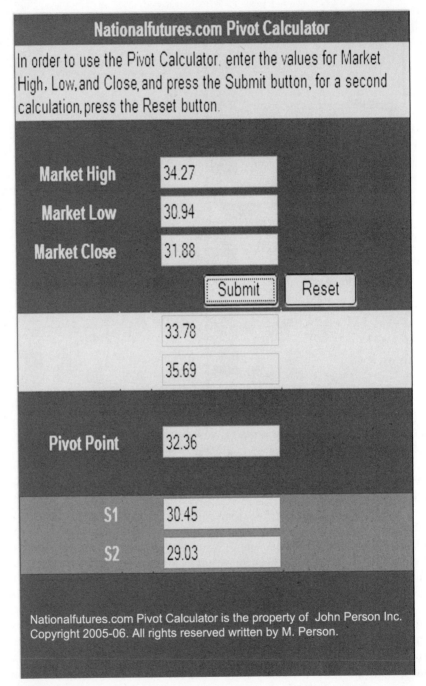

FIGURE 6.15
Used with permission of www.nationalfutures.com.

Daily (Right) DELL - DELL INC Bar Stochastic

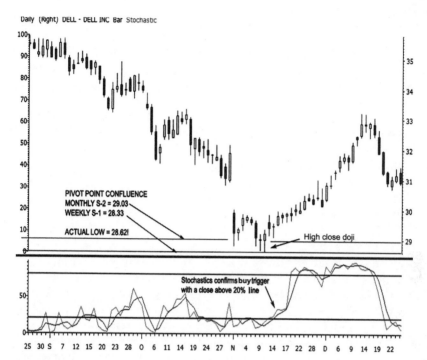

FIGURE 6.16
RealTick graphics used with permission of Townsend Analytics, Ltd.

New Trading Systems and Methods (Wiley, 2005) quoted my work from such magazine articles. Many other educators have come to listen to me teach, have taught my ideas, and have seen improvement in their students. I have had the opportunity to share my work and research with others, and I would like to share it with you. These trading ideas are not new, and they have stood the test of time.

Here is an excerpt from an online interview I had in February 2003 (see www.nationalfutures.com). The concepts I was talking about then pretty much cover what we have gone over so far and will continue to cover in the following chapters. The difference is that I am going over in detail what the specific signals, settings, and rules are for the trading triggers.

Q: How long have you been involved in the markets?
A: I started in the business back in 1979 as a runner on the floor of the Chicago Mercantile Exchange [CME]. I then worked for George and Carrie Lane, the innovator and premier educator for the stochastics oscillator. Back then, we looked for day trading opportunities in agricultural commodities, bonds, and foreign currencies. The best markets that we used

specifically for quick day trading were in the Swiss franc and the German deutsche mark. Floor traders used these numbers and kept them to themselves as a secret formula for their day trading numbers. These are known as the pivot point calculations. I started incorporating them in my trading approach back in 1984 and have been using them ever since.

Q: How do you calculate pivot points?

A: I use the traditional formula. To determine current support/resistance levels, the first step is to find the pivot point [PP] number: PP = (H + L + C) divided by 3

The first resistance level (R-1) = (PP × 2) – L

The second resistance level (R-2) = PP + H – L

The first support level (S-1) = (PP × 2) – H

The second support level (S-2) = PP – H + L

Q: What time frames do you apply to calculate the pivot points?

A: I find it extremely important to use multiple time frames in my research and analysis. For those who are familiar with the "numbers" from the pivot point calculations, the idea of applying them from any time period other than the prior day's session may make little or no sense. However, I apply the daily, weekly, and even monthly target numbers and incorporate these in my traders "tool box." Often traders will comment, "If I am a day trader, why would I want to be concerned with a monthly or a weekly market outlook?" Consider that in every month, there will be a high and a low, and the close will be somewhere in between. In one week, a high or a low will be established; and in one day of the week, the market will form that point of interest. More often than not, in an hour or so, trades will take place that will establish that high and subsequently that low!

Q: What are the various time periods in forex markets from which you take the data to calculate the numbers?

A: For the daily numbers, I take the New York Bank settlement. For weekly numbers, I use the data beginning from the open on Sunday night to the close on Friday afternoon. Monthly numbers are calculated by calendar periods.

Q: What is the main purpose for using the pivot points, and how can traders use them?

A: One popular application of the pivot point concept is to go long or cover any short positions at either of the two support levels or to go short or sell at the projected resistance levels. Knowing these fixed price levels gives the trader unambiguous points to trade off, to enter, or to exit the market or, more important at times, where not to enter a position. For example, you should not buy right at either of the resistance levels. These levels act as boundaries that can turn back price advances or declines, at least on the first attempt. Another technique is to trade the breakout of the first support or resistance levels. If prices do break through the S-1 or R-1 level, traders have a new target at the R-2 or S-2 level to take profits. The benefits of using the both short- and longer-term pivot points for a short-term day trader are numerous: They give a trader a better edge due to the ability to work with predetermined price levels, which lead to precise entry and stop-loss points, all of which give the trader the additional edge in the quest for bigger profits.

Q: You use different technical tools in your daily videos. On which ones do you put more trust or emphasis?

A: Great question! I use stochastics as an overbought/oversold indicator, and I use it to help me determine divergence and convergence signals. I use three-period variable moving averages to help keep me focused on the trend. Moving averages also help me identify potential turning points when the short-term average crosses over or below the longer-term average.

Q: You use candle charts over bar charts. Why is that?

A: Each candle has different characteristics that represent the difference, or the distance, between the high, the low, the open, and the close. These characteristics use colors to differentiate the relationship between the open and the close, referred to as the real body. Candlestick charting acts as an immediate way to illustrate and to help identify the current market's environment and the current time frame's acceptance or rejection of a specific support or resistance level in a clear visual manner. If, for example, on a given trading session, prices move higher from the opening price, establish the high, and then fall, the distance formed from those points of interest is called the "shadow."

Candle charts give me color and depth, which help me almost immediately determine where current prices are in relation to past price levels. Candlestick charting techniques can be used from data for whatever time period you are looking at: hourly, daily, weekly, or monthly. There are 60 to 70 different classifications of named candlestick patterns—from one on up to several candle components. They can signal reversal, stalled, and continuations of a market's price move. Day traders want to focus on a small arsenal of the more consistent and reliable reoccurring formations. Several patterns that a trader wants to home in on and recognize are the more powerful reversal formations at tops and bottoms of price ranges.

Q: How do candlesticks help you in your trading?

A: My trading approach incorporates time-tested techniques but uses the aid of candlestick charts, which help me identify the true condition of the markets. If you believe market prices are simply the reflection of human emotion on perceived *current value* and focus on what the market is doing, rather than on what the market might do, then you are ahead of the crowd in understand how markets function. With that understanding, you will then be able to have the confidence to act swiftly and to execute or trigger into a trade or position in the market.

Q: Which do you favor more—fundamental or technical analysis?

A: I watch what reports are coming out, as some can generate wild gyrations (e.g., monthly unemployment report). I rely heavily on technical analysis. After all, it is the purest and most objective study of price action. It is used for expedience. You can review one, five, ten, or even twenty charts in a matter of seconds or minutes to get a quick overview of the general trends. How long would it take to study the fundamental reports on the economy or interest rates in various countries to develop an opinion to buy or sell a foreign currency? That process could take hours, days, or even weeks to figure out. Specific chart patterns and price actions have a high degree of repetition. They are not 100 percent accurate; however, they do have a high percentage of reoccurrences. Success comes in the simple form of managing risk when applying a systematic method to these principles and being able to quickly identify when and why a particular pattern fails.

Q: You learned that certain candle patterns developed near these pivot points. Which ones do you look for near support or resistance levels?

A: Top reversal or bearish, such as dojis, bearish haramis, harami crosses, dark cloud covers, and evening star formations. And for bottom reversal or bullish candle patterns, I look for bullish haramis, harami crosses, bullish piercing patterns, bullish engulfing patterns, or, my favorite, a rare occurring pattern called a morning doji star.

Q: How significant are doji patterns?

A: Extremely significant, especially if you know what to look for. There are specific criteria that dojis need to meet; but if you know what these are, they can be very powerful in helping your trading decisions. Doji formations help confirm reversals. There are different names and nuances associated with certain dojis. Dojis indicate indecision, the market ends or closes, where it began or opened. Dojis signify that confidence is lost from buyers or sellers after the open as the market made a lot of intraday noise as the range during the day was established. In a bullish or bearish trending market, indecision is the last thing you want to see. Strong rejection or failure from the high and/or the low is a significant telltale sign that changes are coming.

Q: What other considerations can you share with us regarding dojis?

A: In a strong uptrending market, usually the market will close near a high, as larger capitalized traders will hold positions overnight. If the large money traders are not confident the market will move higher in price, then usually the market closes back near the open. I find it uncanny how many times dojis form at or very close to the actual pivot point calculated support or resistance numbers. That is what helps me set up my trades; it is the relation of the next candle's close after a doji that triggers my entries, especially if they are lined up at the pivot points.

Q: What is the shortest time frame that you use for charting?

A: Five minutes.

Q: What other time frames do you track?

A: Besides monthly, weekly, and daily charts, I use the 5-, the 15-, and the 30-minute and even the 60-minute for overnight trend trading.

Q: What is your favorite or most reliable time frame?

A: For day trading, the 5- and 15-minute are equally important; so I watch both.

Q: Do you just use pivot points, or do you use other methods for forecasting support and resistance levels?

A: In my book *A Complete Guide to Technical Trading Tactics: How to Profit Using Pivot Points, Candlesticks, and Other Indicators*, I demonstrate many powerful ways to anticipate support and resistance levels, including Fibonacci retracement, Fibonacci extensions, and projection methods. In fact, in my trading course, I teach specific trade setups and confirm signals to trigger or execute trades, how to manage a trade, and how to know when to exit or even reverse a position.

Q: What signals or rules do you follow for a trading trigger?

A: Without giving away too many of my trade secrets, there is one that can be found in my advanced trading course—a special trading setup that I look for in a bullish setup.

- When the market approaches a key pivot point, buy on the close or on the next open once a new closing high is made above the previous bullish reversal candle pattern or a doji.
- Place your initial risk-management stop below the low of the lowest low point of the bullish candle pattern on a stop-close-only basis.
- Exit the trade on the close or on the first open of a candle that makes a lower low after a prolonged uptrend, especially if it is near a pivot line.
- One can use a "filter," or a back-up process, to confirm the buy signal against a major pivot point number, such as a bullish convergence stochastic pattern.

Remember, a bullish candle pattern can be a harami, a harami doji cross, a bullish piercing pattern, a bullish engulfing pattern, a doji, or a morning doji star.

Q: Tell us about this course and book you have mentioned?

A: The book was published by John Wiley and Sons in May of 2004. I put the course together based on several seminars I conducted, one of which was at the Chicago Board of Trade back in May 2003 and then again in December 2004. I had a huge response from folks who could not attend but were impressed with my methods. I offer it on my web site, which is www.nationalfutures.com. Both the book and the course are available on my site, and I do get asked to autograph and add a personal message when these are prepurchased from my web site.

CHAPTER 7

Candle Charts and Top Reversal Patterns

C andlestick charting is an extremely pronounced and effective method for tracking and examining the four most important price points: the open, the high, the low, and the close. Using candlestick charting helps me visually to better compare current price activity in relation to past price points of interest. The advantage of using candlestick charting in place of bar charting is that you can use the same techniques and analysis that you do with bar charts and have the diversity and unique signals that candlesticks generate. As you learn this method of charting, you will come to see how it is a great barometer of human emotion, namely, fear and greed.

In addition, this is a simple, yet certainly more specialized format of charting. It has gained in popularity in the United States and is currently followed by more and more analysts. My first book covered most of the top formations, and I want to review what I believe are the more frequent and reliable patterns. This chapter will show some statistical evidence that there are certain patterns that develop over and over again. Candlestick charting is extremely easy to learn; and once you remember the sequence of events that form a trending market condition, the candles will certainly be your best tool in spotting market reversals at tops and bottoms. Having that information will certainly stack the odds in your favor for making money consistently in the markets as an independent trader.

CANDLESTICK CHARTING

Candlestick charting gives a detailed depiction of a price graph with almost a three-dimensional effect. What stands out most is that a chartist can see patterns more clearly and distinctly than with other types of charts. There are over 60 candle patterns that form to create certain setups. This book will focus on only a few select patterns and, what matters most, the triggers that initiate a call to action.

If you are not familiar with candlestick formations, I am going over the foundation of how to construct a candle and what it represents. If you wish to become an expert at each of the patterns, several authors have written great books on the subject. One is Steve Nison, who introduced the Western world to candles. (In my first book, on page 44, I wrote about how he discovered candles.) Others are Steve Bigalow and Greg Morris.

For the expert, this section will be a great review. Since each market has a different trading characteristic, such as volatility or price moves, certain candlestick patterns vary and may occur more or less frequently. Each candlestick pictured has a different characteristic that represents the difference or the distance between the high, the low, the open, and the close. Candlestick charting techniques can be used from data for whatever time period you use: hourly, daily, weekly, or monthly. Candlestick charts lend themselves to pattern recognition and trendline support, resistance, and channel lines. Candles also help to corroborate other forms of technical analysis, especially pivot point analysis.

I want to explain the basics, and then I want to show you specific patterns so you can see for yourself how to utilize them. I will also show a few examples of the more popular named candle formations. Moreover, I will explain the psychology of what is behind creating the pattern as it relates to the open, the high, the low, and the close of a given time period. Armed with the knowledge of which patterns have a higher frequency of occurring and with the understanding of what they symbolize, you should be able to trade the markets from recognizing them; and when patterns do develop, you should be able to instinctively act on the signals, thereby increasing your ability to make money as a trader.

The components of a candlestick are derived from the open, the high, the low, and the close. In Figure 7.1, we see a dark candle (in a color charting software package, it would be a red candle). This signifies that this particular time period's close is below the open. It does not indicate whether the market closed higher or lower than the previous time period did. The computer code for this sequence would be C < O—the close is less than the open. We can also assign a negative (–) value or reading to help determine the relative strength of a trend.

In Figure 7.2, the white, or hollow, candle signifies that the concluded

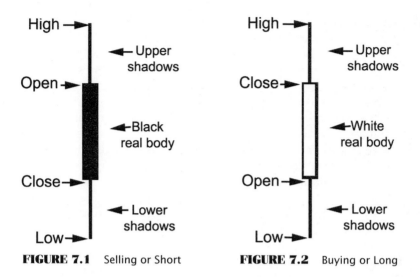

FIGURE 7.1 Selling or Short   **FIGURE 7.2** Buying or Long

time period shows that the close is above the open (in a charting software package, you would universally see this as a green candle). Keep in mind that you can adjust almost any parameter in any software package to your liking. Therefore, you may want the candle to be white. The point is that the color of a "lower close than open" candle should be different from the color of the "higher close than open" candle. The computer code for this sequence would be C > O—the close is greater than the open. We can also assign a positive (+) value or reading to help determine the relative strength of a trend by how many more positive, or "higher close than open," candles exist.

The three main components of candle charts that we need to identify are:

1. *Relationship between Open and Close (Candle Bodies).* With the real candle body colored and representing a negative or a positive reading, we can see what is dominating the market.

     In uptrends, or bullish market conditions, we see buying come in on the open; and as we learned from the stochastics indicator, the market should settle closer to the highs. It should also close above the open; and that is why in bullish market conditions, we see hollow, white, or green candles. This is why I assign it a positive (+) reading. How much the bulls are dominating the market is reflected by the length or the distance between the open and the close. If the market opens on the low and has a large range where it closes at the high of the session, that signifies that the bulls are in strong control. However, if the market has a wide-range session and the market price closes back near where it opened—say, in the middle of the range—that is not a sign that bulls dominate the market for that particular time period.

In a bearish market condition, or a strong downtrend, we would see dark- or red-colored real body candles. This represents sellers entering the market on the open and dominating the session right into the close of that time period. If the market opens on the high and prices decline where the close is at or near the low, this shows that the bears are firmly in control. This is why I assign a negative (–) reading. The distance factors between the open and the close are illustrated in a much more defined way in candle charts than in bar charts due to the shape and color coordination of the candles.

2. *Shadows and Correlations to Candle Body.* The distance of a low and/or a high in relation to the real body as created by the open and the close can really illustrate the market's denial of a support or a resistance level. Long shadows, tails, or wicks, as they are called, that form after a long downtrend indicate a potential that the trend has exhausted itself and that demand is increasing or supply is dwindling. Shadows, tails, or wicks formed at the tops of real bodies, especially after a long price advance, indicate that demand is drying up and supply is increasing. The overall size of shadows is important to watch in relation to a real body and can be easily identified.

3. *Size or Length of the Overall Candle.* Now this is one that is hard to miss using the color-coded method of candle charts. A long candle that opens at the bottom and closes at the high, which would be an abnormal occurrence, has significant meaning. After a long downtrend, seeing this formation indicates that a major trend reversal is taking place. After a long uptrend, seeing an unusually long candle that closes above the open (a positive value) would indicate that an exhaustion or blow-off-top condition may exist.

The reverse is true in down trades. After a long price decline, a tall red- or dark-colored candle, which represents the market close below the open (a negative assigned value), may indicate that a capitulation or an exhaustion bottom has formed. After a long uptrend or price advance, if that same candle was formed, it might indicate that a major trend reversal is occurring.

CANDLE FORMATIONS

The candle development will give us immediate identification of the current market's environment and the market participant's acceptance or rejection or a support or resistance level in a clearly visual manner.

The Doji

There is a special candle that has no real body to speak of and is called the *doji*. The close of this candle is at exactly the same price as the close. I generally am a little more lenient with this formation; if after a long range trading session the close is less than 8 percent of the overall high and low, I consider it a doji. For example, if the Dow has a 100-point trading range and the close is within 8 points of the open, I consider it a doji. In currencies, for example, if the British pound had a 150-point range and the market closed within 12 points of the open, I would consider that a doji formation (Figure 7.3).

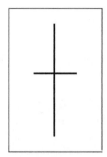

FIGURE 7.3

Doji formations help confirm reversals. There are different names and nuances associated with certain dojis, such as the gravestone, Figure 7.4, which, when formed after a major downtrend, signals that the trend is near an end and that slightly lower prices are expected to come. It is similar in appearance to what is called an *inverted hammer* at market bottoms or a *shooting star* at the top of a prolonged price advance.

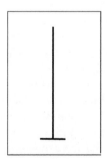

FIGURE 7.4

The *dragonfly*, Figure 7.5, resembles another candle pattern with similar implications, which is a *hanging man* formation. This candle generally develops after a long uptrend and has very bearish implications at market tops.

FIGURE 7.5   **FIGURE 7.6**

Then there is a *long-legged*, or *rickshaw, doji* in Figure 7.6. It has an extremely wide range, which heightens the collective market participant's indecision.

The secret weapon of candlestick charting is knowing the power of what the doji represents. Dojis indicate indecision—the market ends where it began. Confidence is lost from buyers or sellers on the open as the market made a lot of noise as the range was established. In a bullish or bearish trending market, indecision is the last thing you want to see. Strong rejection or failure from the high and/or low is a significant telltale sign that changes are coming.

We use the phrasing of Sir Isaac Newton's law in the markets an awful lot because it really applies to market moves: "A body in motion tends to stay in motion until a force or obstacle stops or changes that motion." I believe and teach that the doji represents that force: It generally stops or changes the motion or momentum due to the uncertainty or indecision that is created at peak and troughs.

In a strong uptrending market, usually the market will close near a high, as larger-capitalized traders will hold positions overnight. If the large-money traders are not confident the market will move higher in price, then usually the market closes back near the open. If large-capitalized traders lose confidence, then it is best to wait before making a trading decision, right? Well, that is the indecision that forms a doji.

Dojis help form two- and three-candle formations that can develop into more powerful and trustworthy signals once identified. A few of these formations are *morning doji star*, the *evening doji star*, and the *bullish* and *bearish harami doji crosses*, which are discussed later in this chapter. With each of these patterns, we need to see a specific sequence of events for these patterns to develop, such as a gap lower open and a gap higher open than a previous close. Due to the electronic age and 24-hour market access, these patterns have several variations. Therefore, I have simplified my search for what really matters most and concentrated my attention on certain high-frequency formations.

That is not to say that other patterns are not worth notice, such as the bullish piercing pattern, the bearish dark cloud cover, the engulfing patterns, the harami, and continuation patterns, such as the rising and falling three methods. There are many combinations that end up becoming great "after the fact" type patterns. There are the fry pan pattern, the advancing soldiers, the towers, the three crows, the separating lines, the tower tops and bottoms, the belt hold, the counterattack lines, the three river bottoms, et cetera.

Other Important Candle Patterns

For practical trading application, it is very difficult to program code for most software trading applications to automatically alert you to a trade signal based on the exact patterns and sequences of a particular formation. It is most important that you be able to act on that signal. However, it is possible to program a few select patterns once you identify what the most frequent and most reliable candle patterns are that reproduce desirable market reactions or price moves, especially when these patterns occur at or near the predicted support and resistance levels derived from pivot point calculations. We have done that in a small sample and a back test, which I will share with you. First, let me give an overall description of what the second-most-important candle patterns are after the dojis and of how to trigger a trade based on the specific relationship of those patterns to the four common denominators to which we all have equal access: the opens, the highs, the lows, and the closes of a respective time period. There is one more element that stock traders have, and that is real-time trading volume analysis. Volume can highlight candle patterns' significance, such as the hammer pattern shown in Figure 7.7.

FIGURE 7.7

- The *hammer* indicates that a reversal or a bottom is near in a down-trend. When a hammer appears at the top of an uptrend, the name changes to a "hanging man" and indicates that a top is near. There are three main characteristics that a pattern needs in order to qualify.

  1. The real body is at the upper end of the trading range; the color (white or black) is not important.
  2. The lower part, or the "shadow," should be at least twice the length of the real body.
  3. It should have little or no upper shadow, like a shaved head candle.

After a long decline, if a hammer forms on higher or increased volume, this adds to the certainty that a capitulation low has occurred.

Hammers can be created both by a closing below the open, which would be assigned a negative change value (shown in Figure 7.8), and by a higher close than the open, which would be assigned a positive change value (shown in Figure 7.9).

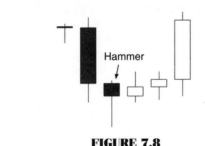

FIGURE 7.8

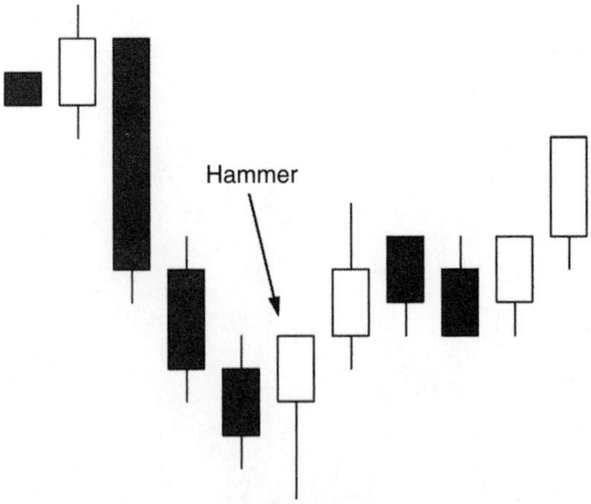

FIGURE 7.9

FIGURE 7.10

- The *shooting star* is the inverted formation of the hammer and forms at tops (Figure 7.10). It usually signals a major reversal. The color does not matter, but the body should be at the lower end of the trading range with a long shadow. Its significance is that it shows that the market opened near the low of the day, then had an explosive rally that failed, and closed back down near the low of the day. Usually there is little or no lower shadow like a shaven bottom. When it is at the bottom of a downtrend, it is called an *inverted hammer*. Figure 7.11 shows a positive assigned candle, or a higher-close-than-open star. Figure 7.12 shows a negative assigned candle, or a lower-close-than-open star.

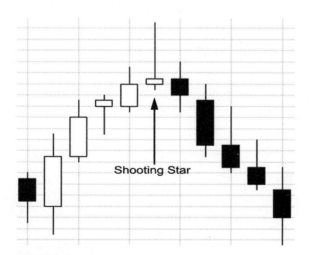

FIGURE 7.11

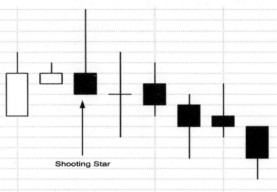

FIGURE 7.12

- The *morning star* is a major bottom reversal pattern that is a three-candle formation (Figure 7.13). The first candle has a long black real body. The second candle has a small real body that gaps lower than the first candle's body. The third candle's body sometimes gaps higher than the second one but does not happen often. It is important that the third candle is a white candle and closes well above the midpoint of the first candle's real body.

  A variation of the morning star doji pattern is shown in Figure 7.14. There are 10 or 12 different variations of this pattern; therefore, I look for the candle following the doji to generate a signal.

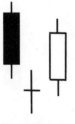

FIGURE 7.13

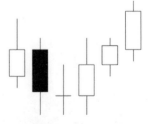

FIGURE 7.14

- The *evening doji star* (see Figures 7.15 and 7.16) is the exact opposite of the morning doji star. It is the second-most-bearish top pattern, next to the *abandon baby* or *island top formation*.

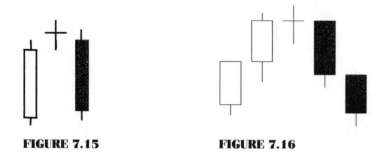

FIGURE 7.15   **FIGURE 7.16**

- The *harami* is a small real body within the body of the prior body's candle (Figure 7.17). This is known as a reversal pattern or a warning of a trend change, especially at tops of markets. It is not important that the colors be opposite, but I notice that the more reliable signals are generated when they are.

FIGURE 7.17

- The *bearish harami doji cross* formation is a long white candle, signifying that the market closed above the open, with little or no shadow at both ends of the candle (Figure 7.18). It was followed in the next time period by a doji within the middle of the real body. This tells me that sellers are entering the market.

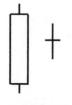

FIGURE 7.18

- The *bullish harami doji cross* would occur in a downtrending market. The first candle is usually a long dark candle, signifying that the market closed below the open, with little or no real shadow at both ends. Then the next trading session, a doji forms (Figures 7.19 and 7.20).

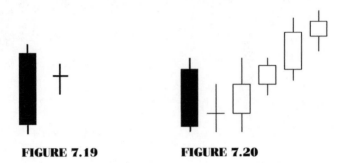

FIGURE 7.19   **FIGURE 7.20**

- The *dark cloud cover* is a bearish reversal signal that usually appears after an uptrend. The first white candle is followed by a dark candle. The important features here are that the dark candle should open higher than the white candle's high and close well below the midpoint of the white candle's real body (Figures 7.21 and 7.22).

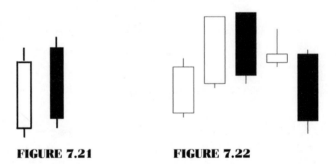

FIGURE 7.21   **FIGURE 7.22**

- The *bullish piercing pattern* is considered the opposite of the dark cloud cover. It requires that the first candle is a long dark candle, that the second candle gaps open lower than the first candle, and that it closes well above the midpoint of the long dark first candle. Look for 50 percent penetration of long dark candle (Figures 7.23 and 7.24).

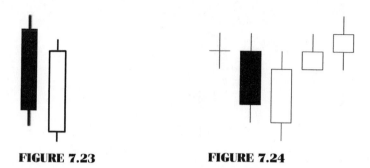

FIGURE 7.23   **FIGURE 7.24**

- The *bullish engulfing pattern* is indicated when a white candle's real body completely covers the previous dark candle's real body. The opening is lower than the first candle's real body, and the close is above the first candle's middle portion of the body. The more "wraps" or past candle's real bodies that are engulfed, the stronger or more significant is the signal (Figures 7.25 and 7.26).

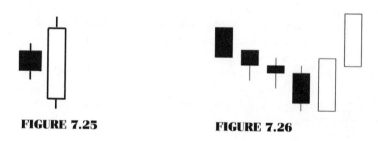

FIGURE 7.25   **FIGURE 7.26**

- The *bearish engulfing pattern* is distinctive. The engulfing bearish line is signaled where a dark candle's real body completely covers the previous white candle's real body. The opening is higher than the first candle's real body, and the close is below the first candle's middle portion of the body (Figures 7.27 and 7.28).

FIGURE 7.27

FIGURE 7.28

- The *bearish falling three methods* is a bearish continuation pattern often associated with a bear flag formation. The three little candles usually remain within the range of the first dark candle, which includes both the real body and the shadow. Some argue that it works with just two candles in the middle, but the actual textbook classification is three white candles. The last portion of this formation is that the next long dark candle closes below the first dark candle's close (Figures 7.29 and 7.30).

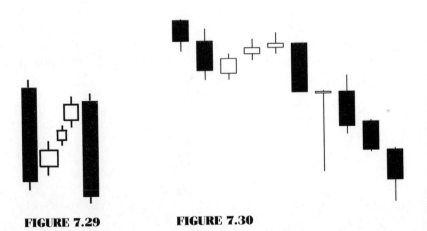

FIGURE 7.29   **FIGURE 7.30**

- The *bullish rising three methods* is a bullish continuation pattern with the same characteristics as in the bearish falling three methods, but just the opposite. During the beginning stages of an advancing price trend, an unusually long white candle is preceded by three smaller dark candles. Again, it can even be just two candles, but the textbook version is that three smaller candles need to stay within the range of the first long white candle. The last white candle shows a powerful, advancing white candle that should open above the previous session's close and should close above the first long white candle's close as well (Figures 7.31 and 7.32).

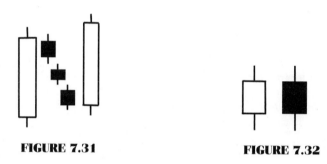

FIGURE 7.31   **FIGURE 7.32**

- The *tweezer tops* or *tweezer bottoms* is a double-top or double-bottom formation that can be disguised by a few variations. The tweezer top forms after an uptrend and then two consecutive time periods making equal highs. This signals that there is strong resistance and a short-term top is in place. One variation is that the first period usually consists of a long body candle with a higher close than open (positive). The second day is usually a small real-body candle that has a high equal to the prior day's high. It can be a positive or a negative open close relationship; but it is more consistent and a better signal that a reversal is forming when the second candle's color is the opposite of the first candle's color. A tweezer bottom would be the exact opposite of this formation.

  Other variations have been called "equal and opposite" or "chopstick" patterns. In Chinese, it would be called the yin (black or red negative close candle) and the yang (white, hollow, or green positive close candle).

  In Figure 7.33, the tweezer bottom looks more like a pair of fat chopsticks and is almost equal in size and in direct proportion to the real body's shape. However, the colors are opposite, which indicates a strong reversal.

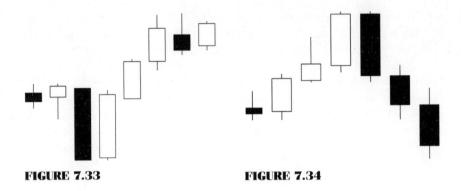

FIGURE 7.33   **FIGURE 7.34**

In Figure 7.34, the tweezer top also resembles a pair of fat chopsticks, but the dark candle exceeds the first candle's real body and engulfs it. That is evidence that a top is in place.

The equal and opposite formations occur with false breakouts and key reversals. They are powerful signals that should be respected. Figure 7.35 shows a bar chart to compare to the candle chart in Figure 7.36.

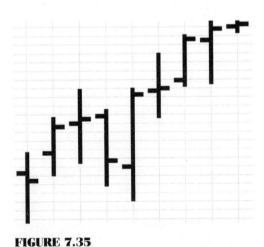

FIGURE 7.35

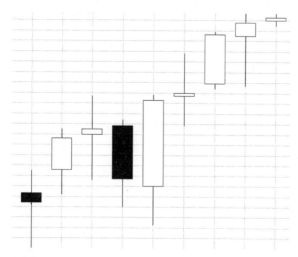

FIGURE 7.36

TRADING TRIGGER STRATEGY

Forex traders note that these candle patterns show up frequently in the currency pairs. Since many times the currency markets trade between the European and U.S. sessions, we see periods of low volatility; and the foreign exchange (forex) markets move in sideways channels, otherwise known as longer-term intraday consolidation periods. We often see false breakdowns and breakouts, which create the equal and opposite formations. Therefore, a trigger to enter a position would be if the market price is near an important pivot point support level: Buy on the close of the second candle's time period or on the open of the immediately next time frame. Place a stop two ticks (or PIPS) beneath the double-bottom low. You should see immediate results as the market moves higher. Adjust your stop accordingly.

Chapter 8 goes into more specific trading rules on entries based on three highly effective and frequently reoccurring patterns. Dojis form more often than not at pivot point support and resistance levels. With that said, the pivot point support and resistance levels will usually be either the exact high, the exact low, both, or darn close to it, which is why I wanted to get statistical information on the doji, the hammer, and the shooting star patterns. Also, I wanted to answer the following questions that apply for the most active day trading markets in futures and forex.

- How many lows of the day are formed by a doji candle pattern?
- How many highs of the day are formed by a doji candle pattern?
- How many lows of the day are formed by a hammer candle pattern?
- How many highs of the day are formed by a shooting star candle pattern?

To find the answers, I conducted a back test using Genesis Software (visit www.nationalfutures.com for more details) with its head programmer, Peter Kilman. Pete came to a seminar I was giving on Advance Trading Tactics for forex markets in Houston in January 2006. It is interesting that, at the time, I was unaware of his preliminary test results when he offered to share them with the audience. In fact, he had thought that he ran the test wrong when the results popped up, so he ran it three times. Pete ran the test from the preceding 255 trading days on a 15-minute time period for each market. Because there are about 255 trading days in an average year, I felt this was a pretty good sample of information. Most people want to see longer-term studies; for some applications and specific studies, that may be a novel idea. However, I would say the markets in 2005 generated enough volatility, with macroeconomic and geopolitical events combined with the Federal Reserve tightening interest rates. Moreover, energy prices were on the move; and we were faced with global terrorist attacks, such as the heinous bomb blast in London that shocked the world in mid-July 2005. That event sent a tremendous price shock to global equity markets. In addition, there are more independent online traders and a new crop of super-traders known as hedge funds trading in the markets. So with these variables and market influences, I would say 2005 was a good representation of a more modern historic test period for determining what influenced market prices.

A 10-year back study would not take into account the more active online trading vehicles or the popular spot foreign currency markets. Even if this were a 2-, 5-, or 10-year study, risk disclosure and the government still would require me to state that past price history is not indicative of future results. So, my study was a back-test study to determine the validity of finding out if dojis, hammers, and shooting stars were really forming at major turning points or were making the actual highs or lows in the more active day trading markets and how often. Here are the parameters Pete and I used to determine the back test and the results of the findings: If a doji is within three ticks of the low, we count it. It could be the low itself, or it could be within one, two, or three ticks of the low. In the same sense, we will include when a shooting star is within three ticks of the high. To create a percentage, we take the number of days when we are within three ticks of the low and divide that by 255.

For example, we found that on 132 of the past 255 days, a doji came within three ticks of the low on bonds. We took 132 and divided by 255, getting 0.528, which is 53 percent. We also found that the hammer pattern was within three ticks of the low 36 percent of the time on bonds. We added the two pattern totals together and found that hammers and dojis formed the low on bonds 88 percent of the time, either making the exact high or coming within three ticks. We must keep in mind that there are many days that have multiple dojis or hammer patterns.

Some days may have four doji patterns where only one of these doji patterns formed the low, while the other three gave false signals. For gold, we used four ticks. For e-mini–Standard & Poors (S&P) 500, we used four ticks (each tick is 12.50, so four ticks is one full point). In the Chicago Board of Trade (CBOT) mini-Dow, we also used four ticks, which may explain why the resulting difference is a lower percentage of occurrences for hammers, stars, and dojis forming at tops and bottoms in the Dow. As you can see, the results are staggering that the highs and lows are formed by these three patterns. If you just focus on when these patterns form, looking for a shift in momentum or the turning point, you may improve your profitability and frequency of winning trades as you may develop a better level of confidence armed with these findings (Figures 7.37 to 7.40).

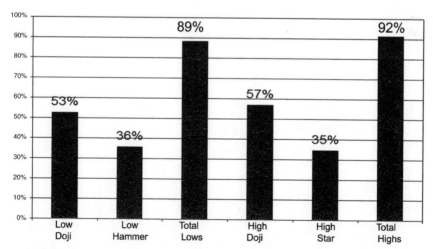

FIGURE 7.37 Bond Lows and Highs
Used with permission of GenesisFT.com.

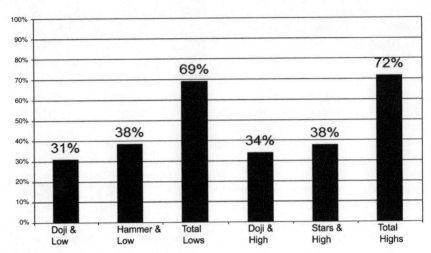

FIGURE 7.38   Gold Comex
Used with permission of GenesisFT.com.

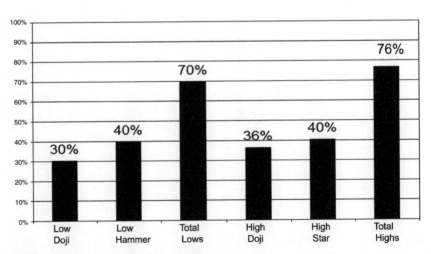

FIGURE 7.39   Mini–S&P Lows and Highs
Used with permission of GenesisFT.com.

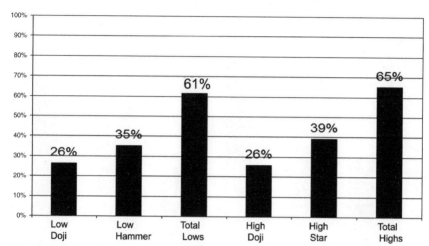

FIGURE 7.40   Mini-Dow Lows and Highs
Used with permission of GenesisFT.com.

As we know, spot forex currency trading goes on 24 hours a day, without a centralized marketplace or exchange. There are many arguments on when the day ends and begins. For our analysis in calculating pivot points, I established that the forex trading day ends with the New York Bank closing at 5 P.M. Eastern time. From a market time period to run a study as to what makes a high or a low, I needed a rigid sample test period with accurate and stable data. We wanted to find the highs and the lows of the day based on trades and real trades. Forex data is not exchange based. Each broker has his or her own set of data. Although the data is parallel to the that of the futures, as we discussed in Chapter 1 (known as the basis), they are not trades; instead, they are bids/asks.

To get a taste for the true highs and lows of the day from a centralized market place that had actual time-stamped transactions (time and sales data), we used the futures markets open outcry session, which is from 7:20 A.M. until 2 P.M. Central time. This eliminates the possibility of the true low being an extra few ticks away on the real exchange markets. Using this trading time period eliminated arguments over what time we should switch from one day to the next based on the forex data. However, since, again, this is a test to find the candle pattern that formed when the market made highs and lows during a specific trading session, it is best to check on the day-session-only highs and lows to avoid possible anomalies with regard to holidays, early bank hours, and market surges in the future (Figures 7.41 to 7.44).

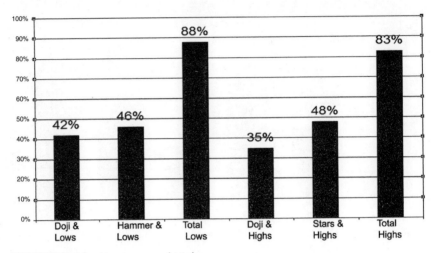

FIGURE 7.41 Yen Lows and Highs
Used with permission of GenesisFT.com.

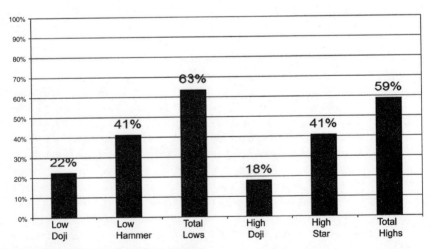

FIGURE 7.42 Euro Lows and Highs
Used with permission of GenesisFT.com.

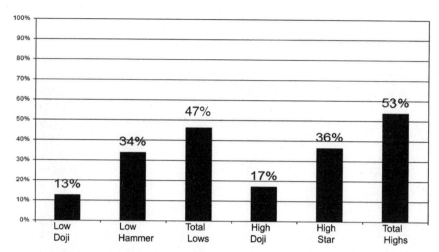

FIGURE 7.43 British Pound Lows and Highs
Used with permission of GenesisFT.com.

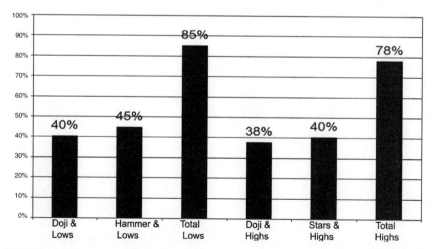

FIGURE 7.44 Canadian Dollar Lows and Highs
Used with permission of GenesisFT.com.

We can dig a bit deeper in the results and say that certain markets respond better than others with the psychological elements that dojis, hammers, and stars represent. Each market has its own character. The Canadian dollar, for example, is a currency that highly correlates to commodities, which would be a good reason why it has a strong percentage of occurrences versus the British pound. The Canadian dollar tracks closer to the moves in gold. In addition, the volume of trading is lower as compared to the British pound, the euro, or the yen, according to the Triennial Central Bank Survey 2004. While most currencies are tradable, the five currencies, including the U.S. dollar (four currency pairs), that represent the majority of foreign exchange trading volume are the euro (EUR/USD), with the majority of volume of 28 percent; the yen (USD/JPY), with estimated 17 percent of market share; the British pound (GBP/USD), with 14 percent; and the Swiss franc (USD/CHF), with an estimated 5 percent share of overall volume activity. The Canadian dollar volume trades comparatively speaking about less than 4 percent.

There are those who will take these statistics and show that there is no evidence that it is reliable information or that there was not enough backtest studies completed. In fact, statisticians and those who understand Bayesian calculations will most likely dispute these findings. Well that's alright, as I see these patterns form over and over and over; and the computer findings substantiate that. In case you wanted to know what Bayesian theory is, it is from the famous mathematician Thomas Bayes. He was born in London in 1702 and died in 1761. One of the few works Bayes published during his lifetime was a defense of Issac Newton against a bishop who had attacked the logic of his calculus, according to the *Encyclopedia Britannica*. Bayes was successful enough as a mathematician to win election to the Royal Society of London. He would have been long forgotten had it not been for his friend Richard Price, who inherited Bayes's papers. Price, himself famous for devising one of the first actuarial tables, came across the "Essay towards Solving a Problem in the Doctrine of Chances" and helped develop the Bayes rule. Statisticians have long recognized the rule's importance, and some high school classes use it to solve straightforward probability problems. But once both data and beliefs enter the picture, the math can become unbelievably complex. Over the past 10 or 15 years, however, computers have become powerful enough to handle Bayesian calculations with relative ease; and the method has won a following. Bayes's formula allows scientists to combine new data with their prior beliefs about how the world works. It is an idea that amounts to heresy in much of the statistical world. After all, the method requires individuals to make subjective decisions about how strongly to weigh prior beliefs. The essence of the Bayesian approach is to provide a mathematical rule explaining how you should change your existing beliefs in the light of new evidence. In other words, it allows scientists to combine new data with their existing knowledge or expertise.

This rule applies to the statistics provided on hammers and dojis forming bottoms, as in the case of the Canadian dollar, saying "40 percent of bottoms are hammers" is not equivalent to saying "40 percent of hammers are bottoms." The Bayes rule can be used to connect these two statements. Therefore, you must be aware that what happened in the past might not repeat with the same frequency or that this data is even reliable. However, the facts are the facts. During this time period, the results speak for themselves.

Now that you are armed with enough information to be dangerous in your trading, let's go over how to find certain setups and explain what triggers a call to initiate a trade based on these findings combined with what we have learned so far with pivot point analysis. In the following chapters, we will also cover the type of risk parameters to use and when and where to exit positions.

CHAPTER 8

Setups and Triggers

Combining Candles and Pivots

There are many methods you can employ to actively trade, including various mechanical trading systems and manual trading tactics. The constant changing of market conditions can require system traders to adapt and update the parameters for their trading decisions. I often prefer the hands-on visual approach, which is more of a manual method, while employing a mechanical trigger to both enter and exit a position with a specific risk management technique. The visual approach is aided by the use of candle charts.

The triggers discussed in this chapter are based on the methodology developed from my 26 years as a trader. I have continually strived to find clearer signals and triggers for short- and even longer-term trade opportunities. I have been doing extensive research regarding the combination of candlestick formations and pivot points; some of the proprietary signals that I have taught traders at seminars and in my course, I am sharing in this book. This chapter details the triggers designed by me, based on my research joining both specific candle patterns and pivot point analysis.

I am going to cover three setups: (1) the high close doji (HCD), (2) the low close doji (LCD), and (3) the jackhammer. Each one has a special set of rules by which to initiate a trade and to exit a trade. These strategies have done well in periods of both bullishness and bearishness, as well as in times of heightened volatility and periods of low volatility.

This is just a small sample of what is taught in my three-month intensive trading school. I have been asked why I would share such high-probability trading signals with the public. Well, I have taught these methods to many people, including my own father and son. Just as they have different results with the same signals, you will, too, due to the very nature of trading. Once my trading concepts are taught by the masses, I do not believe the signals will be diluted or absorbed in the marketplace.

I believe not every trader will implement my methods in exactly the same way as I do. For example, Larry Williams has his OOPS method, Mark Fishers has his method, and Tom Demark had his method let out to the public. And all these systems, to my knowledge, are still highly effective strategies. So I do not believe letting you into my "black box" will hurt or dilute the signals.

There are various markets and various time periods in which to enter a trade, such as a 60-minute, a 15-minute, and a 5-minute time period for swing and day traders. These signals work for futures and stocks, and they work amazingly well in the foreign exchange (forex) markets, as you will see in the coming examples. The premise is to help keep the trader focused on the now, to watch and study the current price action. The candle patterns give a visual confirmation of price momentum, and the pivot points forewarn you of what the potential turning points are. When you combine the two methods, you have a solid trading program. This setup may help you improve your trading performance and allow you to develop a consistently winning trading strategy. This could be your personal trading system that is based off proven and powerful techniques. For a moment, I want you to envision the concept of epoxy glue: It requires two compounds. Separately, they are not very reliable or, in fact, a very strong bonding substance. However, when combined, a chemical reaction occurs and forms an amazingly strong and powerful bond. Using the methods of candlesticks with pivot points can give you that same result if you know what to look for. The implementation of longer-term analysis using pivot points will give a trader a fantastic means by which to anticipate a point where a trend change could occur, thus helping a trader not only to prepare but also to act on a trade opportunity. One can implement this setup using different time frames besides daily analysis. You can include weekly and even monthly pivot point calculations. This method of analysis will alert you well in advance of a potential support and/or resistance level. In the setup process, you will heighten your awareness to enter in a long or a short position against predefined levels and will wait for the trigger or market signal at those levels. It can not only help you define or identify the target area to enter but also establish your risk objective. Another event that occurs with this setup process is that you now can set up your orders to buy on your trading platform with the selected contract amounts—in other words, prearrange the commands on the electronic order ticket. Now all you need is confirmation so you can pull the trigger or click the mouse to establish an entry in the market and establish a position.

In Chapter 7, we covered the importance of dojis and the statistical rel-

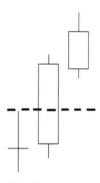

FIGURE 8.1

evance of why I look for them at pivot point support targets. The primary importance in the study of the doji at a pivot is to understand that the doji indicates indecision and is a significant sign that changes are coming. In candle patterns, the morning doji star is one of the most reliable reversal formations that a trader can identify. The problem is that there are about 12 variations, making it hard to write code to program in a trading software package. However, the main component about the doji is the trigger indicating when the next time period's close is higher than the doji's high. This can be a subtle change by just two PIPs in forex or ticks in futures. It cannot be at the exact high of the doji; rather, it needs to close above the doji high. This is a very important point, so make sure you are crystal clear on it. Figure 8.1 demonstrates the definition of a close above the doji high.

HIGH CLOSE DOJI

The most reliable and most common method used to determine support and resistance levels is the mathematical-based calculations from pivot point analysis. Through the years, I have noticed that doji formations form more often than not at these predefined levels. In Chapter 7, we have statistical information that backs up that observation. That is the focus on which we want to concentrate—the market's behavior at support and resistance levels, especially when dojis appear. The key is to watch for confirmation for a transition to take place and to act when there is a shift in momentum. We are looking for a specific conditional change to take place in the market, namely a higher closing high above a doji's high at the pivot point support level. This is the pattern I call the high close doji (HCD) method. It has dimensions of specific criteria that need to fall in place, helping to eliminate and to filter out false signals. It is a simple and basic approach to candlestick chart patterns that is a high-probability winning strategy.

Characteristics

When the market is in an extended trend to the downside and the market condition is oversold, a doji appears, indicating indecision and weakness of sellers to maintain the downward trend. In addition, prices are near a projected pivot point support target level (Figure 8.1).

When a doji appears, you should:

- Buy on the close or on the next open after a new *closing* high is made from the previous doji candle high, especially when the market is against a key pivot point support target number.
- Place stops below the lowest low point of the doji. Stops should be initially placed as a stop-close-only, meaning you do not exit the trade unless the market closes back below the doji's low.
- Sell or exit the trade on the close or on the next open of a candle that makes a lower closing low near a key pivot point resistance number.

You can use a "filter" or backup process to confirm the buy signal, such as a bullish convergence stochastic pattern or a bullish convergence on moving average convergence/divergence (MACD).

Spot Forex Triggers

Now let's put these rules into practice by examining active trading markets, such as in foreign currency markets. Figure 8.2 shows a 15-minute time period candle chart on the spot British pound. Taking the data from September 29 and using the close from the 5 P.M. (ET) New York Bank settlement, we have a high of 177.04, a low of 175.92, and a close of 176.13. Once we calculate the pivot points, we have the first support (S-1) figured as 175.68. The first resistance (R-1) is 176.80.

As you can see, the market trades for almost two hours at the pivot support; but at 4:30, a doji forms. Three time periods later, a close above the doji's high occurs. Note that the market closes above both moving average values. In addition, the COMAS (Conditional Optimized Moving Average System™) method shows the shorter-term moving average cross above the longer-term average, confirming a trigger to go long. The trigger to enter a long position would be on the time period's close or the very next session's

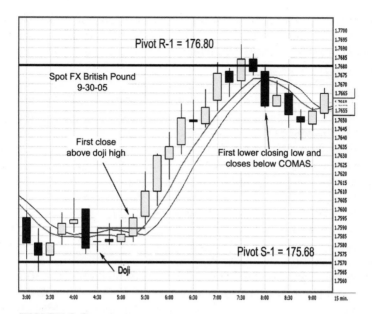

FIGURE 8.2
Used with permission of esignal.com.

open; the entry price would be 175.95. As the market blasts off into trend mode, the money-making sequence of events transpires—higher highs, higher lows, and higher closing highs.

As the trade matures, watch the reaction at the pivot resistance R-1 of 176.80. Observe the bullish momentum dry up; for the first time, there is a lower closing low, and prices close below both moving average values. The moving averages also form a negative cross, confirming a trigger to exit the long position. As a day trader, you have completed your mission to capture money from the market. This example would have had you exit the position at 176.57. For each full-lot-size contract, that would be a 62-PIP profit or $620 gain. Granted, you did not buy the low or sell the high; but you certainly did what you always want to do—capture a nice chunk of the middle of a price move. If you understand that markets move from trend mode to consolidation (or congestion) phase, then you will realize that at this time it is best to walk away and wait for the next setup because you are now vulnerable to getting whipsawed in the market during the consolidation phase. That is why most successful traders make their money and walk away. Other less fortunate traders tend to make money early in the day and lose it by trading it away late in the trading session during the consolidation period.

Let's examine another trading setup in a spot forex market and see how the HCD signal responds. Figure 8.3 is another 15-minute chart on the euro currency with the two indicators stochastics and MACD. So far in this book, you have learned how to spot triggers and how to properly read the indicators. The HCD trigger signals to enter in a position earlier than the MACD does and is confirmed by the stochastics as the %K and %D both close above the 20 percent line. What helps keep you in the trade is the sequence of trading events, such as higher highs, higher lows, and higher closing highs. Note that the %K and %D stochastic readings do not close beneath the 80 percent level until the end of the trend run. Also note that once the market closes below a prior time period's low and a doji forms at the top of the price peak, the stochastics does cross beneath and closes below the 80 percent line. The MACD also signals a zero-line cross. All the indicators lined up with an exit point.

This signal generated a buy at 119.06. If you applied the combined technical tools covered in this book, it would have allowed you to stay with the trade and to capture the bulk of the move as the exit triggered at 120.15. Per 100,000 lot contract in the spot forex market, that would have generated a handsome profit over $1,000 per position. All it takes is a few of those per month to generate a tidy income.

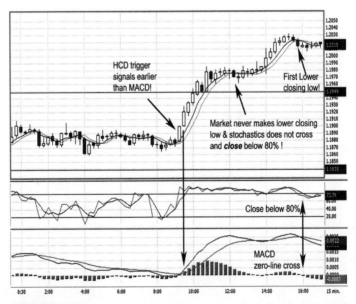

FIGURE 8.3
RealTick graphics used with permission of Townsend Analytics, LTD.

Triggers on Futures Markets

Let's tune our focus to the futures markets. Figure 8.4 shows a 15-minute chart on the Chicago Board of Trade (CBOT) mini-gold contract. Notice the HCD trigger and the small hammerlike pattern that forms on the pivot point support. The trigger to go long is on the close of that time period or the next time frame's open. If the market is to go into trend mode, which in this example it did, we should see the sequence of events unfold, such as higher highs, higher lows, and higher closing highs. As a day trader, your exit is at the least to be calculated by the end of the day; but until the market makes the first lower closing low near a key resistance level, you stay with the position or at least scale out of partial positions at the first sign of a pause in the trending condition.

The long would be entered at 530.50, and the offset was triggered at 538. That would be a $7.50 move per contract and would equate to $250 per contract.

The example in Figure 8.5 is on a five-minute chart. We see confirmation of an HCD trigger with the fast stochastics closing back above the 20 percent line. Here we have the same feature with higher highs, higher lows, and higher closing highs. The trigger to go long here is $113^{15}\!/\!_{32}$, and the trade was still going strong until we see a series of dojis at the top. In this case,

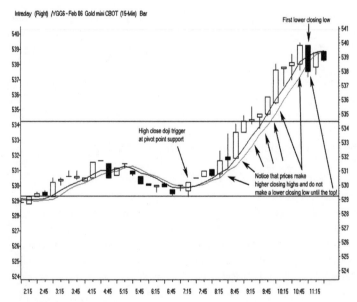

FIGURE 8.4
RealTick graphics used with permission of Townsend Analytics, LTD.

FIGURE 8.5
Used with permission of esignal.com.

especially as a day trader, you may do several things: Liquidate your longs at the last price, 113³⁰⁄₃₂, which equates to a juicy profit per contract of $468.75 (each tick in bonds is $31.25). You would look to get out because you know, based on the research covered in Chapter 7, that dojis form the day's highs or lows in bonds a fair amount of the time; and that is what occurred in this example. Then when you see a doji form after a nice trend run or near a pivot, getting flat is good common sense. If you had multiple positions on, the scaling out of half to two-thirds of them would be another alternative (Figure 8.6).

The trade example in Figure 8.7 shows a 5-minute chart on the CBOT mini-Dow contract. The daily pivot point support lines up at 10836. A doji forms; and the cofirming HCD trigger, which was initiated at 10846, develops. I have three identical studies under the chart: (1) the fast stochastics, (2) the MACD study, and (3) a commodity channel index (CCI) using a 14-period parameter setting. The stochastics closes above the 20 percent line at the same time as the entry on the HCD trigger; the MACD has not yet triggered a signal to go long, even as the market soars to 10861. The CCI makes a zero-line cross signal, triggering to buy or at least confirming that your long position is valid, but also late.

What is important is studying how the indicators work and understanding that if most traders follow lagging indicators, by the time they see

FIGURE 8.6
Used with permission of esignal.com.

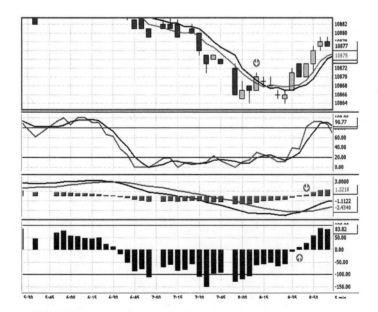

FIGURE 8.7
Used with permission of esignal.com.

a bona fide buy signal, you are already well on your way to profits. This signal gets you 15 points ahead of the crowd, or $75 per contract. That might
be not much money; but on a day trade margin of $500, that is a 15 percent
return and gives you a leading edge over the competition.

Besides the mini-Dow, Standard & Poor's (S&P), and the Nasdaq, there
is the Russell 2000 contract, which had a tremendous run in 2005 and early
2006. This stock index contract responds well with the high close doji triggers combined with the COMAS method. Remember that we do not see a
bona fide doji appear all the time; for example, when the close is not at the
exact same price as the open. A doji can assume the shape of a spinning top
pattern as well, which is why I use my judgment to determine if the close is
less than 8 percent or so of the overall range. I do consider the psychological aspect of the creation of the doji candle pattern. After all, even a spinning top after a downtrend indicates indecision; so a higher assigned value
or a higher closing high takes on the same meaning as a high close doji.
Also confirming a trigger to go long, as the example in Figure 8.8 shows, is
seeing the HCD form at or come near to the pivot point support level and
then look for a close above both moving average components. In addition,
the shorter-term moving average crosses above the pivot point average,

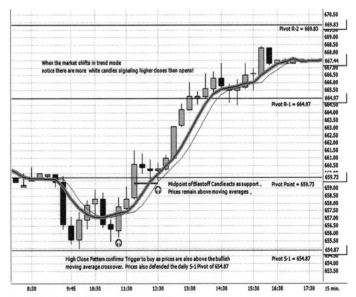

FIGURE 8.8
Used with permission of esignal.com.

confirming a conditional bullish change in the market. A trigger to enter a long was established on the close above the spinning top pattern or the open of the next period, which was at 658.00; and as you can see, higher highs, higher lows, and higher closing highs developed. Examine the market's behavior at the R-1 target resistance level: The market simply paused, but yet still closed above the R-1 price resistance level. After it penetrated the R-1 level, the market consolidated but still maintained a bullish bias because the market did not confirm an exit signal by simultaneously establishing three criteria:

1. A close below a prior low.
2. The moving averages that did not cross and close below each other.
3. A price that did not close below both moving average values.

Fractal Relationships

In Figure 8.9, I want to dissect a daily chart to see what the intraday pattern looked like, as the daily chart formed a textbook high close doji trigger. The trigger to go long was at 208.25, on the close of business on January 24 or on the open on January 25. This example really highlights a fractal relationship as one time period interacts with another.

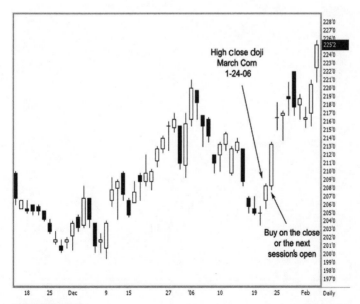

FIGURE 8.9
Used with permission of esignal.com.

My favorite time period for intraday trading is the 15-minute time period because it is divisible by 3, a relatively important number in the field of technical analysis. More important, it is an extremely relevant time period to the grain complex: Since the market opens at 9:30 A.M. (CT) and closes at 1:15 P.M. (CT) there are 15 complete 15-minute time periods to trade.

Coincidentally, the day the doji formed on an end-of-day chart as shown in Figure 8.9, we see that a high close doji pattern formed on the intraday chart on a 15-minute time period as well. Therefore, we sometimes see this pattern develop on smaller time periods, such as the 15-minute period for end-of-day patterns for added confirmation. Figure 8.10 shows the 15-minute chart for corn on January 24, the day the doji formed. This is a great example of what a fractal relationship is with trading signals.

As you look at the 15-minute chart, we see a nice bullish run, complete with the sequence of events we like when in a long position: higher highs, higher lows, and higher closing highs. Quite a sweet setup—no pressure—no hassle—the way trading should be all the time!

FIGURE 8.10
Used with permission of esignal.com.

Intraday Triggers on Stocks

Let's look at a 15-minute chart on IBM, a fairly popular stock, and see how this method applies for day traders. Figure 8.11 shows a double bottom formed with the primary low formed by a doji followed by a hammer. The higher close occurs at 81.24, with immediate results following. Prices peak at 12 noon around 81.50, only to fade back after the crowd decides to take profits before lunchtime. The initial risk target has not been challenged during that time frame. Then, as volume picks up as traders return in the afternoon, another doji forms, followed by a second HCD signal. See how the market hugs the daily S-1 pivot support as well. The market enjoys a nice gain with the very sequence we like when we are in a long position: higher highs, higher lows, and higher closing highs, right up to the daily pivot point R-1 target high.

Let's look at another stock example. For those stock traders not looking to trade commodities but wanting to participate in the action, here is a novel opportunity. One consideration should be to buy stock in the Chicago Board of Trade. That way you will own a piece of the exchange! Figure 8.12 shows a 15-minute chart on CBOT holdings. Notice that the HCD trigger is made by a higher close than open hammer candle pattern; and as you can

FIGURE 8.11
RealTick graphics used with permission of Townsend Analytics, LTD.

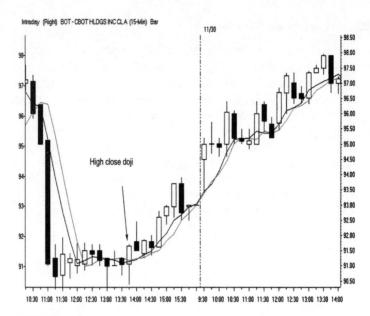

FIGURE 8.12
RealTick graphics used with permission of Townsend Analytics, LTD.

see, the market reacted strongly as the trend sequence developed once again with higher highs, higher lows, and higher closing highs. This stock generated a buy at 91.70, closed at 93.00, and kept following the money trail into the next day's trading session. In fact, the market kept trading higher up to 119 as of February 24, 2006, when I was editing this book. I would imagine that as volume increases, this stock can trade higher for years to come. It has a pretty good track record staying in business; it has been around for over 155 years.

Let's look at another commodity-related stock; this one is Exxon. By now, everyone knows that this company generated the highest profit in a given quarter of any company in the world. As energy prices bounced around, so did this stock. In Figure 8.13, we have a 60-minute chart for a swing trade, showing the weekly and monthly pivot points that are helping to illustrate and uncover the hidden support value. As the market declines, the doji formations develop at these confluence levels of supports. Then, as the moving average crosses and as prices close above the doji highs, we have a confirmed buy signal.

There was never any pressure of loss on the trade; but even if you were bored with the trade, a secondary trigger was generated three days later at 57.00. Notice the trending market condition and the sequence of events that

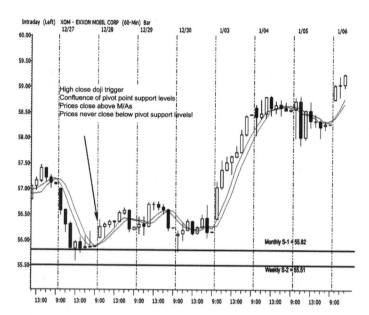

FIGURE 8.13
RealTick graphics used with permission of Townsend Analytics, LTD.

we are looking for when in a long position; higher highs, higher lows, and higher closing highs. Also note that the white candles signify that the market is closing above the open on each time period, demonstrating that buyers are dominating the market. This chart pattern resembles a "W" bottom pattern, which is quite similar in formation to the IBM chart in Figure 8.11. It is interesting that these two stocks showed this formation on different dates as well.

I have illustrated how the setup and signal work for intraday time periods. Let's take a look at how we can apply the methods combining all the techniques, including the pivot point moving average crossovers, pivot point support targets, stochastics, and the high close doji. In Figure 8.14 we are looking at Alcoa; the stock went into a nasty tailspin, as most markets did in October 2005. However, after long price declines, you do not want to get too bearish in the hole, so to speak, especially on high-quality companies implementing the longer-term monthly pivot point methods. We uncovered that there was support at 22.15 and a potential bottom or end of the decline. Granted, the low was 22.28, so we were off by a small margin. But notice how when using my methods, the signal to go long was triggered once the market closed above the moving averages; a high close doji trigger prompted a long position; and the stochastics confirmed the long trigger, as %K and %D both crossed and closed above the 20 percent line. If you

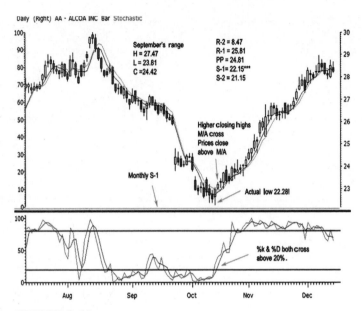

FIGURE 8.14
RealTick graphics used with permission of Townsend Analytics, LTD.

follow the flow of the market, you will see that the sequence of events that transpire is higher highs, higher lows, and the most important feature: higher closing highs! Now, that was a gem of a move! The best part about this method is that it keeps you focused on specific targets and keeps your risk to a minimum, allowing you to be a more relaxed and a more confident trader, letting the trade mature and generating bigger profits.

So far we have demonstrated that dojis form more times than not at pivot point support and resistance targets. In most of the examples, we have not seen a classic morning doji star pattern develop at bottoms; however, high close doji setups have developed. As you have identified the "hidden" support target by calculating the pivot point target levels, you had a much clearer view of timing the market reversal. Stacking the odds in your favor by including analysis from other time frames, in addition to the aid of knowing the right way to read the confirming indicators, will continue to help you with your entries. Combining that with the knowledge of what to look for in identifying trending conditions and what signals a trend to run out of momentum will help you with your exits. That is what will increase your profits.

Figure 8.15 is a chart on Dell. As the market was plummeting, an exhaustion gap developed. For some traders, buying sharply lower gap openings, such as those that occurred at the end of October, is their bread and butter. Most traders buy the lower opens and look for the gap to be "filled" on the charts. In other words, they buy the market looking for prices to move back up to test the prior day's settlement. In this situation, that would have been a bad strategy because the market remained on the defensive for another week and a half. In fact, the market made a lower low. However, instead of playing the "catch the falling knife" guessing game, if you were patient and practiced discipline by waiting to see what the market's behavior was at the confluence of weekly and monthly supports levels, you would have seen a high close doji setup develop. Even the stochastics indicator confirmed the trigger to buy. As you can see, the %K and %D crossed and closed back above the 20 percent line at the same time as the high close doji trigger occurred.

The high close doji helps add simplicity to your trading. Aided by the use of pivot points analysis, stochastics, and MACD indicators and the moving average method, you have a beautiful system that should help generate reliable buy signals for forex, futures, and stock traders, whether they are short-term or long-term in nature.

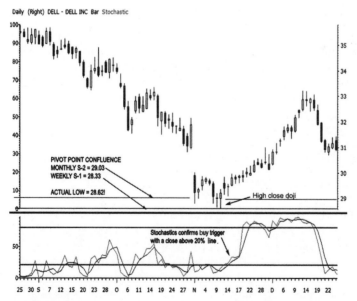

FIGURE 8.15
RealTick graphics used with permission of Townsend Analytics, LTD.

LOW CLOSE DOJI

The next trading signal is the opposite of the high close doji. It is a setup developed on the premise that once the market has rallied and established a high, when a doji forms, it is indicating there is indecision; and once we establish a lower closing low below the doji's low, as shown in Figure 8.16, which establishes that there is a loss in bullish momentum, we can initiate a short position.

FIGURE 8.16

Characteristics

When the market is in an extended trend to the upside and the market is overbought, a doji appears, indicating indecision and weakness of buyers to maintain the upward trend. Pay particular attention if the candle preceding the doji is a tall white candle, which would be a two-candle pattern called a bearish harami doji cross. Watch for increased volume, as this also confirms a blow-off-top formation.

Trading Rules

When a doji appears, you should:

- Sell on the close or the next time period's open once a new *closing* low is made from the previous time period's doji's low, especially when the market is against a key pivot point resistance target number.
- Place stops above the highest high point of the initial doji candle. Stops should be initially placed as a stop-close-only, meaning you do not exit the trade unless the market closes back above the doji's high.
- Buy or exit on the open of the first candle after the previous candle makes a higher closing high than the previous candle.

You can use a filter confirming the signal, such as a bearish divergence stochastic or MACD pattern.

Here is a secondary guideline for the exit and risk management strategy. Get out of half of your positions on the first shift in momentum, which in a low close doji (LCD) trade would be after the initial trigger. The market moves in your favor; and at times we see a consolidation period, similar to a bear flag formation. Covering your shorts and booking profits on half of your positions will keep you in a profitable position for the remainder of the trade. You initially placed a stop-close-only; but for an intraday time period, this would have been a mental stop-close-only because most order platforms do not have that feature for day trading. As the market has moved in your favor, you can place a hard stop above the doji high. There will be times when you have to make a judgment on whether the risk is too excessive by the distance of the proposed entry and the stop-close-only. Therefore, you may want to scale out of two-thirds of a position at the first sign you see the trend lose momentum.

Spot Forex Triggers

Let's examine market price action and how to execute this signal. You have your predetermined pivot point resistance levels already mapped out for you. RealTick has the feature that automatically sets the daily pivot point levels on the charts. Genesis Software has the Person Pivot with the COMAS triggers programmed in a library feature that highlights the buy and sell signals with the red and green arrows. Some charting packages have pivot points available as well. If you do not have either of these two software packages, you can do an Excel program; or at the very least, you can use my pivot point calculator included on the CD or on my web site www.nationalfutures.com to program any market for any time frame you want. The key is that once you have the predetermined support and resistance numbers, it is the second variable that is more important, which is looking for a signal that triggers a call to action. That would be the LCD signal.

The chart in Figure 8.17 is a spot forex euro currency that shows once again why it is important to wait for sell signals at resistance rather than buying breakouts. The euro currency chart shows the market breaking out above the R-1 level. As a standard rule, I do not like to take buy signals at resistance (we have covered that in the pivot point section). I would rather wait for a sell signal to develop and go with the declining momentum. I believe that one reason why this signal works so well is that many traders are trying to trade breakouts of pivot point resistance and, therefore, go long once they see the breakout above the R-1 level. Once there is little follow-through and prices start to retreat, then they are trapped and scramble to

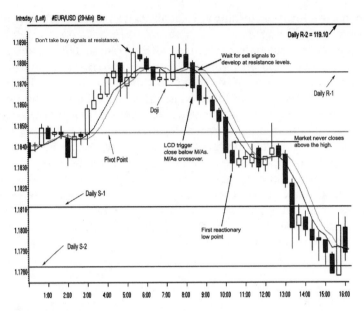

FIGURE 8.17
RealTick graphics used with permission of Townsend Analytics, LTD.

sell to get out of their losing trade. In this example, notice where we have a moving average crossover—not only do prices close below the doji, but also below both moving average values.

The trigger to sell short was executed at 118.67, and we saw an immediate reaction as prices plunged. The sequence of events that we want to see once we are in a short position, as in this example, is lower highs, lower lows, and the most important lower closing lows. Finally, the market pauses at 118.30, where we would look to cover half to two-thirds of our position, banking a quick 37-point (or PIP) gain per position. Now we can make a decision instead of placing a hard stop above the initial doji high. We could decide, since the move was a decent distance away from our initial entry, to place a stop at breakeven on the balance of our position. As the market enters a consolidation phase, we see that prices never close above the high of the first reactionary low's high. That keeps prices contained in a sideways channel, which is similar to a bear flag formation. As we follow the flow of the market, notice how the market declines by the end of the day to the S-2 of 117.80. As a day trader, there is no question on where you need to exit the position. It is the end of the day, and you have managed a trade all day and rode a very nice trending market condition.

Using a half-position scale-out method, you obviously need to trade at least a minimum of two contracts. In this example, when you cover half of your positions at 118.30, you pick up $370 per 100,000 full-size contract. You can now afford to ride the balance. That generates the bulk of your profits, as you would be covering the other half of the trade at the 118.00 level for a 67-PIP gain, or $670. Combined, you have a profit of $1,040 on just a two-lot position.

In Figure 8.18, I want to look at a textbook setup in the Japanese yen. This is a 5-minute chart without the pivot point moving averages overlaid to help you see the progression of the trade and the sequence of the open/close relationship that candlestick charts display.

As the market advances toward the projected pivot point daily R-2, traders may assume the market conditions are in a bullish mode. When you get in that mindset, you tend to forget about looking at the current market conditions. The top pattern is not a traditional or classic morning doji star formation because the third candle does not close below the midpoint of the tall white candle. However, it does close below the doji's low; that is the conditional change that takes place giving us the clue that the bullish momentum has dried up and that a reversal is imminent. First, there is a lower closing low; then, the market closes below the open; and finally, prices reversed direction—all after the market tapped the pivot point resistance level. Therefore, we want to sell on the close or on the very next time pe-

FIGURE 8.18
Used with permission of esignal.com.

riod's open, placing our stop (*initially*) as a mental stop-close-only above the high of the doji, which is 118.18. That is just three PIPs above the daily pivot point resistance level, too.

Again, what we want to see is almost instant follow-through for the price to decline. As you can see with this trade, there was immediate follow-through. Notice the progression of the market as it declines from the entry price at 118.07 straight down to 117.87, for a quick 20-PIP gain. The market then trades back and forth, creating small-range candles, which form a sideways channel. If you look carefully at each candle's close, you will see that it does not close back above the high of candle that established the first reactionary low. As a trader, you may want to hold all positions at this time or at least cover half of your positions for small gain. One reason to do that is because, as powerful and reliable as these triggers are, we still do not know how far prices can or will actually move. Remember that the patterns recur; the outcome is what is different each time.

The markets could easily reverse back and challenge the highs. By taking money out of the market immediately on half of your positions, you have profits; and more important, you reduce your risk exposure in the market.

Always remember that every time you are in the market, you face risk. So by establishing a profit and following the flow of the market, you can manage the balance of your trade with less stress, knowing you have made money. See how the candles in Figure 8.18 show the true direction of the market: The dark candles reflect closes below the open. For the most part, there are more of the dark, or negative assigned, candles, which are establishing lower closing lows, than there are white, or positive assigned, candles. Not only do they have smaller ranges, but they do not make higher closing highs. This shows that every time the market rallies just a little bit, sellers are present. Long real-body, or negative assigned, candles represent sellers, who dominate this market. Therefore, staying short on the balance of the position is warranted. Now, as the market price disintegrates, demonstrating the conviction of sellers, we can place a hard stop at breakeven on the balance of the position and start to adjust the stop to protect profits accordingly. This is what managing the trade is about and what we will go over in Chapter 9.

As a short-term trader, it is imperative to trade with the current flow or momentum of the market. Because there are so many variables that can influence your trading decisions, using the methods described here will help you keep focused and will alleviate the problem of trading on emotional impulses.

When you are armed with what the potential resistance levels are, then once you identify a low close doji signal and then apply trade management techniques, you can certainly increase your chances to consistently capture profits. It is literally up to you to pull the money out of the markets. In Figure 8.19, we have a 10-minute chart, just to illustrate that dojis form on various time frames as well. As you can see, the market starts to rally and closes above the pivot point resistance. By not allowing emotions to interfere with your better judgment, just by applying one mechanical rule—do not take buy signals at resistance—you will have eliminated the greed factor that often causes a trader to chase after a market. Therefore, just wait, and practice patience to look for a sell signal to develop. As you can see in Figure 8.19, after the long white candle forms, a doji forms. Then, as the method dictates, you do not enter a short position until you see confirmation of a breakdown in the bullish momentum by a lower closing low below the doji's low. Once that occurs, you enter a short position on the close of that period or on the next open. Remember that this does not tell you how much money you will make on each trade. Every outcome is different. There is a strong possibility that, based on historic reference, you should see a decline in prices; the question is by how much.

In this chart, you see an immediate reaction, as you would have entered a short from 122.94; and the bears take over almost immediately. There is a sequence of lower highs, lower lows, and lower closing lows. In

FIGURE 8.19
Used with permission of esignal.com.

fact, using the moving averages, notice the confirmation of a negative crossover and prices closing below the moving averages. This short-term downtrend ends when you see a change in conditions once the moving averages cross back up and prices start to close above both moving average values. This is a sign that the negative momentum, or selling pressure, is fading and that it is time to exit your position. Also, notice that a doji forms at the bottom of this downturn; it is the candle that closes above the doji's high that makes you commit to exiting all positions. This trade results only in an 11-PIP gain; but not all outcomes will be grand-slam home runs. The key is in being able to identify true conditional changes that will make you act on facts, triggering a call to action by a set of rules rather than by emotional impulses. If you have the discipline to trade by a set of rules and to follow those rules, you will reap some juicy trading profits consistently over a long period of time.

Triggers on Futures Markets

Let's look at implementing a confluence of pivot points and see how the market behaves at these longer-term resistance projections. In Figure 8.20, we have the daily, weekly, and monthly numbers all concentrating near 115 in the bonds. This chart is a 5-minute time period that illustrates again why it is important to look for sell signals at resistance and for buy signals at support.

Many traders fail to see the bigger picture and get caught up in the excitement of a trending market condition. As prices trade above the daily R-2 pivot point, some traders look at their R-3 numbers and think they are on a "cash cow" train ride that will never stop climbing higher. By examining the higher-degree time periods, such as the weekly and monthly numbers, you can get a better idea that the market may soon run out of steam as there is hidden resistance from longer-term pivot analysis. Practicing discipline by not following the herd mentality and demonstrating patience to wait for a sell signal will lead to a more fruitful opportunity.

As you can see, once the market closes below the double doji formations triggering a short position, the moving averages cross and the market closes below both values. Once again, here is the market reaction as bulls scramble to sell out their longs. The trigger to sell short was $114^{28}\!/_{32}$, and the market plunged to $114^{15}\!/_{32}$, for a quick $^{13}\!/_{32}$-point decline (each point is $31.25), or a gain of nearly $400 per position. Notice how the market pauses or consolidates forming a bear flag. Here is where tightening your stops and covering half or two-thirds of your positions would again come into action and be a wise and profitable decisison.

The LCD signal works on most active markets, as long as there is volatility and price movement. In late 2005, as commodity markets came

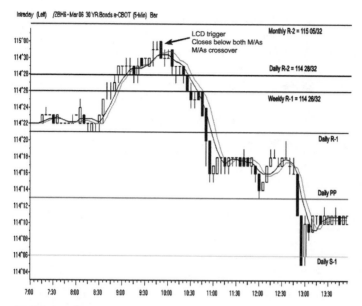

FIGURE 8.20
RealTick graphics used with permission of Townsend Analytics, LTD.

alive, the Chicago Board of Trade's electronic gold contract allowed easy access to take advantage of some pretty good intraday moves. With the statistical study done in Chapter 7, it makes good sense to diversify in other markets that respond to certain technical patterns, such as dojis, hammers, and shooting stars. It is also rewarding to see how robust this method is, as it works in no- to low-correlation market relationships and in various time periods. In Figure 8.21, as bullish as gold was in 2005, there were periods of consolidation. No market ever goes straight up. A sector or market segment trading with such high interest as gold attracted many traders. In this example, a sell signal was triggered at 559.70, and we started to see a progression of price deterioration down to the pivot support of 544.00.

Utilizing the stock index futures is one of the better markets for day traders, as we have discussed. The low close doji trigger is a highly effective pattern in these markets. Figure 8.22 displays the e-mini–Standard & Poor's (S&P) on a 15-minute candle chart illustrating an entry based on the close below the doji low, a negative crossover from the moving averages, and confirmation that prices closed below both moving average values. Here we have a trigger to sell short at 1239.25. Prices continue to follow the same progression of a pause or consolidation, and then continuation of

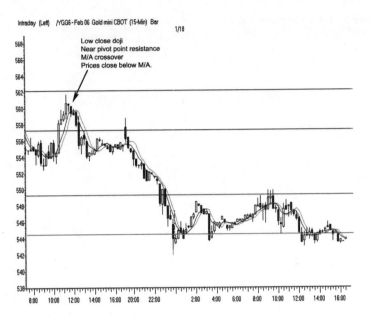

FIGURE 8.21
RealTick graphics used with permission of Townsend Analytics, LTD.

FIGURE 8.22
Used with permission of esignal.com.

the downtrend resumes. During the consolidation period, notice that prices do not close above the high of the last reactionary low point. In fact, notice the doji as the sideways channel develops; prices do not close above that high either.

The low close doji pattern, when combined with the three elements using pivot point analysis, is a very effective trading system. You are not simply relying on predicting a top, but rather waiting to see a conditional change occur in the market. By following the flow of the markets—lower highs, lower lows, and lower closing lows—you can really stay in the trade and, more important, on the right side of the market. Examine Figure 8.23, which is a 5-minute chart on the CBOT mini-Dow contract. You will notice that it is not the same chart as in Figures 8.19, 8.20, or 8.22 and that the signals are triggered at different points in time and in different time periods, just to prove the frequency and effectiveness of this pattern. Here we see the market trade up just past the daily projected pivot resistance target. While the high was actually formed by a shooting star, the real trigger to sell occurred at the time period that established a close below the doji's low. Notice the three elements that help confirm a trend reversal: price close below both moving average values and the two moving average components crossed, with the short-term moving average below the longer-

FIGURE 8.23
Used with permission of esignal.com.

term moving average. The trigger to sell short occurred at 10523, and the exit was confirmed with the high close doji signal at 10483, for a tidy gain of 40 Dow points, or $200 per contract, based on a day trading margin of $500. (Day trading margins vary; initial margin requirements to hold a futures position overnight is $2,632 as of 2/1/2006.) That is a trade setup I watch and wait for, day in and day out; and it works on most markets in most time periods.

The low close doji setup combined with pivot points and the moving average component really allows you to see the change in price momentum. As a screen-based day or swing trader, you have superior advantage over floor traders or other traders when using charts, pivot points, and the progression of a moving average component. In Figure 8.24, we have a 60-minute e-mini–S&P chart showing the price deteriorating once the trigger was made by a close below the doji low. Notice, too, that the moving averages crossed and prices closed below the moving averages as well. This signals a trigger to sell short at 1278; and by the end of the day, the market was at 1264. There was never a signal to exit the short position, which resulted in a 14-point gain, or $700 per contract. Now, this is over 140 percent gain on a 500 margin in a single day.

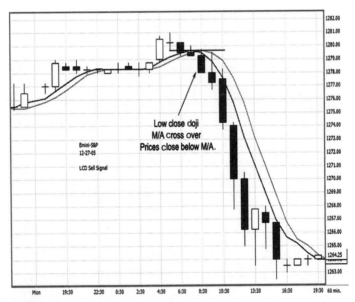

FIGURE 8.24
Used with permission of esignal.com.

Case in Point

Combining the statistical data that we went over in Chapter 7 (which indicated the frequency with which dojis, hammers, and shooting stars form) with the correlating markets (such as the S&P, the Dow, gold, and currency) gives you high-performing patterns; and trading using these patterns should not be ignored. If the markets outlined here have both a high frequency and a strong tendency to form tops and bottoms by the developing doji candle and if you learn to wait for that specific setup and act on a trigger rather than guessing or anticipating when a market is ready to turn, you may see a significant improvement in your trading results.

Triggers on Stocks

In Chapter 1, I gave an example of how an exchange traded fund may not react as much or at all compared to a stock in that group or sector. One such stock I showed was in Figure 1.15—Toll Brothers. If you broke that monthly chart down to a weekly and then a daily time frame and used the combination of the techniques taught so far with pivot point analysis in conjunction with these specific candle patterns, you would have been alerted to a top in the market in the summer of 2005.

Why don't traders act on these signals? Most traders do not realize what pivot point calculations are and how the markets react to them. The resistance target levels are "hidden," meaning you cannot see a projected high because it is not drawn from a past chart pattern; rather, it is derived from a mathematical calculation. This gives a projected price expansion on a measured-increase based on the previous time period's range according to the pivot point formula. Using the monthly pivot point method, taking the trading data for Toll Brothers from June would have helped predict the high for July. Figure 8.25 shows the Pivot Point Calculator with the high, the low, and the close from the month of June. Notice that the R-2 target number was 58.12. The exact high in July was 58.67!

The chart in Figure 8.26 illustrates the low close doji trigger. In addition, we had the moving averages cross over, and prices traded beneath both moving averages to help confirm that the market had lost its bullish momentum.

To some traders, the tall white candle at the top may have appeared to look like a buying opportunity, especially as the market made a slight correction. The low close doji against the longer-term monthly pivot point resistance told a different story. Identifying the doji at or near a pivot point is a great guideline to alert you almost every time that there is a potential price change or reversal coming. Once the market makes that lower closing

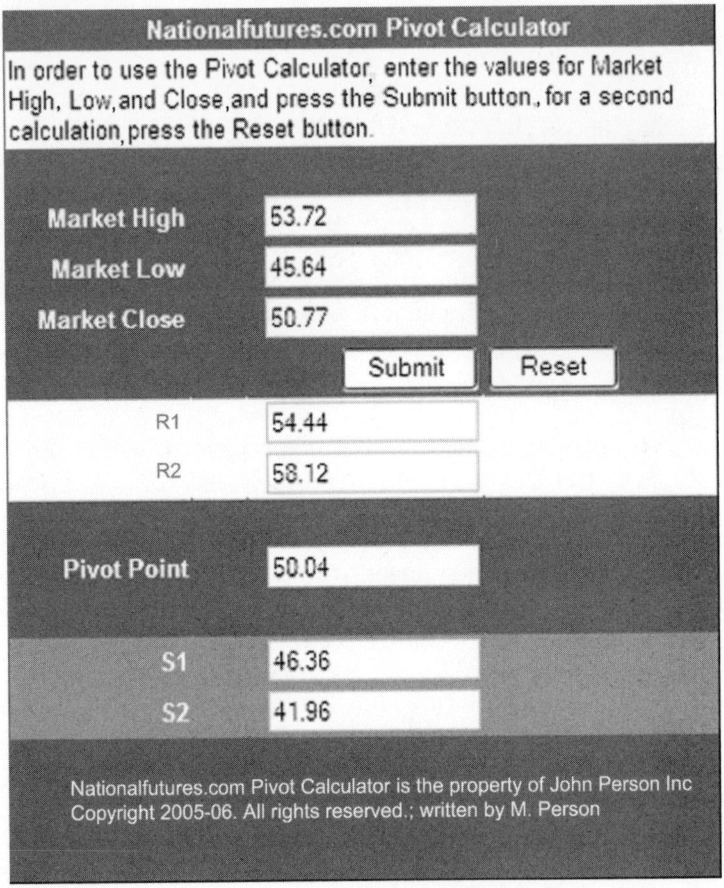

FIGURE 8.25
Used with permission of www.nationalfutures.com.

low, that is the trigger to sell. That will hold as a valid statement until the market closes back above the doji's high.

The Best Predictive Indicator

The best predictive market analysis tool is the pivot point, especially when using the higher time periods, such as the monthly and weekly time frames. We did cover the power of confluence, which should never be ignored. Using the monthly time frames, any investment vehicle like forex, futures, and stocks, especially after a market starts to form a doji on a daily chart,

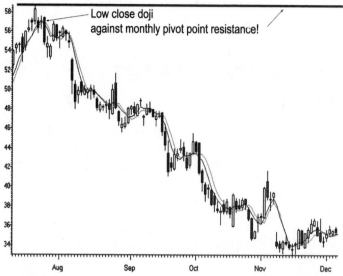

Daily (Left)   TOL - TOLL BROTHERS INC Bar

Low close doji
against monthly pivot point resistance!

FIGURE 8.26
RealTick graphics used with permission of Townsend Analytics, LTD.

is a sure sign that there is a strong possibility that a price or trend change is about to occur. A great example of using this method to help uncover a potential disaster in the stock of clothing retailer American Eagle Outfitters was used in mid-July. Taking the trading data from June as shown in Figure 8.27, the Pivot Point Calculator shows the monthly R-1 was 32.86 and the R-2 was 35.07. The actual high was 34.04, right in the middle of the target resistance levels.

One thing interesting here is that in Figure 8.28, the variation evening doji star does create the low close doji setup and indicates that the bullish momentum, or uptrend, had stopped. However, the market traded in a consolidation range for two weeks before the trend reversal occurred. The trigger to go short was not elected because there were two elements missing: (1) The market did not close below both moving average values; (2) the shorter-term moving average did not cross below the longer-term moving average. Those variables came later, as you can see on the chart. But the fact is that the monthly pivot point kept the market from establishing further gains; and the low close doji trigger was a significant warning to exit longs, buy put options, or at least tighten stops or move stop orders up to protect profits from long positions. The initiative to sell short was also a

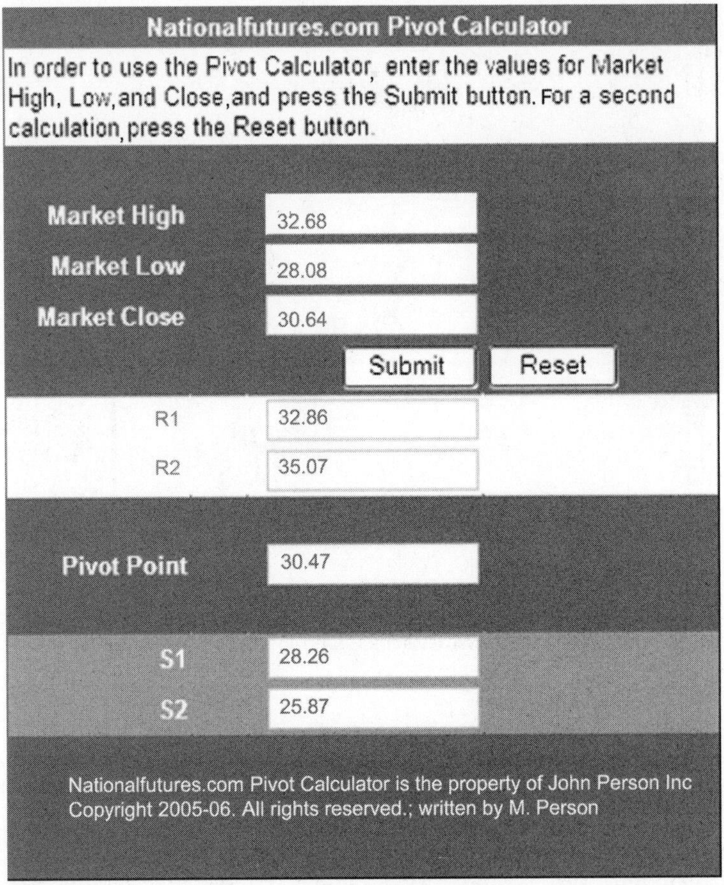
Nationalfutures.com Pivot Calculator
In order to use the Pivot Calculator, enter the values for Market High, Low, and Close, and press the Submit button. For a second calculation, press the Reset button.
Market High
32.68
Market Low
28.08
Market Close
30.64
Submit
Reset
R1
32.86
R2
35.07
Pivot Point
30.47
S1
28.26
S2
25.87
Nationalfutures.com Pivot Calculator is the property of John Person Inc
Copyright 2005-06. All rights reserved.; written by M. Person

FIGURE 8.27
Used with permission of www.nationalfutures.com.

very viable action. Using a stop-close-only above the doji's high, a trader would not have been knocked out of the short position at any time.

One of the more popular stocks in 2005, which mystified traders as it made a stratospheric rise, was Google. Figure 8.29 shows the price move that many thought would never end. Stock analysts were making upgrades calling for 600 per share in the first week of January 2006, and some were claiming as high as 2000. As you can clearly see, the low close doji pattern foretold of the market top; more important, it traded near the monthly R-2 resistance level of 466.95. Once again, here was a high-profile stock that formed a major top with an LCD trigger at a monthly pivot point target resistance number.

FIGURE 8.28
RealTick graphics used with permission of Townsend Analytics, LTD.

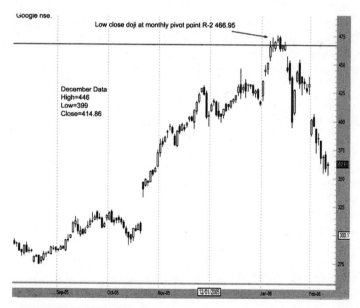

FIGURE 8.29 Google rise
Used with permission of www.GenesisFT.com.

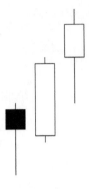

FIGURE 8.30

THE JACKHAMMER

In my experience, the one candle pattern that is associated or synonymous more than any other with the word *capitulation* is the hammer as Figure 8.30 shows. In Chapter 7, we identified the frequency or the percentage of times over a course of the year on a 15-minute time interval when the hammer candle pattern formed at or near the low of a given day. The jackhammer, however, develops in the middle to the end of the trading session. Usually immediately following the hammer is a bullish candle, or a *marabuzo*, a tall green positive (+) assigned candle.

What specifically describes the jackhammer? The *jackhammer* pattern is a hammer candle, but it occurs in the middle to the end of a trading session. I call it "the search and destroy" stop-loss order pattern. The general market characteristics of this pattern starts off with the market establishing a low, then consolidates or trades sideways for a bit, and then without warning sells off abruptly. It is generally that particular sell-off that creates a hammer pattern. Therefore, anyone who had intraday stops too close, under what is considered the primary low for the day, got "bagged and tagged." In other words, stop-loss orders were elected, and longs were jacked out of their positions and money—as in hit over the head with a billy club and "jacked" (robbed).

Trading Rules Defined

The jackhammer formation is an extremely powerful intraday reversal formation that requires immediate action to enter a long position. The sequence of events that occur for this pattern is:

- The hammer formed is a secondary low with the close at or near the primary low's low.
- It does not matter whether the real body is formed with a higher close than open or positive assigned value; however, it is generally a more solid signal when the close is above the open.
- This action generally completes a bullish convergence in the stochastics or MACD oscillator.
- Buy on the close of the hammer or the next time periods' open; initial risk is a *regular* stop below the hammer's low.
- Give additional importance if this pattern develops near pivot point support targets, especially if there is a confluence of pivot support targets from different time frames.
- Stock traders should watch for an increase or a volume spike, which indicates an exhaustion bottom is confirmed.

Figure 8.31 shows a 5-minute chart on the CBOT mini-Dow. Notice that the "midsession" is defined by the middle of the day. The first intraday low has been established, nearly three hours pass by, and the market makes a nosedive as prices hit a new low for the trading session. In this example, the hammer closes back within the primary low's range. The trigger to go long is on the hammer's close or on the open once the hammer formation is con-

FIGURE 8.31
Used with permission of esignal.com.

firmed. Generally, the jackhammer is followed by a blast-off secondary candle as prices surge ahead. What we also have happen is that the market crosses above both moving average values, thus signaling confirmation that this is a valid buy signal. The trigger to buy was at 10393; as you can see, the market ran straight to 10473 before giving an LCD trigger to exit at 10443 for a 50-point Dow move, or $250 per contract.

So far in this book, I have given you several patterns that work well for great day trading vehicles, such as the stock index futures contracts. The electronic markets offer retail traders a competitive advantage because they can use a home computer with a DSL or a broadband connection to integrate charting software packages and equal access to markets. The stock index futures contract, such as the mini-Dow contract, has what technical and fundamental traders need: News-driven events and other technical trading market participants both provide volatility and liquidity. Many of the chart examples contained in these pages are a great representation of an average day's trading patterns. That's not to say the other stock index markets, such as the e-mini–S&P and the Russell, perform differently; they interact extremely well with each other. In fact, at times I may have a trigger in the mini-Dow and take the trade in the S&P, and vice versa. Most times, when the Dow gives me a trigger, that is the market I will trade in. Consider that the e-mini–S&P have an influence from the tech sector. Dow at times may or may not have a similar dollar value move as the S&P. Both markets are great day trading vehicles, as is the Russell. The Dow more times than not has more distinct trading signals; for that reason, I have illustrated these setups with using the Dow.

As another example of spotting a jackhammer pattern, look at Figure 8.32, which is another 5-minute chart in the Dow. Here you see the secondary low bounce right off a pivot point support; and as the white or positive assigned values show, the candles' closes are above the opens and what is indicated immediately after the hammer forms. Notice the immediate reaction of the market as the sequence of higher highs, higher lows, and higher closing highs occurs. You can also see confirmation of the buy signal with the moving averages crossing over and with the second candle after the hammer is formed—it closes above both moving average values. This is the confirmation that should give you the confidence to maintain a long position. The stop is initially placed below the hammer's low. This should *not* be a stop-close-only as this setup should see an immediate positive reaction. The trigger to go long here was at 10935; the first sign that the bullish drive lost momentum was the lower closing low at 10965, which resulted in a quick 30-point gain.

There are times when we see this pattern late in the trading session. But keep in mind that the CBOT Dow contract trades continuously until 4

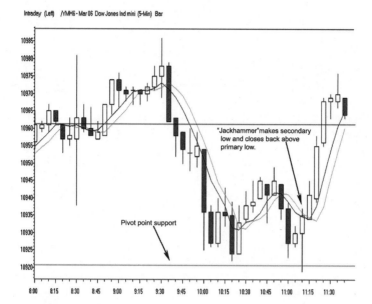

Intraday (Left) /YMH6 - Mar 06 Dow Jones Ind mini (5-Min) Bar

"Jackhammer" makes secondary low and closes back above primary low.

Pivot point support

FIGURE 8.32
RealTick graphics used with permission of Townsend Analytics, LTD.

P.M. (CT), whereas the e-mini–S&P closes at 3:15 P.M. (CT) and reopens at 3:30 P.M. (CT). This offers day traders more time to play those short squeeze plays that tend to occur toward the end of the day. More important, I covered why I do not look to sell at support levels. These short squeeze plays occur as those who may have sold at higher levels look to cover and take profits, as we see at certain times when the secondary low was rejected, which is what the hammer represents. Prices tend to move sharply higher in a very short period of time, signifying a rejection of lower prices. It is that price action that shows buyers attracted to the market, and bears start buying back or covering their shorts.

Therefore, when you are looking for a pattern such as the high close doji or the jackhammer in this situation, it is a more fruitful venture. One great example is in Figure 8.33, where the jackhammer forms near the end of the session. The trigger to go long was at 10784, which we see as almost an immediate reaction for prices to move sharply higher to nearly 10830. This was another quick 40-point-plus gain, or $200 per contract. Again, this does not sound like big money; but when you consider that the day trading margin is $500 at most online brokerage firms, that is a healthly percentage gain.

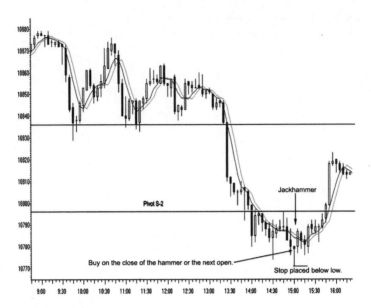

FIGURE 8.33
RealTick graphics used with permission of Townsend Analytics, LTD.

Trading Tips

- If the stop level is too great a distance, lower or reduce your contract size.
- Place hard stop below the low of the hammer candle.
- Scale out of positions when the market gives you a windfall profit, and move stops on balance of position above your entry price.

Bullish Convergence Pattern

In Chapter 4, we went over how the market price makes lower lows, but not by significant measures, and that when prices are at oversold extremes, we should be cautious for market reversals. We went over the market condition of bullish convergence and how to use the stochastics and MACD indicators to confirm buy signals when that market condition exists. The jackhammer is a formation that seems to be present in such a situation. Therefore, it is a great method for setting up a potential buy signal once the pattern is confirmed. Look at Figure 8.34, which is a 5-minute chart on the

FIGURE 8.34
Used with permission of esignal.com.

e-mini–S&P 500 futures. As you see, the midsession of the trading day at 12:30 shows on the charts that the market takes a secondary decline, forming that spike bottom hammer pattern. Notice that the very next candle after the hammer is a tall engulfing candle that forms a higher high. Prices then continue on in the sequence of higher highs, higher lows, and higher closing highs, while continuosly trading above the moving averages. If you examine the stochastics at the bottom of the chart, notice that when the price made a new lower low, the reading from the stochastics made a higher low, identifying that bullish convergence existed. If you watched for the stochastics to close back above the 20 percent line to confirm the price reversal and the trigger to go long, you would have had a stress-free trade that resulted in immediate returns.

In Figure 8.35, you see another example of the e-mini–S&P, this time with the aid of the MACD study. The jackhammer occurs past the midsession and actually closer to the close of business. Here we see both the moving average and the histogram components alerting us to the fact that the price action was oversold and that a reversal was likely. The one-two combination of the jackhammer and then the bullish engulfing pattern revealed a forthcoming price reversal.

FIGURE 8.35
Used with permission of esignal.com.

Stocks Get Jacked, Too

The psychological aspect of this formation occurs in stocks as well. Believe me, they are not immune to the ravages of human emotion. The example in Figure 8.36 is Comcast Corporation and is a great illustration of how the stochastics indicator confirms that the jackhammer, or secondary low buy signal, was triggered as confirmed with a bullish convergence signal. The fast stochastics indicator shows the timing of both %K and %D closed back above the 20 percent line, confirming a bottom was in place. The trigger to go long here is on the close of the hammer at 26.63; and before the close at 4 P.M. (ET), the market price is at 26.84.

The Jackhammer's One-Two Punch

Figure 8.37 shows a 30-minute chart on United Technologies that illustrates, depending on the time period, that the jackhammer pattern can exist from one day to the next, like a one-two knockout punch that attacks the stops and immediately pops up. Since many traders look at the obvious low point to place their stop-loss order, as this example shows, the jackhammer took out the prior day's low; and then once again, the one-two pattern develops with the hammer and then the next candle being the tall white, or

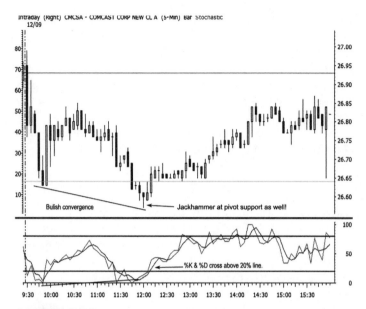

FIGURE 8.36
RealTick graphics used with permission of Townsend Analytics, LTD.

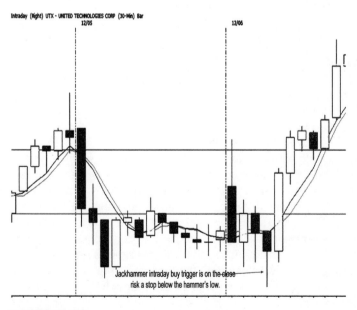

FIGURE 8.37
RealTick graphics used with permission of Townsend Analytics, LTD.

bullish, engulfing candle. This starts the immediate price reversal, with the sequence of higher highs, higher lows, and higher closing highs. See how the market also closes above and continuously trades above both the moving average values.

If you know what to look for, trading for a living is a great opportunity; but with opportunity comes responsibility. Prior to entering a trade, you should have your "pregame" setup, complete with your market analysis and rules for entering a trade. Certain rules should start with the techniques covered in this book so far, which include:

- Identifying what the market condition is—overbought or oversold bullish, bearish, or neutral.
- Identifying the levels that the pivot points lines are at, using the various time frames—monthly, weekly, and daily periods.
- Setting up your charting software parameters with these specific pivot points moving average values.
- Experimenting with variation settings on your own.

Then you need to watch and identify when and at what price points the dojis, hammers, and shooting stars develop. Knowledge of these items will arm you with critical information that can help provide protection from overtrading as well as from adverse moves and such pitfalls as reacting on emotions rather than on actual trading signals.

SUMMARY

The method of market analysis described in this book is designed so you will be educated on the importance of developing your personal trading system and so you can apply the techniques on a consistent basis, which will allow you to make decisions in a mechanical and nonemotional way. Common mistakes that traders make are not testing a strategy and not making a logical determination of whether the strategy is viable for their trading style. Many traders adopt a new strategy, trade with it, and immediately start tweaking different components of the strategy. The best approach that I have found in trading is to establish trading rules and to test those rules until an outcome is determined based on a reasonable number of trades. Also, I have several different trading strategies for different markets or conditions. The high close doji, the low close doji, and the jackhammer patterns are just a few of my proprietary setups that I watch for meeting these conditions.

If you are in a declining market, once an apparent bottom occurs near a pivot point support target, watch for the high close doji or the jackhammer pattern to develop. In a rising trend, once the market trades at or near a projected pivot point resistance, watch for a low close doji or a shooting star pattern. These specific patterns can be added to your personal toolbox of setups or used exclusively as a day trading plan. By understanding the current market conditions (uptrend, downtrend, or sideways), you can heighten your awareness of specific patterns that can be applied to that trading environment. All that is left after entering a position is risk and trade management, which is the focus of the next chapter.

CHAPTER 9

Risk Management

Setting Stops

This chapter will walk you through the various types of stop orders and when and where to place them. It will also provide a great deal of important information on the reasons for stop orders, the type of stops that should be placed at critical price levels, and identifying these specific price levels. If a trader is to maintain a degree of profitability over time, managing risk and using a system that helps evaluate price changes are essential. When you have finished this chapter, you will understand how to select stops to limit your potential losses and how to let profits ride.

The process in selecting stop placement as a risk management tool starts with the price of where the trade was initiated. Here are some finer points on the rationale for using a risk method, or having a stop-loss system in place.

- Predetermined stops help conquer emotional interference.
- Stops should be part of a system or included in a set of trading rules.
- The risk/reward ratio should be weighed before entering trades, and a stop objective should be set.
- When volatility is low, stops can be placed closer to an entry level.
- When volatility is high, stops should be placed further away from entry level.

One of my favorite bits of advice that I give students and have taught at seminars is that the first rule of trading starts with the premise that it is okay to form an opinion on a gut, or instinctive, feeling—just act on a trade signal that substantiates that opinion. Write your rules down and have them posted on your trading screen on your computer. Before you enter the trade, check your rule list; and make sure you know why, where, and what type of stop to place. As you gain more experience in the business, you will undoubtedly get caught in a news-driven, price-shock event, that is, if you have not already experienced one. These are unavoidable and hard to escape unscathed. It is considered a cost of doing business and should not reflect on your abilities as a trader. Managing risk is your job, and capturing as much profit as possible from winning trades should be your utmost goal. The descriptions of the types of stops and the pros and cons of each should help you make the right decision for the various circumstances or market conditions.

PLACING STOP ORDERS

Stop orders are often referred to as a protection method against losses. These orders can also be placed to enter positions. Specifically, a *stop order* is an order that you place either through a broker or online. If the market trades at a certain price, then the order is triggered and becomes a market order to be filled at the next best available price. The general rules of stop placement are:

- Buy stops are placed above the current market price.
- Sell stops are placed below the current market price.

GENERAL USES OF STOP ORDERS

This chapter will focus on protective stops used to offset a position and to protect against losses and against accrued profits. You can also use a stop to enter a position. There are a variety of stops that can be used depending on your situation, the market you are trading, and what you are trying to accomplish. There are various types of available stops and several techniques that can be used with these stops to help you manage your position and reduce your overall risk.

- *Dollar Limits.* Stops can be based on a dollar amount per position. The dollar amount is categorized under money management for trading systems. If you are risking $250 per futures contract in an e-mini–Standard & Poor's (S&P) contract, then your stop level would be placed at a five-point distance from your entry price. This method is used less frequently by professional traders because it has no relevancy to a mechanical trading model, especially systems that are in the market all the time, such as a moving average system. However, there are benefits to this feature with setting a daily dollar amount on a loss limit for active day traders. Some electronic order platforms allow you to set a daily loss limit. Rather than per trade, it sets an overall loss limit on your account.

- *Percentage Figures.* Most traders hear of using a stop of a certain percentage of the overall account size. Generally speaking, that number can be 2 percent up to as much as 5 percent of the overall account. Unfortunately for most traders in futures or foreign exchange (forex) markets, the average size trading account is $10,000, which means the stop is $200 to $500 dollars per trade. This leaves little room for error. Normally, you want to use at least a two-to-one risk/reward ratio on your trades. So if you risk 5 percent on a $10,000 account, you should expect to risk $500 and make $1,000 per trade.
- *Time Factors.* After a specific time period, if the price does not move in the expected direction or if the velocity of such a move does not warrant holding onto the position, then exit the trade. If you see a low close doji (LCD) or a high close doji (HCD) signal, it is my experience that the market generally demonstrates an immediate reaction within two or four time periods. After a long period of the market not responding to this type of signal, liquidate the position. The timing of the trade did not correspond with the historical tendency and did not generate the desired results in a given period.

  Another consideration in the art of placing stops using a time element is the aid of a moving average. A *moving average* is simply a trend line that is considered a time-driven price-directional tool. One time factor that one can use as a stop placement method is the crossover point of reference created when using two moving average values. Once the shorter-term moving average crosses the longer-term moving average, it reflects a value change in the market. In Figure 9.1, once the market triggers a signal to go long with the high close doji, combining a close below doji low and the crossover point (using both the one-period pivot point and the three-period pivot point moving averages) can act as a stop placement level. Once again, you would want to look at the point of crossover of the two moving average values; and if the market closes below the low of the doji's low and the moving average (M/A) values, then a trigger to exit the position would be warranted. As you can see, a bullish trend develops with the golden sequence of events: higher highs, higher lows, and higher closing highs. The stop-loss was placed at a critical point.
- *Price Levels.* Traders often use basic statistics to measure the degree

FIGURE 9.1
Used with permission of esignal.com.

of price volatility that can occur on a daily basis in a given market. These measures can then be used to place a stop order or a limit order that takes into account these natural daily price movements. Statistics that are often used are the *mean*, the *standard deviation*, and the *coefficient of variation*. The best trailing-stop approach has been explored by many technicians. The various methods include placing a stop using a set price amount, which could be as much as 50 percent of the average true range of a given time period, either above or below the 10- or 20-day moving average.

Why is this an important method? If you place a stop near a specific chart point of interest, such as an old high or an old low, that level is obvious to every chart watcher. Markets do "test" and penetrate from time to time those levels. If you set your stop too close, such as setting a sell stop below an old low point or a buy stop above an old price high, chances are that your order may be executed if it is too close, such as what the jackhammer or shooting star represents. So generally, a certain factor or distance should be calculated for your stop placement. Since most traders believe a market has reached a peak, they will place a stop slightly above an old high or below an old low. Depending on where you place your stop, the market may demonstrate a spike pattern that will hit your order and then proceed to move in the desired direction, without you, of course. Figure 9.2 shows an example of when the market is at a major turning point, how a price spike occurs. You may want to take the average daily range of the most recent 10 or more periods and then use a factor between 20 percent and 50 percent of the 10-day average daily range. When entering a short position you would use a protective buy stop based on a percentage above the 10-day average range. For example, if you take the average daily range for the 10 trading sessions from the low back on October 12 up to the first peak on October 25, you have an average daily range for that 10-day period of 174 PIPs (percentage in points), or points. The first spike top exceeded the prior high by 34 PIPs.

If you established a short position and wanted to place your stop out of harm's way, then using a stop of 20 percent of 174 PIPs above the predetermined high would not have worked out, as that was 34 PIPs, the exact amount by which the market exceeded the high. If you in-

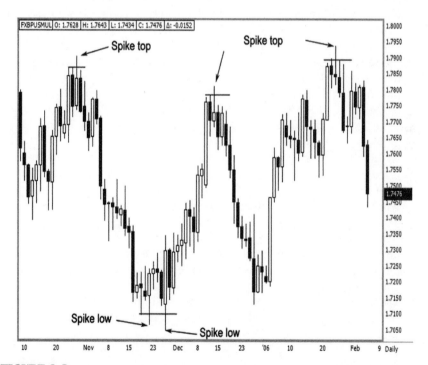

FIGURE 9.2
Used with permission of esignal.com.

creased the stop amount by 50 percent of the 10-day average daily range, then you would have an 87-point stop above the high; and this would have kept you from getting stopped out. By using 120 percent of the average of the last 10-day period range, this method would accomplish the goal of not getting stopped out. Realistically, that may be way too much risk for an individual trader. But examine the risk/reward ratio on that particular trade. A risk of 150 percent of the average daily range from the most recent 10-day period would have been 261 PIPs. The stop would be placed above the high on October 25 at 181.30. The low was at 170.65, made nearly one month later on November 22. Granted, depending on your risk tolerance, this may seem excessive; but you can select and back-test any percentage variable of an average daily range stop placement.

The key idea here is to keep your stops out of harm's way. If a trade is to become profitable, there should be signs, such as in the case of selling short, that you see immediate results with lower highs, lower lows, and lower closing lows. Even in the days where we see spike highs or spike lows, notice where the market closes in relation to their respective highs and lows. The price penetrates the highs but closes back below the prior highs. The reverse is true at the spike lows. This is a good clue that the market has exhausted a trend and is ready to reverse. Keeping a stop out of harm's way will allow you to participate in the move using a variation of an average daily range stop placement.

- *Conditional Changes.* A *conditional change* is defined as a higher closing high in a downtrend or a lower closing low in an uptrend. Such as the case with a spike top, the market does not close above an old high. Therefore, one factor such as the stop-close-only order will be of great use to a trader not looking to get bumped out of a position. There is, as with any stop, the unknown risk that there is not a guaranteed price at which your stop order will be filled. This order has a negative connotation among traders because it spells too much risk. A buy stop will be elected and will knock you out of a position if the market closes above the stop price; and a sell stop will be elected and will knock you out of your position if the close is below your selected price level. The unknown is how far away the market will close from the selected stop price. The key benefit in using a stop-close-only order is that it keeps your risk defined to a conditional change and helps you from getting knocked out of a position from intraperiod volatility. Stop-close-only orders (SCOs) are for end-of-day trading and can be placed on most trading platforms. The SCOs can be used for day trading; however, they must be used manually, as most platforms do not accept intraday SCOs. Some consider these mental stops, which are predefined risk factors. However, many traders violate the rules once a signal calls for an exit but they do not exit, thereby increasing their losses. A trader needs to have a strict disciplinary approach.

The challenge in selecting the right stop is to reduce risk while not being shaken out of the trade by market volatility. It is important to try to maximize your trading results and to stay in profitable trades as long as possible. Employing random stop-losses and profit targets can ruin a trading strategy, making it perform significantly worse than it would have otherwise. One successful method is to use trailing stops that adapt to market volatility so that the stop is placed far enough away, which combines enough sensitivity to price changes with flexibility to fit your risk/reward parameters. Using this combination may provide profitable consistency from a stop-placement aspect for the intermediate-term trader. The trailing stop is used as an attempt to lock in some of the paper profits that could accrue should the market move in the direction desired. Like an ordinary stop, the trailing stop is started at some initial value but then is moved up (in a long trade) or down (in a short trade) as the market moves in your favor.

Testing has demonstrated that a proper combination of even simple exit methods, such as placing a stop below the low of the prior past two trading sessions, can substantially improve the behavior of a trading strategy, even turning a random, losing strategy into a profitable one!

Another less complicated method to use for a bullish trending market condition is placing a stop below the lowest low from the most recent 10-day period. Another method is a trailing stop method using the lowest low from the last conditional change. I define the *last conditional change* as a higher closing high. This is a much more important event than a higher high. Buyers who stepped in on the open have a strong conviction that price should expand to new higher territory once the market established a new high ground. Therefore, if the lows are violated, then the market is demonstrating weakness. In Figure 9.3, we are looking at the daily chart on gold. Starting from the low on November 4 near 465, the market does not make a lower closing low. On December 1, we see a close at a doji low but not below the low of the doji. The trend then continues higher with a sequence of higher highs, higher lows, and higher closing highs.

It is not until the shooting star develops that the intermediate top is made. A stop placed beneath the low of the candle prior to the star would be the last conditional change or the last higher closing high that occurred. That would be where you would want to place a sell stop. Using the two-period lowest-low method, you would have been stopped out at 528. If you used a stop-close-only below that low, your fill was the next time period's close; and that was not as friendly or as profitable, as the market closed at 514. However, using the lowest low

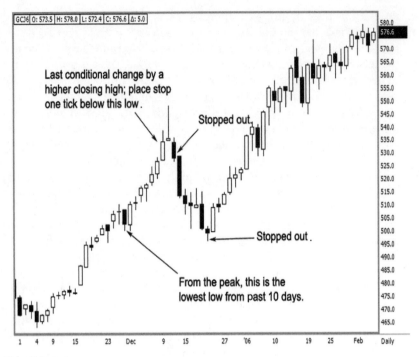

| GCJ6 | O: 573.5 | H: 578.0 | L: 572.4 | C: 576.6 | Δ: 5.0 |

Last conditional change by a higher closing high; place stop one tick below this low.

Stopped out.

Stopped out.

From the peak, this is the lowest low from past 10 days.

FIGURE 9.3
Used with permission of esignal.com.

for the most recent 10 periods, your stop-out point was all the way down at 497.

Let's examine this method with a day trade using a chart example on the spot forex British pound market from 2/6/2006 using a 15-minute time frame. Figure 9.4 shows a low close doji trigger to sell short at 176.07. The initial stop per the LCD trigger states to use a stop-close-only above the doji high. That would be 176.28. As you can see, the market stalls in a traditional sideways channel, as forex markets are known to do. But, sticking with your trading rules, as the market starts to deteriorate, you would change the stop from a stop-close-only to a regular stop one tick above the high of the second conditional lower closing low candle. You now have the option to move stops above the highs of the last reactionary high points; and if you follow the trail of the market, you will notice the high from the last conditional lower closing low. This failed reactionary high was the perfect spot to move your stop down to just one PIP above that high point. At the end of the run, you want to trail the stop to the point one PIP above the high of the

FIGURE 9.4
Used with permission of esignal.com.

second-to-last candle that made a conditional change, which would be a lower closing low.

Let's explore this method further for day traders in the stock index futures. Figure 9.5 shows a 15-minute candle pattern showing another low close doji trigger to sell short. The fill would be 1279.25, and the initial stop would be a mental stop-close-only above the doji high at 1283.5. As we want to see when short, immediate results materialize with the sequence of events such as lower highs, lower lows, and, best of all, lower closing lows. We now have the option to change and trail a hard stop above the high of the second conditional change candle. Here, a conditional change is a candle that makes a lower closing low. Prices now decline to 1270.75; we have over an eight-point gain, or $400 per contract. We can do several things, such as taking profits on half of our positions, because the market has reached a move equal to the average daily range from the most recent 10 trading days, or moving stops down to lock in profits and letting our winners ride. We should now place a trailing stop above the high of the last conditional change or an SCO to exit the balance of positions.

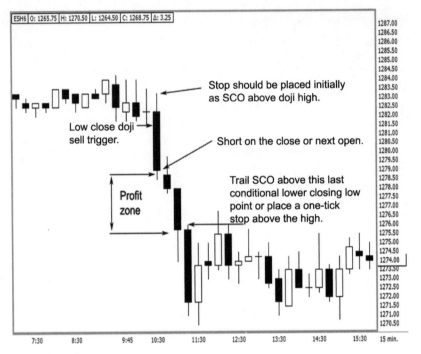

FIGURE 9.5
Used with permission of esignal.com.

In this example, you would not have been able to sell the high or buy the low using a set of trading rules. However, a solid chunk of middle of that trading session was captured with having little-to-no risk pressure. The trailing stop method would allow you to stay with the trade until the bearish conditions changed. The chart in Figure 9.5 is also a great illustration of how a market moves from a trending condition to a consolidation phase. Once you have captured the profit, it is time to wait for another trade setup.

There are many different variations to placing stops. The key is watching for conditional changes; for example, in a declining market, you should watch for the last reactionary high as the peak at which to place a trailing stop once you are in a short position. You should use a stop-close-only above a conditional change candle especially on a two-period time count. These methods will help you limit losses, prevent you from being prematurely knocked out of a trade, and reduce emotional stress, while capitalizing on letting your winning trades ride.

THE BOTTOM LINE

The bottom line is this: *Stops are not for sissies.* You just need to know when changes in a market's condition occur to help determine when to exit a trade. If you are in a trending condition for too long, chances are that you may be overextending your welcome; therefore, tightening stops is a good way to protect profits. After all, it really counts most when you get out of the trade. All traders struggle with stop placements. There is no one single best method. The concept is to develop a consistent method that helps you define cutting your losses and letting winners ride.

CHAPTER 10

Projecting Entry and Exit Points

Learn to Scale Out

W hat are some of the most important things that successful traders do? They have:

- A system or a method that provides an accurate daily market forecast, helping them define where the market might go each day.
- A set of rules for when to get in and out of the market and a bit of discipline to follow these rules.
- A set of timing indicators to help them pull the trigger at the key areas.

The legendary basketball coach Bob Knight often says, "Most people have the will to win; few people have the will to prepare to win." This is true in many aspects of a person's life, be it in athletics, academics, business, a profession, or trading.

Trading is about making money, not about being correct in market analysis or being a great prognosticator. Traders must be consistent in their approach and strive to completely remove emotion from trading decisions. This is often best achieved by having and sticking to a plan for every trade. We trade in the *future* markets, not in the *past* markets. Hindsight is always 20/20. Keep in mind that you will never trade as well in real time with real money as you will by looking at or trading in the past. Trading in the past is an exercise in futility that will only harm your psyche going forward. You should view every trade you make as the best trade you could make at the time with the information available. That is why I like to scale out of my positions as a short-term trader at market points that signal when a trend has a loss in momentum. The reason I like to keep a portion of positions on is simple: As good as my triggers can be, I cannot predict the future. I do not know if a market will develop into a consolidation phase or if it is simply pausing before continuing the trend or getting ready to reverse the trend entirely. Therefore, it is crucial to take money off the table when given the opportunity, while letting a trade mature and potentially develop into a larger profit. There is only one way I know to manage such a feat, and that is by scaling out of partial positions. The question some traders ask is, "What is the formula or percentage that I use to take positions off?" I normally use the 50 percent rule, but at times the one-third rule works as well. In order to define what the percentage figure is, I need to judge what condition the market is in. I do that by using the diagnosis described in this book. In the trade process, there are three critical stages:

1. Gathering information on which to make decisions.
2. Using that information to help formulate a trading idea.
3. Planning the actions to be taken.

The gathering of information involves collecting past data and then applying it to a specific means of market analysis, such as what I have covered in this book using pivot point analysis. In formulating ideas, you may look at the pivot point moving averages to help determine a market's ability to make a certain price range. This step helps you to predict where the market might head and then gives you information so that you can decide where it should be going. Planning action involves thinking creatively about alternative courses of action, evaluating their feasibility, and making decisions on implementation of the plans. This step involves helping you decide if you should be in multiple contracts or if you should scale back on your normal position size. If the risk is not worth the reward, then trade with fewer positions. In other words, scale back your normal position size.

STEPS TO SUCCESS

The steps outlined here are a review of the overall purpose of the trading methods discussed in this book. Pivot point analysis helps give me a "heads up" on the potential range of a session. The moving average of the pivot point helps give me a truer reflection of the market's value, and that helps me define the market's condition and possibly the correct direction. Candlestick charts help illustrate and define the trigger, which enables me to carry out a systematic process of arriving at optimum plans and strategies for my trades. With that, I am now aware of the full range of issues to be considered in a systematic thinking process before entering a trade. By examining a set of relevant questions, such as how low the market can go, what the next support target is, how high the market can go, and what the next resistance level is, I can formulate a trading plan with a clear, concise strategic idea. Exiting the positions and taking money off the table should be the easy part. However, as it turns out, that is the hardest part for most traders.

Let's take a trade example as shown in Figure 10.1. The hammer forms; I buy on the close, as the market closed above the moving averages; and I have immediate results. I entered at 10765; and the bullish momentum carried the market higher, as indicated by higher highs, higher lows, and higher closing highs. The market has lost the bullish momentum, as I see a lower-close-than-open pattern develop on two time periods followed by a doji. That is the definition of price action demonstrating a loss in bullish momentum. Therefore, that dictates for me to liquidate half of my position, which is at 10780. Hardly a profit to speak of, considering the mini-Dow is $5 per point, which is only a $75 profit. But it is a profit.

FIGURE 10.1
Used with permission of esignal.com.

Now what about the balance of my positions, and where do I place my stops? In this example, I would suggest either moving stops up to my break-even point or, as just discussed, placing the stop on a close below the low of the most recent conditional change candle (a higher closing high), which occurs at the 6:15 time period. At this point, I do not know if the market will move higher or lower, but I definitely have a loss of momentum. In this situation, prices established a pause, or consolidation; and then the market did break out and continued the uptrend. With scaling out of half of the position, I have a profit and am continuously participating in a tremendous trending condition, as the market ends up more than 10870. That equates to more than a 110-point gain, or $550 per contract, on the balance of positions. As a day trader, did I do wrong in liquidating half of my position? Not if you follow rules. In this situation, I did not have a classic sell signal, just an indication of a loss in momentum. Therefore, it was a prudent measure to get paid on partial positions and let the balance ride. So in this example, there was a reason or a call to action, but not a signal for a reversal of the long.

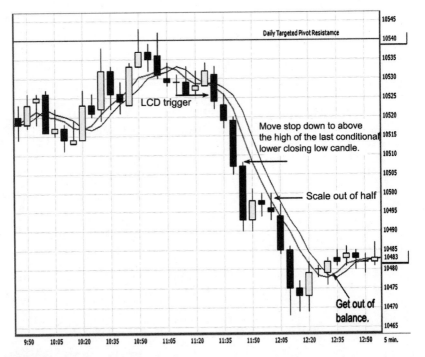

FIGURE 10.2
Used with permission of esignal.com.

Ever heard of the saying "Character in great and little things means carrying through what you feel able to do"? Covering half of your positions when markets signal a loss in momentum is carrying through what you are able to do. You made money and stayed with the trade.

In Figure 10.2, we have a low close doji trigger, a classic crossover of the moving averages, and prices closing below both moving averages. A trigger to sell short was generated at 10523. We see a beautiful event unfold—immediate results with lower highs, lower lows, and lower closing lows—until the 11:50 time period; and the market moves sideways in a consolidation pattern. It does take on the form of a bearish descending triangle; however, we do not know what the outcome will be. As the market is at 10490,. we are staring at a 30-point mini-Dow move, which translates into a $150 profit per contract. At this time, it is prudent to cover half of the position and put the stop in at breakeven. The market in fact happens to move in the direction of the original trend as the bearish triangle indicated. By following the market flow, we finally see a specific reason to cover the balance of the position with the high close doji signal at 10483. Here we have a 40-point gain on the second half of the trade for a $200 gain. We have, in essence, captured the majority of the trend and kept disciplined in our trading approach while scaling out of half of the position.

DO SOMETHING GREAT

I am sure you have read or heard this expression sometime in your life: "I'd rather attempt to do something great and fail than to attempt to do nothing and succeed." By scaling out, you have a profit in your trading account while letting the trade mature. You have accomplished a great thing, a true sense of following a business plan—and you made money.

Scaling out of positions is the most apropriate method when the market gives you a clue that the trend momentum is slowing. It allows you to capture a profit while participating in a potential market move. As a day trader, you are not so much concerned with long-term macroeconomic situations as you are with riding a momentum wave. Granted, it helps to have a good understanding of fundamental conditions; but for the most part, you are looking to ride a move and profit from it. That is your job. In short-term trading, conditions change; and you need to capture opportunities as they become present stocks. Foreign exchange (forex) and futures markets are ideal for momentum trades. Traders need assistance with capturing the profits while letting the balance of the position ride or, better stated, with an execution plan. The foreign currency markets also tend to trend well over the course of 7 to 10 days, allowing swing traders opportunities to capture larger price swings over a given period of time. One of the greatest ben-

efits here is that you have access to the markets on a 24-hour basis, unlike
the equity markets.

SCALE AND TRAIL

The euro currency chart in Figure 10.3 demonstrates a nice swing trading
opportunity and how scaling out of half of your positions is a great mechanism to capture profits while staying with a potentially longer-term trend.
As you can see, the sell signal triggers at 124.80. Immediately we see the sequence of events develop: lower closes than opens, lower highs, lower
lows, and lower closing lows. This is what we want to see each time we
place a short position in the market. As the price declines, a hammer forms;
and as you know, that generally gives a clue that a market reversal is developing. The market does make a higher closing high, which would give
you reason to scale out of half of your positions at 122.65. Not a bad trade,
which took place over 11 trading sessions.

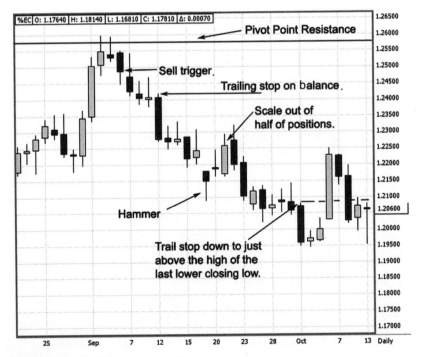

FIGURE 10.3
Used with permission of esignal.com.

The market has not given any confirmation of a trend change; therefore, you would want to move a stop down on the balance of the positions to just above the high of the candle that made the last major conditional change of a lower closing low. Trading with scaling out of the balance of half of your positions combined with the trailing stop method we went over in Chapter 9 will help you capture profits while participating in the majority of a trending market condition.

INTEGRATE PIVOT POINTS TO HELP TIME OUR EXITS?

We have gone over how to move the stops and why it is good to scale out of positions. We can integrate pivot points to help us trigger our entries and use the pivot point support or resistance levels to help us target our exits. As shown in Figure 10.4, we have a 15-minute candle chart showing a classic sell signal with a low close doji at pivot resistance, and we see how the

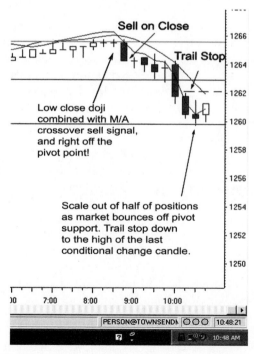

FIGURE 10.4
RealTick graphics used with permission of Townsend Analytics, LTD.

moving averages have crossed and the market is trading below both values. We have a call to action to sell on the close or on the next open. This chart is the e-mini–Standard & Poor's (S&P), and we would be filled at 1264.25. The market declines in the perfect order—lower highs, lower lows, and lower closing lows—right until we see the market trade down to the pivot support target. This is a perfect opportunity to scale out of half of your positions. Remember that in Chapter 2 we went over the fact that once a market goes into trend mode, it will then go into a consolidation phase. We do not know if the trend will continue or reverse; so at this point, it makes sense to trail a stop on the balance of positions.

I use the point just above the last conditional change, which is the candle that made the last lower closing low. We cover half of the positions at 1260.75 for a 3.5-point gain, or $175 per contract. We would lower our stops on the balance to 1262.25 to lock in profits on the balance of positions. Using the pivot point target levels will help you identify when and where to scale out of positions.

BUY SUPPORT, SELL RESISTANCE

Throughout this book, I have made many references to why I look for buy signals at the predetermined pivot point support levels and take sell signals at predetermined resistance levels. This also falls along the lines of not knowing the outcome of the trading signal and market trend conditions, which can and do change. As a day trader looking to capture a portion of a day's potential trading range, you have to use a plan. Scaling out of positions is such a plan of action. Take a look at Figure 10.5. We have a spot forex euro currency versus the U.S. dollar. Notice that the market breaks below the targeted pivot point support several times; however, prices do not seem to decline very far or carry any momentum. In fact, a low close doji pattern develops, which means, if you follow my rules, you do not take sell signals at support. This helps filter out the false trading signals. Once we have a high close doji trigger to go long at 119.83, we now can place our stop and follow the developments as the trade matures. We see higher highs, higher lows, and higher closing highs. The market closes closer to the highs of each successive candle, and the closes of each candle are above the opens. These are all very bullish signs, and the market blasts beyond the first resistance (R-1) point. So far, we do not have a reason to liquidate the position or scale out of the trade. Then as the market trades at the R-2 level, we see a doji form; and that will be the clue to scale out of half of the position near 120.20. At this point, we trail our stop on the bal-

Intraday (Right) #EUR/USD (5-Min) Bar

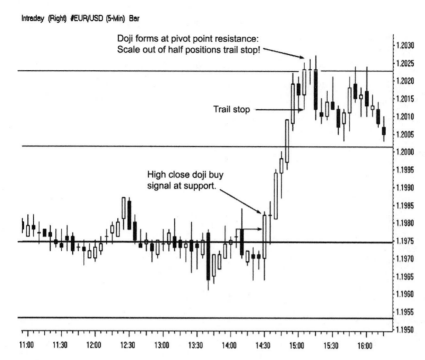

Doji forms at pivot point resistance:
Scale out of half positions trail stop!

Trail stop

High close doji buy
signal at support.

FIGURE 10.5
RealTick graphics used with permission of Townsend Analytics, LTD.

ance of positions to the low of the last conditional change candle, which is
the one that made the last higher closing high. We do get knocked out of
the trade, as the market develops into a consolidation phase. This trade resulted in capturing a nice chunk of the middle of a beautiful intraday trending market condition. Scaling out of the first half of the position would
have generated a 40-point profit, or $400 per $100,000 contract lot value;
and the balance would have made nearly 30 points, or $300. There was lit-
tle to no pressure once the trade was initiated. Pivot points helped you target the entry and scale out of the exit. As an interesting note, remember the
statistic that stated that dojis form close to the highs and/or pivot point resistance levels. Figure 10.5 is just another chart to help visually validate
that claim.

Most people use scale trading as a means to stagger positions to enter
as well as exit a market. There are many variations and specific techniques.
It can be argued that rather than scaling out of half of the positions, you

should actually add on to trades to really pyramid profits. I personally do not use this style of trading. I encourage you to explore any and all methods, but I like to stick to the methods that work for me. When I have a projected entry price based on pivot point analysis, I never have a "guaranteed" profit until I liquidate the trade. By scaling out, it is the finest method I know of that puts cash in my account while allowing me to further participate in gains on the balance of positions.

CHAPTER 11

The Sample Analysis

The Proof Is in the Back-Testing

S hort-term system traders make their money, leave the game, and wait to execute the next setup; they don't have to worry about being an economist. They get in when the signals indicate and get out when the signals dictate. It has been stated many times and proven by history that traders who consistently make money are those who follow a program or a set of predefined rules. These rules have been tested, and they correspond in a variety of time periods and with diversified or noncorrelated markets.

You may have made observations on changes in the market, such as when the stock index futures are trending up by 10:30 A.M. (CT) on a Friday, the market has a tendency to trade higher through the end of the day. Actually, that was a casual observation of mine as described on page 212 of my first book, *A Complete Guide to Technical Trading Tactics* (Wiley, 2004). With that said, once you have a trading idea about the way a market moves, through your own observation, you can apply it to computer code and have a computer generate an alert to inform you when a signal is generated.

Through the proficiency of computers, we can take historical data and back-test the results to see how reliable and accurate the theories are. Not all systems work well. Some are good in trending market conditions, and others will work well in nontrending market environments. Therefore, it is important to back-test a methodology for various time periods and in various noncorrelated markets to see if the principles are sound and stand the test of time. So far, with what we have gone over, you can develop your own rules based on pivot point and candlestick patterns.

One such example is if we assign a positive (+) value to a candle with a higher close than open, if you have a sequence of three positive values after a succession of, say, five negative (–) values, and if the low of a given candle is within two ticks, or 5 percent of, the average daily range on a 10-day average, then a buy signal is triggered. Another way of stating this is:

- For a positive assigned candle:
  Close (C) is greater than open (O) (C > O)
- For a negative assigned candle:
  Close is less than open (C < O)
- For a doji candle, with a neutral (=) assigned value:
  Close is equal to open (C = O)
- You can program your own system to generate an exit strategy based on an average holding period of, say, seven or eight periods or until the market forms a lower close than open (C < O) or a negative assigned value and if that time period closes below the prior time period's low.

Another methodology or system that is a simpler program would be to combine a three-period pivot point moving average with a five-period pivot point moving average. After a series of lower closing lows, once the three-period moving average crosses above the five-period moving average and if the market was within five points above or below a pivot point first support level (S-1) target number, then a buy signal would be generated. For added optimization, you could add a filter that if the stochastics indicator was below the 20 percent line, once %K and %D crossed and closed back above the 20 percent level, a buy signal would trigger.

Using the value of the pivot point resistance target of R-1 while combining the three-period pivot point moving average with the five-period pivot point moving average, once the three-period crossed and closed below the five-period pivot point moving average, within five points either above or below the R-1, a sell signal would be generated. For added fine tuning, you could add another element, such as a stochastics reading, so if both moving averages were above the 80 percent level and once %K and %D both closed back below the 80 percent level, a sell signal would be triggered.

The hard part in coding is comprehending or understanding the software language and then thinking like a computer. You can't just state "sell" when stochastics gives a sell signal. The software or computer program does not know what your interpretation of a sell signal is.

If you recall, in Chapter 1, I suggested that traders need to ask more questions. That is what a system trader does. In order to develop a trading plan or a mechanical system, you need to search for answers to question such as:

- Will this be for day or position trading?
- Will volume studies be used and, if so, how?
- What will be the average holding period?
- What methods do we want to use and what parameter will we choose?

A trader needs to use various tools to get the job done, so to speak. That is why I have several trading platforms and quote services. Genesis Software allows me to develop my own "black box" of algorithms and indicators and to back-test the program. In order to develop a good system, you need to decide if the trading concepts are valid. Once you have come up with your set of rules or criteria, then you can start to optimize the program. You have heard of the "Keep It Simple" rule? Leonardo da Vinci is credited with saying "Simplicity is the ultimate sophistication." If Leonardo liked things simple, well then, it is good enough for me, too!

A trading system should be designed from simple yet effective rules that blend key concepts of momentum changes and trending conditions. A well-defined trading strategy can be developed to generate buy and sell signals in most markets in various time periods. Believe it or not, designing a trading system is easy to do once you have an idea of what the call to action, or the trigger, will be to enter a position. In this book, we have gone over several good techniques with which you can start, such as when indicators correspond near pivot points like the stochastics 80 percent/20 percent close line technique or the moving average convergence/divergence (MACD) zero-line cross signal. You can develop a system based on these two indicators and then determine how many time periods, or the length of time, a position should be in the market. Now all you need to determine is how many holding periods (such as 4 or 8 periods) are needed before an exit strategy is triggered. You can develop a trigger on moving average crossover to initiate a signal, just like the pivot point moving average we went over in Chapter 6 or a simple moving average using 5-period versus 10-period parameters. You will want to test the system over a lengthy time frame and with various noncorrelated markets. If there is any validity to the rules or methods, then you should see positive performance across the board.

Not all systems that show results of extremely high profit levels are best. A system also depends on drawdowns, or periods of equity loss. Also, it is important to have software that will show you a trading system's weakness or will help point out specific time periods or time frames in which you should not trade. Being able to closely follow your drawdown patterns is a huge benefit to the computer-friendly active systems trader, finding answers to such questions as: What is the recovery period to gain back losses? What is the depth or magnitude of the losses? These are very important questions because if a system has great returns but absurd equity drawdowns for long periods, then it is most likely a poor system for an average investor to trade. When you are designing your system, ask yourself what you want this system to do. The obvious answer is to make money; but you also want to know how long and how deep the drawdown periods are or whether there are consistently more winners than losers. As a trader you need to evaluate new techniques, especially ones that increase your profitability while reducing your risk and exposure in the market. Systems need to be developed with the idea of triggering a turning point in the market earlier than other indicators and other traders do. Considering that most indicators are lagging, you need a signal that identifies turning points as they occur, and you need to use indicators to confirm that the position is valid. Pivot point analysis does just that, especially when combining support and resistance levels and by implementing a moving average approach

One of the best features or benefits to using mechanical trading systems is that they alert a trader to initiate a trade or to act on a signal as it occurs, rather than on a hunch or on the two main destructive emotional elements, fear and greed. Based on a system that is tested, you have statistical evidence to validate the entry; and that should help eliminate trading on a hunch, a rumor, or a feeling, which is what drives most trading decisions from inexperienced traders. As this book has demonstrated, it is not my intention to portray the ability to buy the exact low or sell the exact high. In most cases, I am looking for a definitive trend or price reversal to occur; and then I act on that signal and carry a position until the market demonstrates a loss in momentum, the time to exit the trade. The keys to winning are the ability to practice patience and wait for the setup to develop and the discipline to act on the trigger. Mostly, it is the ability to exit a losing trade as the signals dictate, not to hang onto the loser. So when using a system, you will know and understand that the mechanics are never 100 percent right and that you will have a certain number of trades that do not work out. Once you come to grips with that fact, it will be easier to embrace your losses rather than become emotionally wrangled when they occur. Hopefully, you can learn from a trader with long-term positive experiences. Good advice will get you ahead more quickly than if you have to learn everything on your own, and it will help you avoid costly mistakes. Take my advice: Learn a system, back-test it to see the strengths and weakness of the method, and then trade on these testable signals.

SEASONAL STOCK SYSTEM

Jeff Hirsch and his father, Yale, who publish *Stock Trader's Almanac* (Wiley, 2004, 2005), reveal many top-notch statistical studies based on past historic price action. Many of their strategies are based on seasonal factors that help stock pickers time the markets. One of the methods they promote is using a simple MACD developed by Gerald Appel to better time entries and exits during the best six-month period for stocks, which starts in October. Once a market bottoms out and develops in an uptrend, the MACD indicator triggers confirmation that a price reversal is underway. The MACD signals help traders time their entries. However, as we uncovered in prior chapters, it is a lagging indicator. With that said, I believe what can make that buying program or system more effective is to add and apply a weekly and/or monthly pivot point study. This may give a trader an edge by adding another dimensional element that combines the seasonal factor for timing with targeting a price level from pivot points. Using this approach can help light the path to a trading system that a trader can back-test on his or her own through software such as Genesis.

HISTORY LESSONS

I want to combine the lessons on how to choose the right pivot point support and resistance numbers with how those values relate to the market direction number. This can help you determine if the market has departed too far from the mean or too far from what I call the "fair value" of the market. Start by examining the past price history. Once you see where the market was and how far the market has moved in a given length of time (pace of price change), you can possibly determine the realm of reality of where a target level of support may be located. You can use this information to determine if a market is significantly overbought or, as we will show in this example, oversold and ripe for a buying opportunity. When a market is significantly oversold, the conditions exist for a consolidation phase and a reversal of trend, especially when we have a seasonal condition. This concept applies in commodities, stocks, and foreign exchange (forex) markets as well.

Let's take a look at how the bottom formed in the stock market in October 2005 as we review and expand on the *Stock Trader's Almanac* MACD signal. Figure 11.1 is my sheet from the week ending October 14. We use this sheet as a quick reference so I can see what the past week's high, low, and close were. The pivot point is displayed in the far right column. We see that in the prior week, the high in Standard & Poor's (S&P) was 1239. The pivot point is 1208, and the pivot point moving average is 1220.58 (round down to 1220.50). The indication is that the market is bearish, so we would look at the Bearish Target column and see 1155. Here is where back-testing software may help you determine what the largest price range is in a given

John L Person, CTA   Week Ending 10-14-2005

Commodity		Target Key No		Bullish Target		Bearish Target		Market Direction		Previous Range			Pivot
Symbol	Month	Resistance	Support	High	Low	High	Low	Direction		High	Low	Settle	
S&P 500	Dec.	1230.75	1177.50	1261.50	1177.50	1230.75	1155.00	Bearish	1220.58	1239.00	1185.75	1200.00	1208.25
DOW	Dec.	10560.33	10164.33	10797.67	10164.33	10560.33	10005.67	Bearish	10488.22	10639	10243	10323	10401.67
NASDAQ	Dec.	1612.83	1531.83	1661.67	1531.83	1612.83	1499.67	Bearish	1590.00	1629.50	1548.50	1564.00	1580.67
Russell	Dec.	651.83	638.63	656.57	638.63	651.83	630.17	Bearish	656.59	648.10	634.90	647.10	643.37
BONDS	Dec.	114 28/32	113 13/32	115 17/32	113 13/32	114 28/32	112 19/32	Bearish	114 20/32	114 22/32	113 7/32	114 8/32	114 2/32
T-NOTES	Dec.	110 5/32	109 7/32	110 18/32	109 7/32	110 5/32	108 22/32	Bearish	110 6/32	110 2/32	109 4/32	109 23/32	109 20/32
YEN	Dec.	0.8906	0.8800	0.8966	0.8800	0.8906	0.8754	Bearish	0.8931	0.892	0.8814	0.8846	0.8860
EuroFX	Dec.	122.90	119.88	124.21	119.88	122.90	118.17	Bullish	121.22	122.49	119.47	121.60	121.19
Crude Oil	NOV.	65.25	59.30	68.87	59.30	65.25	56.97	Bearish	64.59	66.55	60.60	61.62	62.92
Gold	Dec.	483.03	469.83	487.67	469.83	483.03	461.27	Bullish	471.43	479.1	465.9	478.4	474.47
Silver	Dec.	791.00	748.50	806.00	748.50	791.00	721.00	Bullish	749.13	778.5	736.00	776	763.50
Soybeans	NOV.	581.00	553.00	597.50	553.00	581.00	541.50	Bearish	571.42	586.00	558	564.5	569.50

Copyright © 1999-2005 by John L Person, CTA Palm Beach, FL 33480 The opinions presented, are for informational purpose only. There is no warranty of profits as a result of using these calculations. Past performance is not indicative of future results. The use of "stop loss" or "stop limit" orders will not necessarily limit your losses to the intended amounts, since market conditions may make it impossible to execute such orders. Any decision to purchase or sell as a result of the opinions expressed in this report will be the full responsibility of the person authorizing such transaction.

FIGURE 11.1

Used with permission of www.nationalfutures.com.

week in the S&P on a historic basis. Why is that relevant? Because I want to know if 1155 is an unrealstic number to hit if the market was at 1239 and the standard range was 40 points. From the prior week's high to the projected bearish S-2 target low, that would be an 84.00-point price decline. Not unheard of but not realistic, at least not in one week's trading period. At the very least, we need to see how the market reacts at the S-1 target support number, 1177.50, labeled as the Target Key Number, which is the S-1 pivot number.

On further examination, we see the market closed the week ending 10/07/2005 at 1200. So sometime in the following week, I want to heighten my awareness or program a system to alert me to when or if the market reaches that level and if a buy signal exists at or near 1177.50, such as if a hammer or doji is present within five points above or below that level. After all, we have a decent sample of statistics that reveal that these two candle patterns form at or near the lows in e-mini–S&Ps a high percentage of the time on an intraday 15-minute period.

The low was made on 10/13/2005 at 1172; it closed that day back above the pivot support at 1178.25. The next session formed a high close doji (HCD). Using the HCD pattern and trading by the rules, you would have bought at 1189.75; and your risk was a stop on a close below the doji low, which was at 1172. The most pressure you took on a futures position trade was from your entry price to the lowest low on a pull-back was when it retested the low at 1174, which is 16 points. The stop-close-only order was the correct risk mechanism for this position trade. Using a seasonal factor combined with pivot point analysis helped traders pinpoint both the time and the price of a particular market; and in using historical seasonal information, traders would possibly want to employ a longer-term risk-and-reward strategy. Even if you are a one-day or swing trader, seasonal factors can help identify the side of the market to be on, like in a bullish environment to look to buy breaks. My point is that if you are a position trader, your risks and reward objectives should be greater than those of a day trader. Here we have a trading opportunity based on several factors. All we need to do now is select a strategy.

WHICH STRATEGY TO SELECT?

If buying the futures markets seemed too risky, you at least have a situation where you can explore longer-term low-risk/high-reward options strategies such as S&P call options. That was my recommendation in my weekly newsletter. You could apply this analysis to buy Standard & Poor's Depositary Receipts (SPDRs), Diamonds, Nasdaq QQQs, or options on those exchange traded funds. That is one reason why I spent time going over those products in Chapter 1. Seriously, if you are just a day trader in futures or forex or simply a stock trader, diversification is a trader's best friend. Anyone who is after profits and making money can apply these techniques. To any investment vehicle, a trading system can be programmed to alert you when dojis form near pivots support or resistance levels. Moving average crossover features using various parameter settings can also be applied. This form of market analysis is adaptable and very versatile for integrating in a trading system.

WHAT ABOUT THE MACD?

Pivot point analysis enhances what *Stock Trader's Almanac* reveals. Looking at the chart again in Figure 11.2, you see how the MACD indicator gave a buy signal triggered by the zero-line crossover and a moving average crossover on October 24. This was generated on the close at 1202.25. Not

FIGURE 11.2
Used with permission of esignal.com.

knowing the risk you want to take with the MACD seasonal buy signal, if you bought at that price at that time, the most pressure you took on the trade was 22 points, slightly more than the high close doji trigger signal. Also the MACD signal came a bit later. This is why all traders can use pivot point support and resistance analysis to help time trades better with both elements, time and price.

I went over how to use the pivot point as a moving average in Chapter 6. In Figure 11.3, I took the liberty of highlighting the pivot point to illustrate the slope (or direction) of the moving average. Once the market hits the pivot support, the market moves in a consolidation phase; but the pivot point average is sloping higher, indicating a bullish bias. Granted, you always want to see immediate results as a trader; but using the seasonal factors identified by *Stock Trader's Almanac* combined with pivot point support targets and a pivot point moving average component gives you a much better timed entry and method to identify a trend reversal.

One more advantage of incorporating the pivot point average is that as the market finally blasts off, the moving average component generates a sell signal and the histogram makes a negative zero-line cross. However,

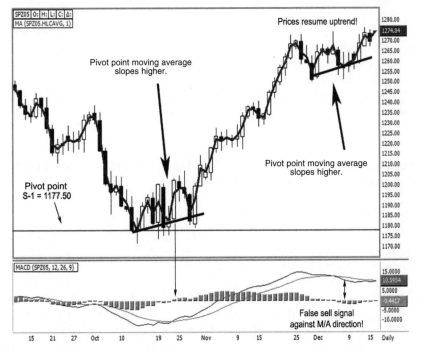

FIGURE 11.3
Used with permission of esignal.com.

that is the opposite of what prices are showing from the candle patterns, as we do not see a succession of lower closing lows. In addition, the pivot point moving average is sloping higher, once again indicating a bullish bias. From a systems programmer looking for a defined set of rules, when you develop your own system, it is important to make sure that your set of criteria or the series of conditions that exist all need to be in sync, such as all must be generating sell signals, before making your entry or exit triggers.

In Figure 11.4, the Genesis Software has my algorithms programmed with variations of what was covered in this book to show you how you can develop your own personal "black box" system. As this illustrates, for my day trading program, I use both the 5-minute and the 15-minute periods with the e-mini–S&P, the Chicago Board of Trade (CBOT) mini-Dow, 30-year Treasury bonds, euro currency, and the spot forex British pound. Except for in this figure, the one chart that is second from the right is a 5-minute chart on bonds; and under it is a 15-minute chart on the euro currency.

I use this system to help confirm buy and sell signals, as indicated with the arrows. When we are at the projected support targets, which the software indicates by green support lines, arrows appear, indicating to go long. The chart on the left is the e-mini–S&P; the 5-minute is on top and the 15-minute is beneath it. See how arrows point up simultaneously, which indicates a buy signal, especially as the market is near support. The chart second from the left is the mini-Dow with the 5-minute on top and the 15-minute beneath it. The 5-minute time period generates a buy signal against the pivot point support targets simultaneously with the e-mini–S&P. This corroborates the buy signal, as it has developed in both markets. It is also confirmed in the 15-minute chart beneath it.

WHAT IS THE BEST DAY TRADING CONFIRMATION TRIGGER TO PROGRAM?

The most reliable trading signal is when the 5-minute time period triggers a buy when the 15-minute time period is also in a buy mode; in other words, the best signals are when the 5-minute period is in sync with the 15-minute time period in a pivot point moving average crossover system. We see this occur as it applies to day trading the spot forex British pound as the chart in Figure 11.4 shows. Look on the right-hand side of the chart; in the upper right-hand corner is the 5-minute period, and directly below it is the 15-minute chart. See how the 5-minute generates the sell signal first, as it is against the projected pivot point resistance targets; and the 15-minute chart beneath it confirms that sell signal. This is exactly what we want to see—a

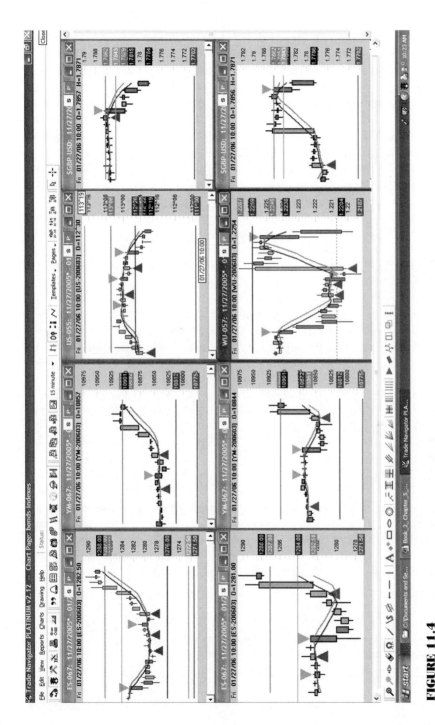

FIGURE 11.4
Used with permission of www.GenesisFT.com.

sell signal triggered against resistance; and the higher time period, such as the 15-minute component to the 5-minute sell signal, confirming that action.

SHOW ME THE PROOF

As a systems trader, once you have set your variables or your best selected set of rules or criteria and have defined the parameters such as time periods, then you can go and back-test the method. I want to show you that any system worth following needs to show sizable profits with reasonable risks. No system is 100 percent accurate, at least none that I know of in reality. If one existed, I would believe through the laws of probabilities that it was due for a breakdown. There are several categories on which you want to focus that will enlighten you as to the true validity of the methods. In essence, back-testing allows you to closely examine your system's inefficiencies so you can correct the flaws. Looking at the back-test results will also help you understand when to increase position sizes, when to avoid trading, and how to facilitate improvements.

You want to see if the reasons you make decisions to execute a trade consistently generate more profits when you are right than losses when the system or trade fails. If less than 70 percent of trades result in winning trades, you want the winners to outgain the losses. It makes no sense to have a 70 percent winning system that generates more losses than winners and longer holding periods. Imagine what that will do to your psyche, not to mention your trading account.

It is important that you understand what elements trigger a trade when the transaction is entered or exited. This helps in determining another way to account for slippage. For example, if the system generates buy and sell signals on the close or on the next open, if this is a day trading program, then there may be less chance for price gaps. However, if the system executes based on the closing price or on the next open, such as what we have disclosed in the high close doji pattern or the low close doji pattern, then on overnight positions you may experience poor entry or exits. With that knowledge, you can change your program to include the next available open, which would include night sessions.

Let me clarify what the *night session* is for various trading vehicles. As we know, there is no official close in spot foreign currencies. Therefore, you need to assign a daily close and then an open. In Chapter 1, I revealed that I use the New York Bank settlement of 5 P.M. (ET) and use the open as the next five-minute interval. As for futures, different exchanges on which various markets trade have specific official closes and reopens for their after-hours trading markets. The Chicago Mercantile Exchange (CME) has

GLOBEX, the CBOT has the e-CBOT, and the New Mercantile Exchange (NYMEX) started using the CME's electronic trading platform in June 2006. The partnership between the CME and the NYMEX begins a 10-year deal that allows the NYMEX to use the CME's GLOBEX platform to electronically trade both energy and metal futures and options. This promises to give better access to traders worldwide for those specific markets.

If you are reading this book, I assume that you already know the various market hours; but if not, visit www.nationalfutures.com, where they are listed under Trading Tools, which has the current margin requirements, contract specifications, and trading hours listed. In Table 11.1, I have a description of the categories that are important in helping to determine a system's validity.

In Table 11.2, we have results from a pivot point moving average system I developed with the help of Pete Kilman at Genesis. It is what I call the "Defcon" day traders' program system. As I stated before, this is not 100 percent accurate. I do not know of any system that is; but it is a

TABLE 11.1 Determining a System's Validity

Total net profit	This number tells you how much the system made after slippage, commissions, fees, and losses.
Payout ratio	This tells you based on a profit/loss the percent that winners outpace losers.
Avgerage number of bars for winners	This category shows what the average time period was before the trade was offset in order to establish a profit.
Win percent	This figure shows how many winners versus losers were generated.
Kelly ratio	A math calculation used to derive the number of contracts to trade in relation to the ratio of winning trades to losing trades.
Largest win	This figure shows the largest single winning trade. We look at this number to see if profits on a single trade are larger than 20 percent of the overall net profit. If it is, it indicates the trade signals may be invalid.
Largest loss	This category helps traders identify if single losses are bigger than winners so they can implement a better risk management approach.
Average win trade	This shows what to expect on the average-size winning trade.
Average losing trade	This shows what the average-size loss is.
Return percent	This is the percent of profit on the initial size starting account.

TABLE 11.2   E-mini–S&P All Trades, from 01/08/2003 to 01/10/2006

Total net profit:	$39,538	Profit factor ($wins/$losses):	2.06
Total trades:	258	Winning percentage:	63.6%
Average trade:	$153	Payout ratio (average win/loss):	1.18
Average # of bars in trade:	78.89	Z–score (W/L predictability):	0.8
Average # of trades per year:	85.7	Percent in the market:	74.4%
Max closed-out drawdown:	–$4,063	Maximum intraday drawdown:	–$4,350
Account size required:	$7,913	Return percent:	499.7%
Open equity:	$100	Kelly ratio:	0.3266
Total winners:	164	Total losers:	94
Gross profit:	$76,963	Gross loss:	–$37,425
Average win:	$469	Average loss:	–$398
Largest win:	$2,100	Largest loss:	–$1,825
Largest drawdown in win:	–$1,663	Largest peak in loss:	$1,938
Average drawdown in win:	–$271	Average peak in loss:	$276
Average run-up in win:	$708	Average run-up in loss:	$276
Average run-down in win:	–$271	Average run-down in loss:	–$716
Most consecutive wins:	9	Most consecutive losses:	7
Average number of consecutive wins:	2.60	Average number of consecutive losses:	1.49
Average number of bars in wins:	76.68	Average number of bars in losses:	82.73

fairly reliable and robust system with a 63.6 percent overall win ratio in the e-mini–S&P 500 futures. The sample testing period was conducted during open outcry session only, from 9:30 A.M. (ET) until 4:15 P.M. (ET). There were no stops or loss parameters; this was simply a reversal system, which means we were always in the market and out on the close of business. The trades were all done on just one single contract; so we did not have a money management position scale-up program designed, which means we did not increase lot size as profits accrued. This system is based on pivot point analysis and the principles outlined in this book; the trading signals were based on a 15-minute time period, and the testing period was three years.

All trade signals were taken from 01/08/2003 to 01/10/2006. This time period was one of the most active trading times in recent decates, so I feel this was a good sample period to back-test. A starting account was set up with $10,000, taking one contract per signal. A $50 commission and slippage were assigned per trade. Generally, the electronic commission rates are as low as 3.50 and as high as 25, depending on which brokerage firm was used; so again this was an adequate figure to use. With those variables, the system generated close to a 500 percent return. As we examine the system closer, we see it generated 258 trades, of which only 164 were winners. That means we must have bigger winners than losers, and we do. The average win is $469, compared to $398 per loss on average. The neat feature in this system or with this sample back-test model is that the largest drawdown in wins is 1,663. This is the kind of information that will give you a statistical edge in trading. You now know that you have a system that generates buy and sell signals with a 64 percent win ratio. This information should help you stay emotionally grounded by achieving two things: (1) not getting too upset when losses occur; (2) not overpositioning yourself in trades if and when you have a win streak with more than eight or nine consecutive trades.

Most people lose big as they see their systems or methods generate huge profits many times in a row. They get this feeling that their trading is invincible or impervious to losers. And then, wham, that's when a drawdown period occurs! Generally, it is at this point that a trader goes from trading 10 contracts to 50 contracts. All it takes is one bad trade, and you have wiped away your trading profits or, worse, your entire trading account.

MONEY MANAGEMENT IS THE KEY TO SUCCESS

Using the Defcon trading system, we started with a trading account balance of $10,000. The overnight initial speculative margin for the CME's e-mini–S&P, as of 2/15/2006 was $3,938 per contract. Therefore, with trading just one contract, we had committed 39 percent of our trading capital at any one time. Since our account starts with $10,000 and the system only generates less than two trades per week, we need to define when it is apropriate to increase our lot sizes. Aha! This is a novel idea and is what truly helps traders get wealthy—knowing when to fold, hold, or add on.

If you look at Figure 11.5, you see a chart with an equity curve showing some pretty good gains with an occasional bump in the road. Recoverable as it is, a drawdown in profits occurs. Using system analysis can help you determine most consecutive wins and losses and what the largest loss is. Armed with that information, you can now go on to trading like a true megastar professional fund manager—or simply a downright happy camper. Why? Because that information will help you determine the next level of profits you have to build in order to increase your lot size. If you do not manage your money properly and double or quadruple your position size before doubling your account size, you could be in for a rude awakening. As you can see, the maximum drawdown experienced is –4,062.50 on 11/10/2004. If that was the day you decided to mistakenly increase your lot size, it may have potentially wiped your account out.

In Table 11.2, observe that the largest loss is $1,825. By increasing your lot size prematurely or or by having an imbalance to largest loss in relationship to account balance, such as having four or more contracts on at any one time, you could wipe out not only your gains but also the majority of your account. Using statistics and mathematical formulas is what will

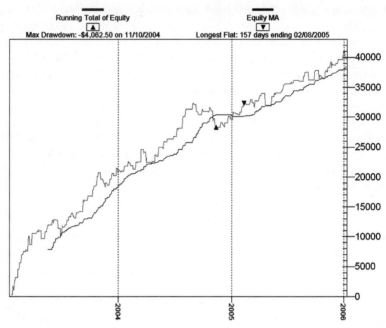

FIGURE 11.5
Used with permission of www.GenesisFT.com.

give you an edge in the markets, from both a business stance and an emotional stance. You will be better prepared, and that should help make you a better trader.

In conclusion, one of the greatest values of data derived from back-testing a system is that it will reveal hidden intricacies about the system. Simply having a rudimentary knowledge of placing stop-loss orders is not the definition of knowing sound money management techniques. You must expand your knowledge in managing your money properly by either under- or overleveraging your trading capital. We went over a seasonal trading strategy that *Stock Trader's Almanac* uses in the equity markets using the MACD indicator. I showed you how you can optimize that method by introducing the use of pivot point analysis. With the ability of back-testing a strategy, we can back-test this theory on our own; and more important, we can learn if our system or trading method has a seasonal factor that performs best or worst at certain times of the year. Then, you can also determine, based on your equity size, the number of positions you should have on while maintaining a proper risk/reward ratio.

WHEN IS THE BEST TIME TO TRADE?

Remember I stated in Chapter 1 that traders need to ask more questions? Well, the more you learn, the more you know what to ask. As a systems trader, asking how a system performs during different times of the year is a novel idea, especially as seasonal forces can impact a market. Ask questions such as, "When is the best or the worst time to trade?" From a simple yet elegant standpoint, the answer for day traders in equities is lunchtime. This is substantiated by volume levels generally declining during that time frame. Forex traders note that trading activity is light from 10 P.M. (ET) until 1:30 A.M. (ET), as we discussed in Chapter 1. What about on a weekly or monthly basis? When does our system perform best?

By tracking trading performance, as shown in Table 11.3, from a historical perspective, we can form an opinion of when the system is at peak performance or when the market we are trading is in sync with seasonal factors. There is never a guarantee that past performance is indicative of future results, but we can and do benefit from studying history. Without a doubt, I do not want to go on a major tangent here; but we are trading in a new frontier environment. The new age of technology has more people trading online, and more people are more computer savvy. We have an intricate globalization of our economy. Trading partners with China and even India is not like what we had just five years ago. So with that perspective, my opinion is that looking at seasonal tendencies of a market starting from 2000 up through 2005 would not be a huge statistical event, but it would be more relevant than a testing period in 1990 through 1995. With that in mind, we ran a test, as the results show in Figure 11.6, to see which months perform best with the "Defcon III model."

Using the Genesis Software product and asking the right questions (e.g., When is the best time to trade?), I can get a reasonable answer. In fact, I wanted to know which months are the best and which months are the worst in which to trade. Using the Genesis Software, I can run back tests to see what the performance from a seasonal perspective with the Defcon system looks like on a monthly performance basis. Using a test period over the past three years, I am able to conclude that April is a month to avoid trading! Based on a three-year average, this is the month that consistently delivers drawdowns. With that statistical information, I have a slight edge in the market, as it relates with my system. I can make a decision either to lower my contract sizes or to avoid trading entirely. Figure 11.7 shows the yearly breakdown of the compiled results.

The more statistics I have, the better prepared I am; and with that knowledge, I have stacked the odds in my favor. This is the ultimate in trading tools and system designs: being able to identify opportunity and discover the weakest link in my chain of trading system. Table 11.4 dissects

TABLE 11.3 By Month Report

Jan 28, 2006 21:25:39
Name: John Person Defcon III
Symbol: ES1-067
Statistic to chart Profit, Position selection, All trades, From date 01/08/2003, To date 01/10/2006.

Month	Trades	Win Pct	Win Avg	Loss Avg	Run Up	Run Down	P/L	P/F	Average Trade	C/L	Max Loss	Profit	Average Bars
January	27	66.67%	$488	-$369	$734	-$635	1.32	2.64	$202	1	-$1,175	$5,450	65.70
February	22	68.18%	$408	-$273	$597	-$754	1.49	3.20	$191	2	-$650	$4,213	68.00
March	21	66.67%	$690	-$732	$1,075	-$1,113	0.94	1.89	$216	2	-$1,475	$4,538	87.95
April	19	57.89%	$414	-$609	$656	-$922	0.68	0.93	-$17	2	-$1,825	-$325	91.37
May	19	78.95%	$418	-$256	$649	-$619	1.63	6.11	$276	1	-$500	$5,238	87.79
June	21	66.67%	$371	-$393	$575	-$946	0.95	1.89	$117	4	-$1,413	$2,450	86.38
July	23	65.22%	$453	-$117	$697	-$309	3.86	7.24	$254	2	-$338	$5,850	70.22
August	19	63.16%	$502	-$516	$720	-$782	0.97	1.67	$127	2	-$1,325	$2,413	100.21
September	21	47.62%	$376	-$267	$630	-$545	1.41	1.28	$39	6	-$1,375	$825	90.29
October	20	65.00%	$476	-$554	$669	-$946	0.86	1.60	$116	3	-$1,750	$2,313	62.45
November	23	47.83%	$508	-$413	$733	-$647	1.23	1.13	$28	3	-$1,313	$638	75.39
December	23	69.57%	$502	-$300	$736	-$536	1.67	3.83	$258	2	-$650	$5,938	70.43

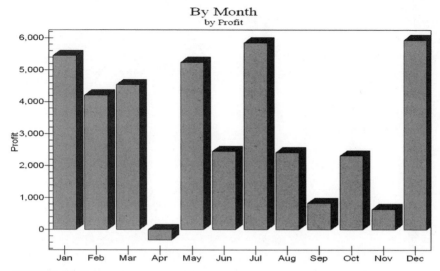

FIGURE 11.6
Used with permission of www.GenesisFT.com.

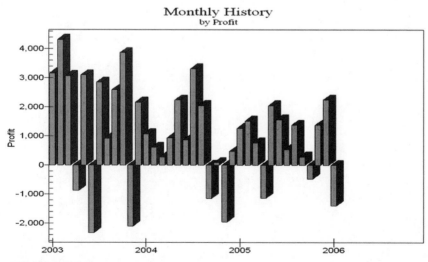

FIGURE 11.7
Used with permission of www.GenesisFT.com.

TABLE 11.4 Monthly History Report

Name: John Person Defcon III
Symbol: ES1-067

Statistic to chart Profit, Position selection All trades. From date 01/06/2003, To date 01/10/2006

Monthly	Trades	Win Pct	Win Avg	Loss Avg	Run Up	Run Dn	P/L	P/F	Avg Trade	CL	Max Loss	Profit	Net Profit	Avg Bars	ROI%
Jan	5	80.00%	$956	-$663	$1,253	-$88	1.44	5.77	$633	1	-$663	$3,163	$3,163	78.00	39.97%
Feb	8	87.50%	$620	-$13	$613	-$913	49.57	347.00	$541	1	-$13	$4,325	$7,488	67.38	54.66%
Mar	6	66.67%	$1,169	-$800	$1,613	-$1,288	1.46	2.92	$513	1	-$1,400	-$875	$10,563	81.00	38.86%
Apr	5	60.00%	$258	-$925	$913	-$1,219	0.31	0.47	-$175	0	-$1,263	-$675	$9,688	110.40	-11.06%
May	7	100.00	$443	$0	$639	$0	442.86	999.00	$443	4	$0	$3,100	$12,788	91.14	39.16%
Jun	8	25.00%	$419	-$527	$613	-$1,129	0.79	0.26	-$291	2	-$1,413	-$2,325	$10,463	73.25	-29.38%
Jul 2003	8	75.00%	$521	-$138	$613	-$500	3.79	11.36	$356	2	-$263	$2,850	$13,313	57.00	36.02%
Aug	7	57.14%	$461	-$333	$766	-$686	1.44	1.93	$132	1	-$380	$925	$14,238	95.86	11.69%
Sep	6	80.00%	$734	-$350	$1,066	-$686	2.10	8.39	$518	2	-$538	$2,588	$16,825	95.25	32.70%
Oct	8	87.50%	$519	-$100	$761	-$575	5.66	39.63	$483	4	-$100	$3,963	$20,688	78.25	48.81%
Nov	7	28.57%	$329	-$548	$556	-$923	0.58	0.23	-$300	1	-$1,075	-$2,100	$20,750	85.57	-26.54%
Dec	8	75.00%	$252	-$146	$427	-$425	1.05	3.14	$270	1	-$263	$2,163	$20,825	74.00	27.33%
Jan	9	62.50%	$433	-$517	$713	-$725	1.73	3.46	$119	2	-$660	$1,075	$21,438	53.11	13.59%
Feb	8	57.14%	$619	-$733	$875	-$1,067	0.84	1.40	$7	1	-$883	$613	$22,713	71.88	7.74%
Mar	8	62.50%	$395	-$348	$695	-$613	0.84	1.13	$89	2	-$588	$275	$23,650	68.43	3.45%
Apr	8	66.67%	$658	-$256	$931	-$638	1.14	1.90	$117	2	-$1,475	$938	$26,750	70.00	11.85%
May	5	60.00%	$317	-$44	$756	-$444	2.68	5.37	$373	1	-$313	$2,238	$28,588	91.50	28.28%
Jun	5	85.71%	$588	-$213	$756	-$338	7.24	10.86	$173	1	-$75	$563	$29,563	106.00	10.90%
Jul 2004	9	60.00%	$669	-$225	$778	-$313	2.76	16.59	$473	1	-$213	$3,313	$32,113	82.00	41.86%
Aug	9	11.11%	$938	-$281	$1,038	-$444	3.59	0.45	$410	6	-$225	$2,050	$30,963	61.33	25.91%
Sep	8	40.00%	$356	-$288	$513	-$600	1.71	1.14	-$128	5	-$1,050	-$1,150	$31,050	94.60	-14.53%
Oct	6	33.33%	$638	-$288	$883	-$586	0.79	0.40	$18	3	-$600	$86	$29,100	100.33	1.11%
Nov	9	37.50%	$638	-$192	$542	-$418	2.22	1.33	-$325	2	-$1,750	-$1,950	$29,575	57.00	-24.64%
Dec	8	66.67%	$506	-$138	$628	-$454	1.60	3.20	$59	2	-$488	$475	$30,838	57.00	6.00%
Jan	9	66.67%	$447	-$138	$628	-$869	3.25	6.50	$140	2	-$225	$1,263	$32,350	65.25	15.95%
Feb	8	62.50%	$433	-$467	$628	-$621	0.93	1.54	$95	2	-$263	$763	$33,113	65.25	19.11%
Mar	8	66.67%	$213	-$994	$544	-$1,306	0.21	0.43	-$190	2	-$900	-$1,138	$31,975	72.17	9.64%
Apr	8	66.67%	$566	-$106	$731	-$325	5.32	10.65	$342	2	-$200	$1,975	$34,025	106.67	-14.38%
May	8	100.00	$195	$0	$445	$0	196.31	999.00	$195	0	$0	$2,050	$35,588	69.38	25.91%
Jun	8	50.00%	$228	-$94	$403	-$231	2.43	2.43	$67	2	-$338	$1,563	$36,125	69.25	19.75%
Jul 2005	7	71.43%	$293	-$44	$550	-$275	6.69	16.71	$196	2	-$75	$538	$37,500	111.71	6.79%
Aug	7	85.71%	$269		$481	-$1,488	0.20	1.22	$41	3	-$1,325	$1,375	$37,788	77.29	17.38%
Sep	7	42.86%	$467	-$489	$592	-$1,034	1.00	0.75	-$68	3	-$1,375	$288	$37,313	83.00	3.63%
Oct	10	60.00%	$452	-$334	$633	-$513	1.35	2.03	$138	2	-$913	-$475	$38,688	45.40	-6.00%
Nov	7	85.71%	$458	-$125	$723	-$450	3.17	19.00	$221	2	-$125	$1,375	$40,938	91.00	17.38%
Dec	7	60.00%	$125	-$825	$81	-$1,044	0.15	0.15	$321	1	-$125	$2,250		45.40	28.43%
Jan	4	50.00%	$125	-$825	$81	-$1,044	0.15	0.15	-$350	1	-$1,175	-$1,400	$39,538	38.50	-17.69%

Used with permission of www.GenesisFT.com.

each month's performance from the three-year test period that really shows the poor seasonal performance made in the month of April for those years back-tested.

DOES THIS WORK FOR FOREX?

Since currency trading is a large component of my trading, I wanted to op-timize a system for forex. The Defcon model was tested to stand up against a noncorrelated investment vehicle to the equity markets. I chose the euro currency market to run a performance test. As we discussed in Chapter 7, due to the computers' inability to test the forex markets' data because there is no centralized market and prices are quoted in bid/ask form, we ran the test using the euro currency futures, which trades parallel to forex markets. The test period was conducted using 15-minute intervals during the U.S. open outcry trading session from 8:20 A.M. (ET) until 3 P.M. (ET).

The winning percentages were not as great as in the S&P; but, boy, the bottom-line results showed a healthier profit! Table 11.5 shows the rate of return with 365 percent, but it was based off a recommended starting bal-ance of $16,770. The overall gross profit was $61,275, based on a test period that went back three years. We had 310 trades—the system generated slightly more trades here than in the S&P. This may indicate that the mar-

TABLE 11.5   Euro Currency—All Trades from 01/03/2003 to 01/09/2006

Total net profit:	$61,2758	Profit factor ($wins/$losses):	1.49
Total trades:	310	Winning percentage:	60.3%
Average trade:	$198	Payout ratio (average win/loss):	0.98
Average # of bars in trade:	64.24	Z–score (W/L predictability):	−0.9
Average # of trades per year:	102.7	Percent in the market:	74.0%
Max closed-out drawdown:	−$13,163	Maximum intraday drawdown:	−$14,475
Account size required:	$16,770	Return percent:	365.4%
Open equity:	$825	Kelly ratio:	0.1981
Total winners:	187	Total losers:	123
Gross profit:	$186,625	Gross loss:	−$125,350
Average win:	$998	Average loss:	−$1,019
Largest win:	$6,038	Largest loss:	−$4,313
Largest drawdown in win:	−$2,713	Largest peak in loss:	$2,113
Average drawdown in win:	−$405	Average peak in loss:	$397
Average run-up in win:	$1,450	Average run-up in loss:	$397
Average run-down in win:	−$405	Average run-down in loss:	−$1,630
Most consecutive wins:	10	Most consecutive losses:	7
Average number of consecutive wins:	2.63	Average number of consecutive losses:	1.76
Average number of bars in wins:	59.78	Average number of bars in losses:	71.03

ket is more volatile, not less, as some people believe. As for the test period, I believe this was a good time frame because it represents a great sampling of various market conditions, considering that we had several market conditions exist: bull trend, to a consolidation phase, and then a trend reversal or downtrend.

In January 2003, the euro was valued at 1.0500 to the U.S. dollar. It went as high as 1.3660 in December 2004; and as of February 2006, the euro was back at 119.00. During that time, the market conditions changed from bullish to bearish and went into a consolidation phase as well. We want to see how a trading system performs in various market conditions. Notice the three market conditions as indicated by the trend lines drawn in the weekly euro currency chart in Figure 11.8. According to the test results, the system fared pretty well.

Let's examine both the volatility and the margin requirements. As of February 15, 2006, the daily initial margin requirement to trade one euro currency with a 125,000 contract value (margin requirements are set by the exchanges and are subject to change without notice) was $2,835.00. As you can see, we are trading a highly leveraged market that has an average daily

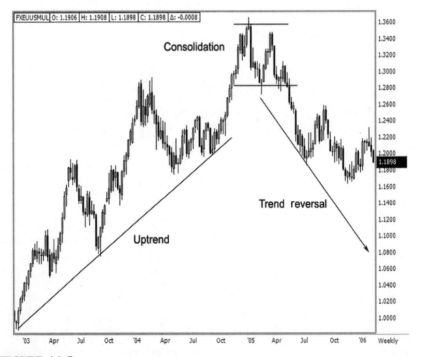

FIGURE 11.8
Used with permission of esignal.com.

range of approximately 86 PIPs (percentage in points) per day. In the futures, each PIP is $12.50. That computes to a daily trading range of $1,075 per day. In using strict money management guidelines, we are using only 28 percent of our investment capital. So in the spirit of being a great trader, I want to ask why I would trade only one contract with a starting account of $10,000. The answer is clear, and another great example of why it is important to know what you are doing before you do it. By back-testing a system, I can determine what the worst to expect is. Granted, we did not implement any means for risk management. The Defcon system solely generates a trade triggered by the pivot point moving average approach. You will see that by going back and validating the methodology, we had a single loss in the amount of $4,313. That is the bad news; and more than likely, as with any severe and sudden market loss, it was generated by a shocking news event. The monthly unemployment report on August 6, 2004, was one such event where the euro currency moved almost 260 points in a single day. This was a good definition of a news-driven price shock. As the data in Table 11.3 shows, the profits were bigger in the euro than they were in the e-mini–S&P; but so were the risks. So we have a bigger profit; but along with that greater profit came greater risks. How many times have you heard that before? The bigger the risk, the bigger the rewards. I have heard that a bunch of times, but it is great to see it put in front of me based on a defined set of rules. So if I get the feeling one day to go "all in" like a poker player and use 100 percent of my margin, in the euro currency I could easily do three contracts. In one bad day, not only would I wipe my account, but I could be deficit, meaning I could actually lose every penny in my account and owe money.

Using the back-tested results of a system allows me to see my program's strengths and weaknesses. That is the edge I have against the market—knowing when to raise my positions and when not to. Besides learning that my system can make money, I also found out that I need to double my account if I want to double my positions. Using a computer product like Genesis allows me to identify and validate the methods employed. As we look at the equity curve in Figure 11.9, we can see a solid performance; and that should help maintain your confidence to stick with trades generated by the signals. Figure 11.9 also highlights a negative $13,162.50 maximum drawdown from peak profits. Imagine increasing your lot or contract size prematurely during that negative phase. It would certainly ruin your trading day, year, or even career!

In the stacked bar graph in Figure 11.10, we see the results of peak performance; and more important, we see the kink in our armor, the weakest point in our system from a seasonal perspective. By back-testing the system, our diagnosis shows a seasonal weakness in the markets that occurs in January and February and continues into March. We know from the table

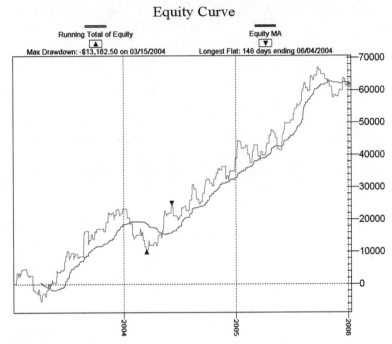

FIGURE 11.9
Used with permission of www.GenesisFT.com.

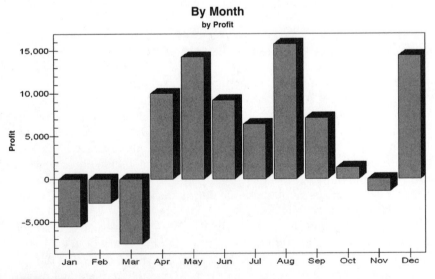

FIGURE 11.10
Used with permission of www.GenesisFT.com.

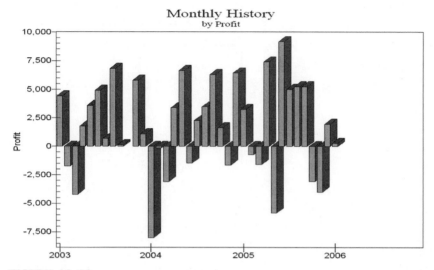

FIGURE 11.11
Used with permission of www.GenesisFT.com.

in Figure 11.1 that we have a string of winners that last on average 10 in a row. Therefore, if at the end of October I have 10 winners in a row, I think I will be more selective in my trade signals in November! As you can see, the statistics show small drawdowns in November. According to the three-year test period, April through August is the most profitable trading time period (Table 11.6). We can enhance our performance by not trading in April, though, as that was one of the worst-performing months as indicated in Figure 11.6 on page 297.

As you break down the numbers by the statistical results, it is by that data that you can determine the validity of your methods (Figures 11.11 and Table 11.7). When we look at a month-to-month breakdown of the euro currency, we see January 2004 was a whale of a disaster, as shown in Figure 11.11! With this information, we can determine if the cause of the disaster was the system, the methods, or one heck of a wild trading period. The answer should not surprise you: It was the last. There were only two days that had daily trading ranges over 250 points. On January 16, 2004, the market dropped like a hot sack of potatoes, with a high of 1.2610 and a low of 1.2351, for a range of 259 points. Then two days later, it reversed higher, with a low of 1.2345 and a high of 1.2599, for a 254-point range. The market gained back what it lost; but overall, it was simply a very violent trading period, as Figure 11.12 shows. Without some type of intraday risk management method, such as a trailing stop, all traders at some point will be

TABLE 11.6 By Month Report

Jan 28, 2006 21:34:14
Name: John Person Defcon III euro
Symbol: EU-067
Statistic to chart Profit, Position selection All trades, From date 01/03/2003, To date 01/09/2006.

Month	Trades	Win Pct	Win Avg	Loss Avg	Run-Up	Run-Down	P/L	P/F	Average Trade	C/L	Max Loss	Profit	Average Bars
January	22	59.09 %	$601	-$1,481	$1,054	-$2,383	0.41	0.59	-$251	4	-$3,350	-$5,513	71.45
February	19	57.89 %	$1,048	-$1,791	$1,547	-$2,486	0.59	0.80	-$147	3	-$3,800	-$2,800	81.37
March	28	42.86 %	$1,033	-$1,245	$1,460	-$1,899	0.83	0.62	-$269	4	-$3,375	-$7,525	65.36
April	24	66.67 %	$1,053	-$858	$1,502	-$1,597	1.23	2.46	$416	2	-$1,975	$9,988	63.25
May	26	53.85 %	$1,702	-$798	$2,339	-$1,451	2.13	2.49	$548	5	-$3,288	$14,250	66.62
June	31	64.52 %	$747	-$520	$1,240	-$883	1.44	2.61	$297	7	-$2,550	$9,213	52.06
July	29	72.41 %	$698	-$1,030	$1,007	-$1,795	0.68	1.78	$221	2	-$2,838	$6,413	58.07
August	34	73.53 %	$977	-$958	$1,294	-$1,347	1.02	2.83	$464	4	-$3,138	$15,788	50.35
September	30	56.67 %	$1,038	-$809	$1,557	-$1,297	1.28	1.68	$238	4	-$4,313	$7,138	57.10
October	19	57.89 %	$808	-$941	$1,478	-$1,584	0.86	1.18	$72	3	-$1,838	$1,363	83.95
November	18	50.00 %	$1,082	-$1,242	$1,790	-$1,931	0.87	0.87	-$80	2	-$3,763	-$1,438	84.00
December	30	60.00 %	$1,330	-$795	$1,617	-$1,294	1.67	2.51	$480	3	-$2,738	$14,400	62.90

TABLE 11.7 Monthly History Report

Name: John Person Defcon III Euro
Symbol: EU-067
Statistic to chart Profit, Position selection All trades, From date 01/03/2003, To date 01/09/2006,

Monthly	Trades	Win Pct	Win Avg	Loss Avg	Run Up	Run Dn	P/L	P/F	AvgTrade	C/L	Max Loss	Profit	Net Profit	Avg Bars	ROI%
Jan	10	80.0	$806	-$1,019	$1,109	$1,531	0.79	3.17	$441	1	-$1,200	$4,413	$4,413	49.00	26.31%
Feb	6	50.0	$188	-$763	$683	$1,288	0.25	0.25	-$288	3	-$1,063	-$1,725	$2,688	84.00	-10.29%
Mar	12	41.6	$815	-$1,184	$1,065	$1,559	0.69	0.49	-$351	4	-$3,800	-$4,213	-$1,525	45.58	-25.12%
Apr	10	70.0	$914	-$1,542	$1,520	$2,158	0.59	1.38	$178	2	-$1,975	$1,775	$250	59.80	10.58%
May	11	45.4	$1,37	-$548	$2,165	$1,173	2.51	2.09	$326	2	-$1,075	$3,588	$3,838	50.00	21.39%
Jun	8	75.0	$869	-$150	$1,406	$819	5.79	17.38	$614	1	-$175	$4,913	$8,750	68.00	29.29%
Jul 2003	12	66.6	$708	-$763	$934	$1,600	0.57	1.14	$56	2	-$2,838	$675	$9,425	45.33	4.03%
Aug	8	75.0	$1,39	-$1,247	$1,598	$2,225	1.83	5.48	$853	1	-$1,238	$6,825	$16,250	74.00	40.70%
Sep	11	72.7	$738	-$1,925	$1,517	$2,458	0.38	1.02	$11	1	-$4,313	$125	$16,375	54.00	0.75%
Oct	4	50.0	$556	-$656	$2,106	-$900	1.00	1.00	$0	1	-$863	$0	$16,375	134.25	0.00%
Nov	4	75.0	$2,13	-$613	$3,250	$1,488	3.49	10.47	$1,450	1	-$613	$5,800	$22,175	120.25	34.59%
Dec	12	58.3	$786	-$880	$1,007	$1,375	0.89	1.25	$92	1	-$2,200	$1,100	$23,275	49.42	6.56%
Jan	4	0.00	$0	-$2,000	$0	$3,634	0.00	0.00	-$2,000	4	-$3,350	-$8,000	$15,275	134.00	-47.70%
Feb	6	50.0	$1,42	-$1,475	$2,321	$2,413	0.97	0.97	-$23	1	-$1,988	-$138	$15,138	87.33	-0.82%
Mar	8	50.0	$1,10	-$1,875	$1,547	$3,022	0.59	0.59	-$388	3	-$2,425	-$3,100	$12,038	63.00	-18.49%
Apr	6	83.3	$870	-$963	$1,450	$2,950	0.90	4.52	$565	1	-$963	$3,388	$15,425	91.83	20.20%
May	9	77.7	$1,34	-$1,381	$1,830	$2,225	0.97	3.41	$739	1	-$1,613	$6,650	$22,075	59.78	39.65%
Jun	9	22.2	$1,82	-$732	$2,575	$1,134	2.49	0.71	-$164	7	-$2,550	-$1,475	$20,600	67.89	-8.80%
Jul 2004	8	75.0	$613	-$713	$1,031	$1,194	0.86	2.58	$281	1	-$1,250	$2,250	$22,850	57.00	13.42%
Aug	8	75.0	$1,31	-$2,219	$1,806	$2,700	0.59	1.78	$433	2	-$3,138	$3,463	$26,313	80.00	20.65%
Sep	9	66.6	$1,31	-$525	$1,756	$1,029	2.50	4.99	$699	2	-$1,013	$6,288	$32,600	70.33	37.49%
Oct	9	55.5	$818	-$616	$1,313	-$919	1.33	1.66	$181	2	-$1,225	$1,625	$34,225	60.89	9.69%
Nov	7	57.1	$697	-$1,475	$1,063	$2,029	0.47	0.63	-$234	2	-$3,763	$1,638	$32,588	72.43	-9.76%
Dec	7	57.1	$1,96	-$483	$2,391	-$850	4.07	5.43	$918	2	-$1,213	$6,425	$39,013	85.14	38.31%
Jan	5	60.0	$1,87	-$1,200	$2,708	$1,681	1.57	2.35	$648	2	-$1,950	$3,238	$42,250	96.60	19.31%
Feb	7	71.4	$920	-$2,663	$1,888	$3,531	0.35	0.86	-$104	3	-$2,875	-$725	$41,525	80.43	-4.32%
Mar	8	37.5	$1,57	-$1,260	$1,633	$1,828	1.25	0.75	-$198	3	-$3,375	-$1,588	$39,938	65.63	-9.47%
Apr	8	75.0	$1,30	-$206	$0	$631	6.30	18.91	$923	6	-$375	$7,388	$47,325	77.75	44.05%
May	6	0.00	$0	-$975	$0	$1,431	0.00	0.00	-$975	6	-$3,288	-$5,850	$41,475	74.00	-34.88%
Jun	14	78.5	$877	-$158	$1,303	-$538	5.54	20.32	$655	2	-$363	$9,175	$50,650	47.71	54.71%
Jul 2005	9	88.8	$698	-$588	$1,078	-$1,800	1.19	9.51	$556	1	-$588	$5,000	$55,650	59.11	29.82%
Aug	18	72.2	$625	-$578	$839	-$873	1.08	2.81	$291	4	-$1,463	$5,238	$60,888	32.11	31.23%
Sep	10	50.0	$1,52	-$475	$1,925	$1,038	3.21	3.21	$524	1	-$938	$5,238	$66,125	60.60	31.23%
Oct	6	33.3	$425	-$978	$738	$1,981	0.43	0.22	-$510	4	-$1,188	-$3,063	$63,063	80.17	-18.26%
Nov	7	28.5	$881	-$1,155	$1,800	$1,815	0.76	0.31	-$573	4	-$3,375	-$4,013	$59,050	80.86	-23.93%
Dec	11	63.6	$729	-$788	$1,084	$1,163	0.93	1.62	$177	2	-$1,838	$1,950	$61,000	48.82	11.63%
Jan	3	66.6	$1,19	-$2,113	$1,363	$2,763	0.57	1.13	$92	1	-$2,113	$275	$61,275	30.67	1.64%

Used with permission of www.GenesisFT.com.

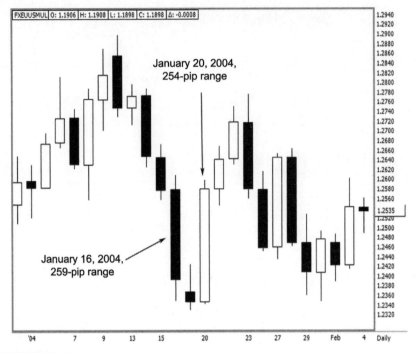

FIGURE 11.12
Used with permission of esignal.com.

subjected to news-driven price-shock market environments. No one is immune to them. The good news is that they do not occur frequently, as this data shows.

To summarize, the essence of back-testing is validating your methods and showing the strengths and the weaknesses of your system. Moreover, it will help you define your goals and expectations for performance. Therefore, it can help you achieve the highest trading profits with the lowest risks in most trading market conditions. I want to elaborate that by studying a system, in all market conditions, you at least will be better prepared and less shocked when an eventual negative situation develops in your trading career. The main goal in trading is consistency and staying in the game. Statistics show this!

CHAPTER 12

Confidence to Pull the Trigger Comes from Within

Successful trading is all about diligence and hard work and having a winning attitude! Great traders take the trades that were developed with thought and with keen observations that were based on predefined trading signals. This mentality will help you develop the confidence to execute when a trading opportunity presents itself. Lack of confidence and fear are your enemies. Trading on a rule-based system will help you overcome most emotional issues as long as you are trading based on a signal or trigger. *Never* take action on *anticipating* the signal. If the rule states to buy when X crosses over Y, you have to wait for the cross rather than anticipating that the cross is about to occur. That is what *trigger* means: It is a call to action based on a conditional change.

Many experienced losing traders who have come to me for help have a common problem—they try to jump the gun and try to outguess the market. They have this feeling that they will miss the opportunity if they don't act. By now, you know what a candle chart is; and you have read many times that it is imperative that you wait for the close of the time period for which you are trading to *close* before acting on a buy or a sell signal. Look at Figure 12.1—the candle on the left may have given an impression that a bullish breakout would materialize. However, keep in mind that unless you waited for the close, it really formed a doji. Imagine getting all wrapped up emotionally, thinking you were missing a great buying opportunity only to experience buying the high of the time period because you failed to be patient and disciplined in waiting for the time period to conclude, assuring you of the buy signal, or of the higher close.

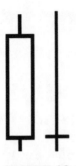

FIGURE 12.1

If you anticipate a signal, you might be right; and there are times when you can anticipate taking a trade based on a formulated, educated guess. One such scenario would be to make a buying decision based on what I call a "gap band" play. That is when the market departs too far from the pivot point moving average, which for a buying opportunity would be defined as a potentially overstretched price extreme or oversold market condition. Armed with the longer-term numbers, such as a monthly second support (S-2) target, I would look to go long but with partial positions; or I would simply scale into a position with from one-quarter up to one-third of my normal lot size or positions.

Here is where it might seem like I would be playing the "catch the falling knife" game, which I am. But when the market has the capacity to make a major price reversal, especially when several indicators line up, such as stochastics warning of bullish convergence, the Commodity Futures Trading Commission (CFTC) Commitment of Traders (COT) report shows a major imbalance, as discussed. Then if the market has been in a long-term downtrend and shows that prices have departed too far from the mean, that is what spotting a buying opportunity is about. That is also when, under these certain conditions, it is apropriate to anticipate a trade. You should cut back on your initial position size and set a risk factor such as a conditional setup if the market, for instance, makes a lower closing low. You can also add a time element, such as "If the market does not reverse in X amount of periods, then get out." In a situation like this, you could implement a longer-term option strategy, such as buying call options. (I did not go into options in this book because that subject matter was covered in my first book on page 217.) Options are a great investment vehicle that offers traders peace of mind and confidence to pull the trigger in highly volatile and precarious situations, such as picking longer-term tops and bottoms, especially in the bullish scenario just described. Remember, I have stated many times that as traders, we "look for opportunity and then apply a strategy." That is how we capture potential profits on big reversals.

Anticipating trades is a dangerous game, so you need to take that into consideration. If you ask yourself the right questions, then you can develop a solid trading plan. One such question is, "Is the risk worth the reward?" If it is, take the opportunity.

WAIT FOR THE TRADE SIGNALS

For day, short-term, or swing trading, you need to wait for signals and trade by those signals. That seems easier said than done. But it is a common mistake that I have helped traders with, especially when they have jumped the gun, anticipating a buy signal from an indicator such as stochastics. We went over the stochastics %K and %D 20-level line-cross signal. Figure 12.2 shows a detailed description of how to apply the 20 percent line closing signal properly, using the market's price action while waiting for the close of a time period to keep you from anticipating a trade. It also demonstrates when it is more apropriate to enter a long. If you learn what a true signal is, based on the close of a time period, and if you repeat that successful action, then you will develop the skills needed to have the confidence to consis-

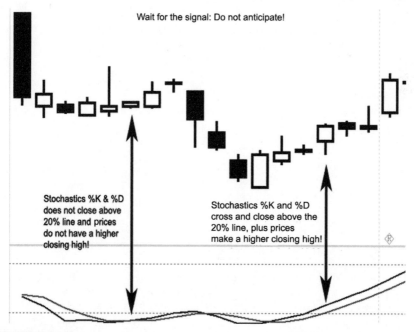

Wait for the signal: Do not anticipate!

Stochastics %K & %D does not close above 20% line and prices do not have a higher closing high!

Stochastics %K and %D cross and close above the 20% line, plus prices make a higher closing high!

FIGURE 12.2
Used with permission of www.GenesisFT.com.

tently apply this method. Ultimately, your performance and trading results will improve.

We discussed in Chapter 3 how to use the stochastics oscillator properly. It is so important. Let's review: If you anticipated a buy signal based on the stochastics %K and %D hook crossover the first time, you should notice how either of the two closed above the 20 percent line in Figure 12.2. In addition, you did not see a higher closing high collaborate a buy signal. Anticipating without confirming factors or misreading a signal can and usually does result in losses. Notice that the second signal where both %K and %D cross and close above the 20 percent level is confirmed with a higher closing high. This is a confirming signal and will put you in a better mindset and more often than not on the profitable side of the ledger. Remember, your mind can and does play tricks on you when you are trading. That little subconscious voice will tell you to just hang in there, to just keep holding on to the loser, because the market will bounce back. Odds are that fear takes over and you sell out of a long, right on the low of the move. You cannot act on emotional impulse. If you act on impulse and you are wrong, you need to get out immediately once and if the market breaks further against you, because the emotional state of greed got you into the trade and the emotional state of fear will get you out. Usually it is on the low. If you wait for a true buy signal based on the closing price action, you are trading with the current flow of the market. This method of trading, once you see consistent results, will increase your confidence; and that will give you what it takes to become a successful trader consistently over time.

THE RIGHT FRAME OF MIND

Many times traders subconsciously sabotage themselves inadvertently. Avoid putting yourself in a situation that will cause you to be skeptical or afraid before you trade. A better way to state it is, do not trade while undergoing a major personal setback. This would include stressful events like buying or selling a house, moving, sickness, a change in careers or a loss of a job, a death in the family, or loss of a friend. A breakup in a relationship or a divorce can also cause undue stress. Try to make educated decisions, and make sure you have the time to invest in your work before putting on any trades. Remember that it is alright to be wrong; just don't be wrong all the time, making the same mistakes over and over again. If you follow a proven strategy, you are already aware that there will be losses. We discussed this in Chapter 11. If you are trading on the edge, not in the right frame of mind, angry, or upset, then you have lost the emotional edge that is needed to stay focused and disciplined.

If you are not trading with an indicator, a plan, or a software program, then write your rules down on your computer screen. This is one method that can help keep you on track when you start trading out of impulse or from an emotional state of mind.

TRACK AND CHART YOUR TRADES

A trading diary is a great way to check and confirm your trading execution entries and exits. In fact, most charting software has the capability to go back to see when you executed a trade. Think what this can do for a trader. If it is followed properly, it can and most likely will help you to improve to a new level of self-discipline and ultimately lead to increasing your self-confidence. How? If you execute when the signals call for action, you can validate whether you responded when called to do so. You can check your work. You will find out if you hesitated when your methods called for you to exit and if you timed it per the system or not. One lesson we teach our students at Trading Triggers University is to save a chart and print it out with the entry scale-out and exit. Printing the chart out helps you to see clearly how you respond or react to the trade signals. It will reinforce the validity of your system or any system, including my Defcon program with Genesis Software. By printing out and cataloging your trades by a chart, you will gain more experience in identifying the patterns that drive your trading signals. It also keeps track of or "inventories" what went right or what went wrong with a trading plan. It will allow you to study and examine the results in black and white. On successful trading days, it will be good to capitalize on your successes so that they can be repeated. Of course, on bad days, it can allow you to focus on what went wrong so that you can understand and improve on it so that you stop repeating the same mistakes over and over again.

TWO CASES IN POINT

If you map out a game plan, trade off the "numbers," or have a trading system, when you print out your chart and examine your trades, you are grading your own homework. I have posted on my web site a daily Dow Report to which the Chicago Board of Trade links. Every day after the market closes, I post two numbers based on my teachings and on what we went over in this book. Those numbers are what I believe the high and/or low of the session will be; and then, based on the market direction number, I will post a trade recommendation. Figure 12.3 shows a direct quote that was for

FIGURE 12.3
Used with permission of esignal.com.

Monday, February 13, 2006. The initial resistance level was 10983, and my target support was 10865. The exact low was 10865, and a high close doji pattern formed.

This is not rocket science. Why would I state the day before what type of pattern to look for and at what price? We know the reasons why I select a high close doji trigger based on the statistical findings in Chapter 7. When I introduce two other dimensional market analysis approaches, such as a moving average and pivot point analysis, all you need is the patience to wait for the signal to materialize. It is a high-probability setup; and in this case, the trade resulted in a 38-point gain, or $190 per contract, in less than an hour. The only drawback on this trade was that you had to wait until the end of the day for it to materialize. No pressure, no worries, just profits. A nice trade. And if you print out a chart and plot your entries and exits, you will begin to see more clearly how a trade develops; and you will reinforce your subconscious mind on what to look for in the next trade and improve your confidence from within to win.

There are many who visit my site just to see my numbers selection for the market. I also include what the projections are for the week. For day traders and swing traders, it helps them also identify a potential confluence support level based on pivot point analysis. Feel free to visit and check the numbers yourself at www.nationalfutures.com; just click on the link that says Daily Dow Report. Even better: You now have your own Pivot Point Calculator, provided on the accompanying CD to this book.

Another case in point as to why it is helpful to print out and catalogue charts that track your trades is that it will help you to visually back-test the methods. The more you see the patterns recur, the more assurance you will have in the methodology.

The topic I covered in Chapter 5, demonstrating how to filter the pivot point price projections, based on the moving average approach, gives me an edge by reducing the noise or eliminating excess information. It helps me to narrow the field to what the potential range might be of a given market for a specific time frame. If I have a predetermined point of view that the market might see a low of 1257 and a high of 1273, once I identify a pattern and conditional change in the price action, I can enter a position. In Figure 12.4, I have a trade example in the e-mini–S&P (Standard & Poor's) that demonstrates how the market was contained within the bearish target

FIGURE 12.4
Used with permission of esignal.com.

selected pivot point numbers based on the system. Remember, if bearish, then the target low will be near S-2 and the high will be near the first resistance level (R-1). If you stick to the rules and look for buy signals near support and sell signals near resistance, follow the game plan, add the other two dimensional factors such as a high close doji or hammer pattern, with the moving average indicating a conditional change, then you enter a position. As the market starts to show momentum loss as indicated by shadows, scale out of half of your positions, place a hard stop at break-even, and then wait to see the flow of the market. If you print out your chart and plot your entry price, your scale-out price, and then the price where you exited on the balance of your positions, you will not only grade the trading system but also your performance and how you react to market conditions.

SIMULATED TRADING

It goes without saying that the more practice you have, the better you will perform. But if you practice the wrong thing over and over, then there is little hope for improvement. That is not a line for a trader—that was a line from a golf pro to a bad golfer. It just so happens that it applies to trading. Almost any brokerage firm will give you a free trial to a simulated trading account for you to bang around on. With no real money on the line, you really are not putting your time to good use. It is extremely advisable if you never traded or if you switch to a new company to get accustomed to the trading platform that may be unique to that company. That makes all the sense in the world.

A trader needs to take action when a trigger is generated, rather than taking a wait-and-see attitude and then reacting to the market long after the market has moved. As a trader, you need to be quick. A sudden brain spasm spawned by fear, doubt, or greed will most likely not bring consistently good results. Hesitation is a trader's enemy; that is why I say, "Plan your trade, and then trade your plan."

Simulated trading can help you test a trading method, but what about testing your emotional response to market conditions? How will you develop the confidence from within to win? What will seriously help the trader who enters too early or too late and can't hold on to the winner? What can help the trader who hesitates and can't pull the trigger?

For starters, you need to not trade with what we call "scared money." That's the money that you are afraid of losing, that you protect so well that you end up losing it. Remember in Chapter 11 that we went over the performance sheet on the trading system results. The payout ratio is the amount of the average winner versus the loser. If you cut out of a winning trade too early and do so randomly because you need to make a profit, then you are possibly setting yourself up for a financial meltdown because you are not letting your winners ride.

One question that new investors ask me is why they did better at paper trading than they did when they traded with real money. The answer is easy. They let their emotions such as fear, doubt, complacency, greed, anxiety, excitement, and false pride interfere with their rational and intellectual thoughts. When dealing with real money, you are faced with the realization that you and your money can part.

Simulated trading is good to understand the mechanics of a trading execution platform. However, putting real money on the line is what will test your trading skills. Here is a suggestion: If you want to really see if you have what it takes to be a professional trader who can execute a testable trading system, then trade with the smallest lot or position size for a period of six weeks or two months. You may not make lots of money if you are consistently right, but you will develop the confidence to act on your signals when your self-imposed training session is completed. If you trade stocks, instead of trading 200 shares of an $80 or $100 stock, trade 50 shares. This will help you feel more at ease, and it will also put your emotions to the test as you are trading with real money.

Here is another suggestion: Open an ultra-mini-sized foreign exchange (forex) account and apply the trading signal to that market. This is a nifty idea for those who are beginners and still have day jobs. The markets trade 24 hours a day, you can afford to hold positions overnight, and you have money on the line so that you will be more realistic in execution of your trading plan. You can trade at night and execute trading signals in an extremely liquid market. If you have a system that works reasonably well based on statistical back-testing studies, the only confidence that should be in question is your ability to execute the signals. That is what trading a mini-forex account can do for you. It will exercise your emotional intellect. You will learn that when you place a trade, it is an educated decision, not merely a guess. One web site to visit is www.fxtriggers.com to help select a forex account and to open a simulated trading account and develop the knowledge that will give you the confidence to execute and act on the trading signals. Building confidence in yourself and in your trading skills is extremely important in stimulating an optimistic winning attitude. Opening a mini-forex account just may help a newcomer using a technical-based system. Over a period of time, as your trading skills improve, so will your attitude. As Thomas Jefferson once said, "Nothing can stop the man with the right mental attitude from achieving his goal: Nothing on earth can help the man with the wrong mental attitude."

If you want to follow what the moneymakers do, have a good plan, method, or system and execute when a trigger presents a call to action. Maintain a winning attitude!

I believe the principles in this book combining candles and pivots will keep you on the right side of the profit ledger. It is the method I have used for over 25 years. I have taught my own family to use these setups, and they have served us well. My former students have expressed gratitude in seeing a method and applying the concepts whether it is stock, futures, or forex. Some have moved on to open their own brokerage firms, and even other educators come to learn my technique. There is back-tested data to support the validity and frequency of patterns. All you need to do is apply the knowledge and follow the rules.

LIVE BY THE RULES

If you follow the rules of any methodology, then you have a better chance of succeeding. That applies toward any aspect in life, for that matter. As Leonardo da Vinci stated, "Simplicity breeds elegance." Keep things simple.

- Look for buy signals near support.
- Look for sell signals near resistance.
- When the system triggers a signal, act on it.
- When a system says get out, get out!

I wish you well in all your trading endeavors. Remember that if you act on validated signals, your actions are validated. If the method has merit, then your rewards should have merit.

All the best,
John L. Person

Glossary

Actualize The underlying assets or instruments that are traded in the cash market.

Adjustable peg An exchange rate regime in which a country's exchange rate is determined (i.e., pegged) in relation to another currency, often the dollar or French franc, but may be changed from time to time.

Aggregate demand Total demand for goods and services in a country's economy; includes private and public sector demand for goods and services within the country and the demand of consumers and firms in other countries.

Aggregate risk Size of exposure of a bank to a single customer for both spot and forward contracts.

Aggregate supply Total supply of goods and services in a country's economy from domestic sources (including imports) available to meet aggregate demand.

Appreciation Describes the strengthening of a currency in response to market demand rather than by official action.

Arbitrage The action of a simultaneous buy and sell of a similar or like commodity or futures product that may be made in different contract months, on different exchanges, and in different countries in order to profit from a discrepancy in price.

Arbitrage channel The range of prices within which there will be no possibility to arbitrage between the cash and futures market.

Ask The price at which a currency or instrument is offered.

Asset In the context of foreign exchange, the right to receive from a counterparty an amount of currency either in respect of a balance sheet asset, such as a loan, or at a specified future date in respect of an unmatched forward or spot deal.

Asset allocation Dividing instrument funds among markets to achieve diversification or maximum return.

At best An instruction given to a dealer to buy or sell at the best rate that can be obtained in a given time period.

At or better An order to deal at a specific rate or better.

Backwardation   The amount by which the spot price exceeds the forward price.

Balance of payments   A systematic record of economic transactions during a given period for a country. (1) The term is often used to mean either (i) balance of payments on "current account" or (ii) the current account plus certain long-term capital movements. (2) The combination of the trade balance, current balance, capital account, and invisible balance, which together make up the balance-of-payments total. Prolonged balance-of-payment deficits tend to lead to restrictions in capital transfers and/or decline in currency values.

Bank rate   The rate at which a central bank is prepared to lend money to its domestic banking system.

Base currency   United States dollars; the currency to which each transaction will be converted at the close of each position.

Basis   The difference between the cash price and the futures price.

Basis point   For most currencies, denotes the fourth decimal place in the exchange rate and represents 1/100 of 1 percent (0.01%). For such currencies as the Japanese yen, a basis point is the second decimal place when quoted in currency terms or the sixth and seventh decimal places, respectively, when quoted in reciprocal terms.

Basis trading   Taking opposite positions in the cash and the futures markets with the intention of profiting from favorable movements in the basis.

Basket   A group of currencies normally used to manage the exchange rate of a currency.

Bear   An investor who believes that prices are going to fall.

Bearish   A down-trending market or a period in which prices depreciate in value.

Bid   The price at which a buyer has offered to purchase a currency or instrument.

Book   The summary of currency positions held by a dealer, a desk, or a room; a sum total of assets and liabilities.

Bretton Woods   The site of the conference that in 1944 led to the establishment of the postwar foreign exchange system that remained intact until the early 1970s. The conference resulted in the formation of the International Monetary Fund (IMF). The system fixed currencies in a fixed exchange rate system with 1 percent fluctuations of the currency to gold or to the U.S. dollar.

Bullish   Referring to an up-trending market or to a period in which prices appreciate in value.

Bull market   A prolonged period of generally rising prices.

Bundesbank   Central Bank of Germany.

Cable   A term used in the foreign exchange market for the U.S. dollar/British pound rate.

Candlestick charts   Charting method that involves a graphic presentation of the relationship between the open, the high, the low, and the close. Color schemes are used to illustrate the real body of a candle, which is the difference between a lower close than the open (black or dark) and a higher close than the open (white).

Capital risk   The risk arising from a bank having to pay the counterparty without knowing whether the other party will or is able to meet its side of the bargain.

Carrying charges   The cost associated with holding or storing cash or physical commodities and financial instruments. Four variables are involved: storage, insurance, finance charges, and/or interest payments on borrowed monies.

Cash   Usually refers to an exchange transaction contracted for settlement on the day the deal is struck. This term is mainly used in the North American markets and those countries that rely for foreign exchange services on these markets because of time zone preference (i.e., Latin America). In Europe and Asia, cash transactions are often referred to as "value same day deals."

Cash market   The market in the actual financial instrument on which a futures or options contract is based.

Cash settlement   A procedure for settling futures contracts through payment of the cash difference between the future and the market price, rather than through the physical delivery of a commodity.

CBOT   Chicago Board of Trade.

Central bank   A country's head regulatory bank, which is responsible for the development and implementation of monetary policy.

CFTC   Commodity Futures Trading Commission, which is the federal regulatory agency in charge of overseeing the futures and nonbank forex industry.

Closed position   A transaction that leaves the trade with a zero net commitment to the market with respect to a particular currency.

CME   Chicago Mercantile Exchange.

COMAS   Conditionally Optimized Moving Average System, which incorporates two different time-period moving averages with two different variables, such as a simple moving average based on the close and a second value based on the pivot point.

Commission   The fee that a broker may charge clients for dealing on their behalf.

Commodity   A financial instrument or a product that is used in commerce and is mainly traded on a regulated commodity exchange. The types of products are agricultural (such as meats and grains), metals, petroleum, foreign currencies, stock index futures, single stock futures, and financial instruments (such as interest rate vehicles like notes and bonds).

Commodity trading advisor (CTA)   A registered individual or entity that advises others, for compensation or profit, in buying or selling futures contracts or commodity options; also includes exercising trading authority over a customer's account and providing research and analysis through newsletters or other media.

Conversion   The process by which an asset or liability denominated in one currency is exchanged for an asset or liability denominated in another currency.

Conversion account   A general ledger account representing the uncovered position in a particular currency. Such accounts are referred to as "position accounts."

Convertible currency   A currency that can be freely exchanged for another currency (and/or gold) without special authorization from the central bank.

Copey   Traders' slang for the Danish krone.

Correspondent bank   The foreign bank's representative who regularly performs services for a bank that has no branch in the relevant center, e.g., to facilitate the transfer of funds. In the United States, this often occurs domestically due to interstate banking restrictions.

Counterparty   The other organization or party with whom an exchange deal is being transacted.

Countervalue   The dollar value of a transaction in which a person buys a currency against the dollar.

Country risk   The risk attached to a borrower by virtue of its location in a particular country; involves examination of economic, political, and geographical factors. Various organizations generate country risk tables.

Coupon   The interest rate on a debt instrument expressed in terms of a percent on an annualized basis that the issuer guarantees to pay to the holder until maturity.

Cover   To close out a short position by buying currency or securities that have been sold short.

Covered arbitrage   Arbitrage between financial instruments denominated in different currencies, using forward cover to eliminate exchange risk.

Credit risk   Risk of loss that may arise on outstanding contracts should a counterparty default on its obligations.

Cross rates   Rates between two currencies, neither of which is the U.S. dollar.

Current account   The net balance of a country's international payments arising from exports and imports together with unilateral transfers, such as aid and migrant remittances; excludes capital flows.

Day trader   A speculators who takes positions in commodities that are iquidated prior to the close of the same trading day.

Dead cross   A term used when a sell signal is generated when one or more shorter-term moving averages cross below a longer-term moving average.

Deal date   The date on which a transaction is agreed on.

Dealer   A person who acts as a principal in all transactions, buying and selling for his or her own accounts; opposite of *broker*.

Deal ticket   The primary method of recording the basic information relating to a transaction.

Deferred month   The more distant month in which futures trading is taking place, as established from the active nearby or front contract delivery month.

Deflator   Difference between real and nominal gross national product (GNP), which is equivalent to the overall inflation rate.

Delivery date   The date of maturity of a contract, when the exchange of the currencies is made; more commonly known as the "value date" in the forex or money markets.

Delivery risk   A term to describe when a counterparty might not be able to complete one side of the deal, although willing to do so.

Depreciation   A fall in the value of a currency due to market forces, rather than to official action.

Discount rate   The interest rate charged on loans by the Federal Reserve to member banks.

Doji   A candlestick term; used to describe a time period when the open and the close are nearly exact. It is a strong sell signal, but a cautionary warning at bottoms.

Easing   Modest decline in price.

Economic indicator   A statistic that indicates current economic growth rates and trends, such as retail sales and employment.

ECU   European currency unit.

Effective exchange rate   An attempt to summarize the effects on a country's trade balance of its currency's changes against other currencies.

Elliott Wave   Analysis theory developed by Ralph Elliott, based on the premise that prices move in two basic types of waves: impulse waves, which move with the main trend, and corrective waves, which move against the main trend.

Euro dollars   U.S. dollars on deposit with a bank outside of the United States and, consequently, outside the jurisdiction of the United States. The bank could be either a foreign bank or a subsidiary of a U.S. bank.

European Monetary System (EMS)   A system designed to stabilize if not eliminate exchange risk between member states of the EMS as part of the economic convergence policy of the European Union (EU). It permits currencies to move in a measured fashion (divergence indicator) within agreed bands (the parity grid) with respect to the ECU and consequently with each other.

Exchange control   Rules used to preserve or protect the value of a country's currency.

Exchange for physicals (EFP)   A transaction generally used by two hedgers who want to exchange futures for cash positions; also referred to as "against actuals" or "versus cash."

Exercise   The process by which options traders convert an options position into the underlying futures or derivative market; e.g., the buyer of a call option would convert his or her calls for a long position, and the buyer of a put option would convert his or her option to a short futures contract.

Face value   The amount of money printed on the face of the certificate of a security; the original dollar amount of indebtedness incurred.

Falling three methods   A bearish continuation pattern similar to the Western version of a bear flag. It is a four- but mostly a five-candle pattern composition.

Fast market   Rapid movement in a market caused by strong interest by buyers and/or sellers. In such circumstances, price levels may be omitted, and bid-and-offer quotations may occur too rapidly to be fully reported.

Fed   The United States Federal Reserve System. Federal Deposit Insurance Corporation (FDIC) membership is compulsory for Federal Reserve members. The corporation had deep involvement in the savings-and-loan crisis of the late 1980s.

Federal Reserve System   The central banking system of the United States.

Fed fund rate   The interest rate on Federal Reserve System funds. This is a closely watched short-term interest rate because it signals the Fed's view as to the state of the money supply.

Fibonacci numbers and ratios   A series of numbers that when added together continue to infinity. The ratios are the math calculations, which are the sum of the relationships between the numbers derived either from dividing the series numbers or, in some cases, taking the square roots of the numbers. The common ratio numbers are 0.38%, 0.618%, 50%, and 100%.

Fill or kill   An order that must be entered for trading, normally in a pit, three times; is immediately canceled if not filled.

Financial instrument   One of two basic types: a debt instrument, which is a loan with an agreement to pay back funds with interest, and an equity security, which is a share or stock in a company.

First notice day   According to Chicago Board of Trade (CBOT) rules, the first day on which a notice of intent to deliver a commodity in fulfillment of a given month's futures contract can be made by the clearinghouse to a buyer. The clearinghouse also informs the sellers of whom they have been matched up with. Each exchange sets its own guides and rules for this process.

Fixed exchange rate   Official rate set by monetary authorities; often permits fluctuation within a band.

Flexible exchange rate   An exchange rate with a fixed parity against one or more currencies with frequent revaluations.

Floating exchange rate   An exchange rate determined by market forces. Even floating currencies are subject to intervention by the monetary authorities.

FOMC   Federal Open Market Committee, which sets U.S. money supply targets, which tend to be implemented through Fed Fund interest rates, and so on.

Foreign exchange (forex)   The purchase or sale of a currency against sale or purchase of another.

Forex market   Usually referred to as the over-the-counter market where buyers and sellers conduct foreign currency exchange business.

Forward margins   Discounts or premiums between the spot rate and the forward rate for a currency; usually quoted in points.

Forward operations   Foreign exchange transactions on which the fulfillment of the mutual delivery obligations is made on a date later than the second business day after the transaction was concluded.

Forward outright   A commitment to buy to or sell a currency for delivery on a specified future date or period. The price is quoted as the spot rate plus or minus the forward points for the chosen period.

Forward rate   Quoted in terms of forward points, which represent the difference between the forward rate and the spot rate. To obtain the forward rate from the actual exchange rate, the forward points are either added or subtracted from the exchange rate. The decision to add or subtract points is determined by the differential between the deposit rates for both currencies concerned in the transaction. The base currency with the higher interest rate is said to be at a discount to the lower interest rate quoted currency in the forward market. Therefore, the forward points are *subtracted* from the spot rate. Similarly, the lower interest rate base currency is said to be at a premium, and the forward points are *added* to the spot rate to obtain the forward rate.

Free reserves   Total reserves held by a bank minus the reserves required by the authority.

Full carrying charge market   A futures market where the price difference between delivery months reflects the total costs of interest, insurance, and storage.

Fundamental analysis   A method of anticipating future price movement using supply and demand information; also a method to study the macroeconomic factors (including inflation, growth, trade balance, government deficit, and interest rates) that influence currency and financial markets.

G7 (Group of Seven)   The seven leading industrial countries: the United States, Germany, Japan, France, the United Kingdom, Canada, and Italy.

Gann, William D.   An early pioneer in technical analysis who is credited with a mathematical system based on Fibonacci numbers and with the Gann Square and Cycle studies.

Gap   A mismatch between maturities and cash flows in a bank or individual dealer's position book. Gap exposure is effectively interest rate exposure.

GLOBEX   A global after-hours electronic trading system used on the Chicago Mercantile Exchange (CME).

Golden cross   A bullish term used when one or more shorter-term moving averages cross above a longer-term moving average; generally generates a buy signal.

Gold standard   The original system for supporting the value of currency issued. This is where the price of gold is fixed against the currency; it means that the increased supply of gold does not lower the price of gold but causes prices to increase.

Good until canceled   An instruction to a broker that, unlike normal practice, does not expire at the end of the trading day; usually terminates at the end of the trading month.

Gravestone doji   A long range day where the open and the close are near the low of the range.

Gross Domestic Product (GDP)   Total value of a country's output, income, or expenditure produced within the country's physical borders.

Gross National Product (GNP)   Gross domestic product plus "factor income from abroad," i.e., income earned from investment or work abroad.

Hammer   A candlestick pattern that forms at bottoms. At market tops, the same construction is called a "hanging man." The shadow is generally twice the length of the real body.

Harami   A two-candle candlestick pattern that can be seen to mark tops and bottoms. The second candle of this formation is contained within the real body of the prior session's candle.

Hard currency   Any one of the major world currencies that is well traded and easily converted into other currencies.

Head and shoulders   A pattern in price trends that, according to chartists, indicates a price trend reversal. The price has risen for some time, at the peak of the left shoulder; profit taking has caused the price to drop or to level. The price then rises steeply again to the head before more profit taking causes the price to drop to around the same level as the shoulder. A further modest rise or level will indicate that a further major fall is imminent. The breach of the neckline is the indication to sell.

Hedging   The practice of offsetting the price risk inherent in any cash market position by taking an equal but opposite position in the futures market. Hedgers use the futures markets to protect their businesses from adverse price changes.

High wave   A candle that has a wide range with a small real body that develops in the middle of that range. It has significance as a reversal formation, especially if several of these form in succession.

Horizontal spread   The purchase of either a call or a put option and the simultaneous sale of the same type of option with typically the same strike price but with a different expiration month; also referred to as a "calendar spread."

IMF   International Monetary Fund; established in 1946 to provide international liquidity on a short and medium term and to encourage liberalization of exchange rates. The IMF supports countries with balance-of-payments problems with the provision of loans.

IMM International Monetary Market; part of the Chicago Mercantile Exchange that lists a number of currency and financial futures.

Implied rates The interest rate determined by calculating the difference between spot and forward rates.

Implied volatility A measurement of the market's expected price range of the underlying currency futures based on the traded option premiums.

Indicative quote A market maker's price that is not firm.

Inflation Continued rise in the general price level in conjunction with a related drop in purchasing power; sometimes referred to as an excessive movement in such price levels.

Initial margin The margin required by a foreign exchange firm to initiate the buying or the selling of a determined amount of currency.

Interbank rates The bid and offer rates at which international banks place deposits with each other; the basis of the interbank market.

Intercommodity spread The purchase of a given delivery month of one futures market and the simultaneous sale of the same delivery month of a different, but related, futures market.

Interdelivery spread The purchase of one delivery month of a given futures contract and the simultaneous sale of another delivery month of the same commodity on the same exchange; also referred to as an "intramarket spread" or "calendar spread."

Interest arbitrage Switching into another currency by buying spot and selling forward, and investing proceeds in order to obtain a higher interest yield. Interest arbitrage can be inward (from foreign currency into the local one) or outward (from the local currency to the foreign one). Sometimes better results can be obtained by not selling the forward interest amount. In that case, some treat it as no longer being a complete arbitrage because if the exchange rate moved against the arbitrageur, the profit on the transaction may create a loss.

Interest rate swaps An agreement to swap interest rate exposures from floating to fixed or vice versa. There is no swap of the principal. It is the interest cash flows, be they payments or receipts, that are exchanged.

Intermarket spread The sale of a given delivery month of a futures contract on one exchange and the simultaneous purchase of the same delivery month and futures contract on another exchange.

Internationalization Referring to a currency that is widely used to denominate trade and credit transactions by nonresidents of the country of issue. The U.S. dollar and the Swiss franc are examples.

Intervention   Action by a central bank to effect the value of its currency by entering the market. *Concerted intervention* refers to action by a number of central banks to control exchange rates.

Introducing broker (IB)   A person or an organization that solicits or accepts orders to buy or sell futures contracts or commodity options but does not accept money or other assets from customers to support such orders.

Inverted market   A futures market in which the relationship between two delivery months of the same commodity is abnormal.

Island chart pattern   Formed when the market gaps in one direction and then in the next session gaps open in the opposite direction, leaving the prior day's bar or range seeming like an "island" on the chart. At tops, this is extremely bearish; and at bottoms, it is considered extremely bullish. This is a rare chart pattern and is similar in nature to the Japanese candlestick pattern called the "abandon baby."

J trader   An independent electronic trading order entry platform provider by Pats Systems that routes orders to the exchanges trading systems, such as the Chicago Board of Trade's E-CBOT system and the Chicago Mercantile Exchange's GLOBEX system.

Lagging indicators   Market indicators showing the general direction of the economy and confirming or denying the trend implied by the leading indicators.

Last trading day (LTD)   The final day on which trading may occur in a given futures or options contract month.

Leading indicators   Market indicators that signal the state of the economy for the coming months. Some of the leading indicators include average manufacturing workweek, initial claims for unemployment insurance, orders for consumer goods and material, percentage of companies reporting slower deliveries, change in manufacturers' unfilled orders for durable goods, plant and equipment orders, new building permits, index of consumer expectations, change in material prices, prices of stocks, and change in money supply.

LEAPS   Long-Term Equity Anticipation Securities; options that have an extended life as long as five years; generally used for options on stocks.

Leverage   The ability to control large dollar amounts of a commodity with a comparatively small amount of capital.

Liability   In terms of foreign exchange, the obligation to deliver to a counterparty an amount of currency either in respect of a balance sheet holding at a specified future date or in respect of an unmatured forward or spot transaction.

Limit order   A request to deal as a buyer or a seller for a foreign currency transaction at a specified price or at a better price, if obtainable.

Liquidation   Any transaction that offsets or closes out a previously established position.

Liquidity   The ability of a market to accept large transactions.

Long   The condition of having bought futures contracts or owning a cash commodity.

Long-legged doji   A specific doji that forms when the open and the close occur near the middle of a wide-range trading session.

Maintenance margin   A set minimum margin that a customer must maintain in his or her margin account. If the cash amount in a trading account drops below the margin level and a margin call is generated, then a trader must either send additional funds to get the account back to the initial margin level or liquidate positions to satisfy the call.

Make a market   The action of a dealer quoting bid and offer prices at which he or she stands ready to buy and sell.

Managed float   The regular intervention of the monetary authorities in the market to stabilize the rates or to aim the exchange rate in a required direction.

Managed futures   Represents an industry comprised of professional money managers known as commodity trading advisors who manage client assets on a discretionary basis, using global futures markets as an investment medium.

Margin   The amount of money or collateral that must be initially provided or thereafter maintained to ensure against losses on open contracts. Initial margin must be placed before a trade is entered. Maintenance or variation margin must be added to initial margin to maintain against losses on open positions. The amount that needs to be present to establish or thereafter maintain is sometimes referred to as "necessary margin."

Margin call   A claim by one's broker or dealer for additional good faith performance monies, usually issued when an investor's account suffers adverse price movements.

Market maker   A person or firm authorized to create and maintain a market in an instrument.

Market order   An order to buy or to sell a financial instrument immediately at the best possible price.

Market profile   A method of charting that analyzes price and volume in specific time brackets.

Mark to market   The daily adjustment of an account to reflect accrued profits and losses; often required to calculate variations of margins.

Microeconomics   The study of economic activity as it applies to individual firms or well-defined small groups of individuals or economic sectors.

Midprice or middle rate   The price halfway between two prices, or the average of both buying and selling prices offered by the market makers.

Minimum price fluctuation   The smallest increment of market price movement possible in a given futures contract.

Momentum   The measure of the rate of change in prices.

Morning doji star   A bullish three-candle formation in which the middle candle is formed by a doji.

Moving average   A way of smoothing a set of data; widely used in price time series.

National Futures Association (NFA)   The self-regulatory agency for futures and options markets. The primary responsibilities of the NFA are to enforce ethical standards and customer protection rules, to screen futures professionals for membership, to audit and monitor professionals for financial and general compliance rules, and to provide for arbitration of futures-related disputes.

Nearby month   The futures contract month closest to expiration. Also called the *spot month.*

Net position   The amount of currency bought or sold that has not yet been offset by opposite transactions.

Offer   The price at which a seller is willing to sell; the *best offer* is the lowest such price available.

Offset   The closing out or liquidation of a futures position.

Offshore   The operations of a financial institution that, although physically located in a country, has little connection with that country's financial systems. In certain countries, a bank is not permitted to do business in the domestic market but only with other foreign banks; this is known as an "offshore banking unit."

One cancels other   A contingency order instructing a broker to cancel one side of a two-sided entry order.

Opening range   A range of prices at which buy and sell transactions take place during the first minute of the opening of the market for most markets.

Open interest   The total number of futures or options contracts of a given commodity that have been neither offset by an opposite futures or option transaction nor fulfilled by delivery of the commodity or option exercise. Each open transaction has a buyer and a seller; but for calculation of open interest, only one side of the contract is counted.

Open outcry   Method of public auction for making verbal bids and offers in the trading pits or rings of futures exchanges.

Option   A contract that conveys the right, but not the obligation, to buy or to sell a particular item at a certain price for a limited time.

Out-of-the-money option   An option with no intrinsic value; i.e., a call whose strike price is above the current futures price or a put whose strike price is below the current futures price.

Overbought   The condition of a specific move when the market price has risen too far too fast and is set up for a corrective pullback or period of consolidation; the opposite of *oversold.*

Overnight   A deal from today until the next business day.

Overnight limit   Net long or short position in one or more currencies that a dealer can carry over into the next dealing day. Passing the book to other bank dealing rooms in the next trading time zone reduces the need for dealers to maintain these unmonitored exposures.

Oversold   The condition of a specific move when the market price has fallen and is in a position for a corrective rally or a period of consolidation; the opposite of *overbought*.

Par   The face value of a security; e.g., a bond selling at par is worth the same dollar amount it was issued for or at which it will be redeemed at maturity.

Parities   The value of one currency in terms of another.

Pegged   A system where a currency moves in line with another currency; some pegs are strict while others have bands of movement.

Piercing pattern   A candlestick formation involving two candles formed at bottoms of market moves. The first candle is a long dark candle; the second candle opens lower than the dark candle's low and closes more than half way above the first candle's real body.

PIP (percentage in points)   One unit of price change in the bid/ask price of a currency. For most currencies, it denotes the fourth decimal place in an exchange rate and represents 1/100 of 1 percent (0.01%).

Pit   The area on the trading floor where futures and options on futures contracts are bought and sold. It is customary for Chicago markets to refer to the individual commodity trading areas as pits, whereas in New York, they are referred to as "rings."

Pivot points   The mathematical calculation formula used to determine the support or resistance ranges in a given time period. These formulas can be used to calculate intraday, daily, weekly, monthly, or quarterly ranges.

Point-and-figure   A charting style that tracks the market's price action by representing increases with plotting Xs on a chart and downside corrections with Os. Time is not an issue with this method; rather, it is concerned with pure price movement.

Position   The netted total commitments in a given currency; can be flat or square (no exposure), long (more currency bought than sold), or short (more currency sold than bought).

Premium   The dollar value amount placed on an option.

Prime rate   Interest rate charged by major banks to their most creditworthy customers.

Producer Price Index   An index that shows the cost of goods and services to producers and wholesalers.

Profit taking   The unwinding of a position to realize profits.

Put option   An option that gives the option buyer the right but not the obligation to sell an underlying futures contract at the strike price on or before the expiration date.

Quote   An indicative price; the price quoted for information purposes but not to deal.

Rally   A recovery in price after a period of decline.

Range   The difference between the highest and the lowest prices of a future recorded during a given trading session.

Rate   (1) The price of one currency in terms of another, normally against the U.S. dollar (USD); (2) assessment of the creditworthiness of an institution.

Reaction   A decline in prices following an advance.

Real body   The section of a candlestick defined as the area established between the opening and the closing of a particular time period.

Reciprocal currency   A currency that is normally quoted as dollars per unit of currency rather than as the normal quote of units of currency per dollar. Sterling is the most common example.

Relative Strength Index   A technical indicator used to determine a market in an overbought or oversold condition; was developed by Welles Wilder Jr. to help determine market reversals.

Resistance point or level   A price recognized by technical analysts as a price that is likely to result in a rebound but if broken through is likely to result in a significant price movement.

Revaluation   Increase in the exchange rate of a currency as a result of official action.

Revaluation rate   The rate for any period or currency that is used to revalue a position or book.

Rickshaw doji   A doji that has an unusually large trading range.

Risk management   The identification and acceptance or offsetting of the risks threatening the profitability or existence of an organization; with respect to foreign exchange, involves consideration of market, sovereign, country, transfer, delivery, credit, and counterparty risk, among other things.

Risk position   An asset or liability that is exposed to fluctuations in value through changes in exchange rates or interest rates.

Rollover   An overnight swap; specifically, the next business day against the following business day; also called "tomorrow next" (Tom-next).

Round trip   Buying and selling of a specified amount of currency.

Same-day transaction   A transaction that matures on the day the transaction takes place.

Scalper   A trader who trades for small, short-term profits.

Selling rate   Rate at which a bank is willing to sell foreign currency.

Settlement date   The date on which foreign exchange contracts settle.

Settlement price   The last price paid for a commodity on any trading day. The exchange clearinghouse determines a firm's net gains or losses, margin requirements, and the next day's price limits, based on each futures and options contract settlement price; also referred to as "daily settlement price" or "daily closing price."

Shadow   The area on a candlestick between the high or the low in relation to the open or the close.

Shooting star   The candle that forms at tops of markets where the shadow is at least twice the length of the real body and the real body forms near the low for the session with little or no shadow at the bottom. This candle resembles an inverted hammer.

Short   The position in a futures market where a trader sells a contract with the intention of buying it back at a lower price for a profit or if at a higher price for a loss. An option trader would be considered "short the option" if he or she were a writer of that option.

Short sale   The sale of a specified amount of currency not owned by the seller at the time of the trade; usually made in expectation of a decline in the price.

Slippage   Refers to the negative (or depreciating) price value between where a stop-loss order becomes a market order and where that market order may be filled.

Speculator   An investor who is looking to profit from buying or selling derivative products with the anticipation of profiting from price moves by trading in and out of their positions.

Spinning tops   A candle where the real body is small in nature with a large range and with shadows at both ends.

Spot price   The price at which a currency is currently trading in the spot market.

Spread   (1)The difference between the bid and the ask prices of a currency; (2) the difference between the price of two related futures contracts.

Spreading   The simultaneous buying and selling of two related markets with the expectation that a profit will be made when the position is offset.

Sterling   British pound; otherwise known as *cable*.

Stochastics   A technical indicator created by George C. Lane that gives an indication of when a market is overbought or oversold.

Stock index   An indicator used to measure and report value changes in a selected group of stocks.

Stocky   Market slang for Swedish krona.

Stop-limit order   A variation of a stop order in which a trade must be executed at the exact price or no worse than a specific price. The limit side of the order limits the slippage. It also does not ensure execution if the next best price is beyond the limit side of the stop order until the limit or stop price is reached again.

Stop order   An order to buy or to sell when the market reaches a specified point. A stop order to buy becomes a market order when the futures contract trades at or above the stop price. A stop order to sell becomes a market order when the futures contract trades at or below the stop price.

Strike Price   The price at which the futures contract underlying a call or put option can be purchased or sold.

Support   A price level that attracts buyers.

Swap   The simultaneous purchase and sale of the same amount of a given currency for two different dates against the sale and the purchase of another. A swap can be a swap against a forward. In essence, swapping is somewhat similar to borrowing one currency and lending another for the same period. However, any rate of return or cost of funds is expressed in the price differential between the two sides of the transaction.

Swissy   Market slang for Swiss franc.

Technical analysis   The study of price and/or volume to anticipate future price moves. Studies can include price patterns, mathematical calculations, and data regarding the open, the high, the low, and the close of a market.

Thin market   A market in which trading volume is low and in which bid and ask quotes are wide and the liquidity of the instrument traded is low.

Three crows   A candlestick pattern consisting of three dark candles that close on or at their lows. After an extended advance, this formation can be a strong reversal pattern.

Three white soldiers   A candlestick pattern consisting of three candles that close at their highs and can indicate a continued advance. This pattern is a reliable indication that prices are moving higher, especially if they develop after a longer period of consolidation at a bottom; opposite of *three crow's* formation.

Tick   A minimum change in price, up or down.

Tomorrow next (Tom-next)   Simultaneous buying of a currency for delivery the following day and selling for the spot day, or vice versa.

Transaction   The buying or selling of currencies resulting from the execution of an order.

Transaction date   The date on which a trade occurs.

Uncovered   Another term for an open position.

Undervaluation   The condition of an exchange rate when it is below its purchasing power parity.

Uptick   A transaction executed at a price greater than that of the previous trans-action.

Volatility   A measure of the amount by which an asset price is expected to fluctu-ate over a given period.

Volume   The number of purchases or sales of a commodity futures contract made during a specified period of time; often the total transactions for one trading day.

Wash trade   A matched deal that produces neither a gain nor a loss.

Windows   A Japanese candlestick term referred to as the Western gap.

Working day   A day on which the banks in a currency's principal financial center are open for business. For forex transactions, a working day occurs only if the banks in both financial centers are open for business (all relevant currency centers in the case of a cross are open).

Yield   A measure of the annual return on an investment; also referred to as the amount of interest on a debt instrument.

About the CD-ROM

INTRODUCTION

This appendix provides you with information on the contents of the CD that accompanies this book. For the latest and greatest information, please refer to the ReadMe file located at the root of the CD.

SYSTEM REQUIREMENTS

- A computer with a processor running at 120 Mhz or faster.
- At least 32 MB of total RAM installed on your computer. For best performance, at least 64 MB is recommended.
- A CD-ROM drive.
- Internet access.
- Windows Media Player.

USING THE CD WITH WINDOWS

To install the items from the CD to your hard drive, follow these steps:

1. Insert the CD into your computer's CD-ROM drive.
2. Use the CD-ROM interface that appears to explore the contents of the CD in a simple point-and-click way.

If the opening screen of the CD-ROM does not appear automatically, follow these steps to access the CD:

1. Click the Start button on the left end of the taskbar, and then choose Run from the menu that pops up.
2. In the dialog box that appears, type **d:\setup.exe**. (If your CD-ROM drive is not drive d, fill in the appropriate letter in place of *d*.) This brings up the CD interface described in the preceding set of steps.

WHAT'S ON THE CD?

The following sections provide a summary of the software and other materials you'll find on the CD.

Content

There are more than one hour and three minutes of instructions on four presentations.

Along with the Pivot Point Calculator, this CD covers:

- Introduction to pivot points (44:23).
- Tutorial on how to use the Pivot Point Calculator (9:38).
- Examples on how to use confluence of pivot points (11:13).
- How to use a pivot point trading system (7:46).
- Pivot Point Calculator.
- ReadMe.

In order to activate the Pivot Point Calculator, users need Internet access. Any Internet speed will work. Users do not need high-speed DSL.

Applications

The following applications are on the CD:

Adobe Reader—Adobe reader is a freeware application for viewing files in the Adobe Portable Document format.

Customer Care

If you have trouble with the CD-ROM, please call the Wiley Product Technical Support phone number at (800) 762-2974. Outside the United States, call 1(317) 572-3994. You can also contact Wiley Product Techical Support at **http://support.wiley.com**. John Wiley & Sons will provide technical support only for installation and other general quality-control items. For technical support on the applications themselves, consult the program's vendor or author.

To place additional orders or to request information about other Wiley products, please call (877) 762-2974.

Author's Disclaimer

Stocks, futuress, forex, and options trading involves substantial risk. The valuation of futures, forex, and options may fluctuate; and as a result, clients may lose more than their original investment. In no event should the content of this presentation be construed as an expressed or an implied promise, guarantee, or implication by John Person or John Wiley & Sons, Inc., that you will profit or that losses can or will be limited in any manner whatsoever. Past results are no indication of future performance. Information provided in this presentation is intended solely for informative, educational purposes and is obtained from sources believed to be reliable. Information is in no way guaranteed. No guarantee of any kind is implied or possible where projections of future conditions are attempted. There is a risk of loss in trading stock, futures, forex, and options. One's financial suitability should be considered carefully before placing any trades.

Index

**For more information regarding the DVD,
see the About the DVD section on page 335.**

John Wiley & Sons, Inc.